A lively and compelling account of a frie₁
the future of South Africa. – *Geoff Budle₁.*

George Bizos has a remarkable story of his own. A young refugee from Nazi-occupied Greece, he and his family could so easily have settled down to enjoy the privileges of 'whiteness' that were embedded in South Africa. But he chose, as university student, to become involved in the quite stormy politics of the time.

In 1948, his student activism brought him into contact with black activists; that's when he met Nelson Mandela. A strong relationship developed – they remained friends, colleagues, professional and personal – until Mr Mandela passed away in 2013.

Bizos, intuitive as ever, does not attempt to depict Mandela as a flawless, saintly icon. Through a beguiling mixture of anecdote and analysis, he portrays Mandela as a human being willing to recognise his own weaknesses, and address them. He also captures Mandela's most benevolent strength, a willingness to acknowledge the strengths in others, including avowed former enemies. This would help Mandela to negotiate effectively with the apartheid government.

This book, through lucid analyses, and often very humorous anecdotes, vividly and honestly captures the life of Nelson Mandela. It also goes beyond personalities, providing fresh and honest insights into the evolution of the hideous apartheid system, from the late 1940s and beyond, as well as the birth of the 'new' South Africa. – *Achmat Dangor*

No one but George Bizos could have told this tale. He not only witnessed Nelson Mandela's tribulations and triumphs as counsel and friend for more than half a century, seeing history being made close-up, but himself made an important contribution to that history. This richly detailed record of his personal recollections and insights, while highly readable as a moving story of a unique friendship, makes a valuable contribution to our contemporary history. – *Johann Kriegler*

The memoir reveals the extent of a deep trust Mandela reposed on Bizos, how Mandela entrusted his fate in Bizos' hands during and after his lifetime, and how Bizos surpassed the true test of eternal friendship in upholding that trust. – *Vincent Maleka*

My first reaction to the news of a book about a friendship between George Bizos and Nelson Mandela was one of skepticism: they might have once been client and counsel or comrades even, but were they friends? This book not only dispels my doubts, but shows there are different kinds of friendships. I am now a believer. George and Nelson were friends. Dear friends. Theirs was a unique, special kind of friendship. It has transcended race, culture, generation, politics and life itself. It has been timeless. Few could have captured its essence as the intimate and beautiful prose in this book does. – *Tembeka Ngcukaitobi*

In the mid-70s, as a law student at Fort Hare University, to me the Mandela name represented a romantic notion of the struggle for the liberation of black South Africans whereas people like George, Arthur Chaskalson and the Kentridges were starting to register as lawyer role models to follow and emulate. They made my choice of being a human rights lawyer very easy. Therefore, joining the Legal Resources Centre in 1985 afforded me the privilege to work with and learn first-hand from these legal giants. George's impact has been more profound as I was privileged, not only to work with him during the dying days of apartheid, but also, as an attorney in the early days of our new democracy, learning from his razor-sharp mind and incisive cross-examination. Our engagement has continued right up until the present day in my role as chair of the Legal Resources Trust. As he approaches his 90th milestone, he continues with the fight to entrench the culture of human rights and constitutional democracy in South Africa. George's book on his friendship with Madiba will ensure that future generations who read it, will appreciate the deeply personal bonds across racial lines that were forged during our struggle. We would have been poorer if his dad had not chosen South Africa over

India to embark on a new life. As this book shows, we are also the beneficiaries of a strong bond forged in 1948 between George and Madiba that is manifested through the work of the LRC and so sensitively shared in this book. – *Thandi Orleyn*

This is the story of an unlikely friendship between two extraordinary men from different worlds – a Greek refugee and an African freedom fighter. The lifelong bond between George Bizos and Nelson Mandela traced the long walk from the days of early resistance to the apartheid state; passed in the shadow of the gallows in the Rivonia Trial; was tested by decades of incarceration; blossomed when freedom and victory came. I was often privileged to see the two of them together. Their mode was always formal and old-world but their mutual respect and affection always palpable. George Bizos now tells the remarkable inside story of the bond between these two men. – *Wim Trengove*

This is an amazingly warm and encouraging account of the lives of George and Madiba, two caring and committed human beings who were both victims of crimes against humanity and who made a real contribution to the achievement of democracy in our country. Their relationship was based on their shared humanity and understanding of the plight of disadvantaged people who suffered on account of poverty and discrimination. They were both determined to do what they could to rid South Africa of the evil of apartheid.

The greatness of both men lay in their humility, sensitivity as well as their concern for fellow human beings. My respect for Madiba and George was rekindled as I read this book, which reminded me of the long road we need to travel to achieve true equality. – *Zak Yacoob*

Two days after his release, Nelson embraces me at the rally in Soweto, with Cyril Ramaphosa looking on.

GEORGE BIZOS

65 Years of Friendship

A memoir of my friendship with Nelson Mandela

UMUZI

Published in 2017 by Umuzi

an imprint of Penguin Random House South Africa (Pty) Ltd
Company Reg No 1953/000441/07
Estuaries No 4, Oxbow Crescent, Century Avenue, Century City, 7441, South Africa
PO Box 1144, Cape Town, 8000, South Africa
umuzi@penguinrandomhouse.co.za
www.penguinrandomhouse.co.za

The quotation on the back cover is taken from the documentary *Odyssey to Freedom* by
Yannis Katomeris, produced by Mary Economidou.

Every effort has been made to ascertain copyright and license
the material included herein. In the event material protected by copyright is not credited,
kindly notify the publisher.

First edition, first printing 2017
1 3 5 7 9 8 6 4 2

ISBN 978-1-4152-0758-1 (Print)
ISBN 978-1-4152-0886-1 (ePub)

Cover design by Monique Cleghorn
Cover photograph taken in the Johannesburg Fort on Constitution Hill,
the site of the current Constitutional Court, by Oscar Gutierrez.
Back cover photograph by Louise Gubb
Text design by Nazli Jacobs
Set in Linux Liberting

This book was printed on FSC® certified and controlled sources.
FSC (Forest Stewardship Council®) is an independent, international,
non-governmental organisation. Its aim is to support environmentally sustainable,
and socially and economically responsible global forest management.

Printed and bound in South Africa by Novus Print, a Novus Holdings company.

Dedicated to my dear wife
Arethe and to our family,
who shared my trials,
tribulations and happiness

CONTENTS

FOREWORD

Despite his nearly self-effacing denials, Nelson Rolihlahla Mandela, the departed and well-loved first president of our democratic republic, was larger than life. He walked through many storms; through the wind and the rain and has been tossed and blown. And yet more and longer than anyone else, he has walked on, through his dreams, holding his head up and high. His was an arduous, fearless and long walk to a free and re-configured society now expediently rendered as sixty-seven years of struggle and sacrifice.

About one thing though, Nelson Rolihlahla Mandela was insightful. He readily recognised that 'he never walked alone'. Many lifelong comrades in the struggle for freedom and equality within the African National Congress and other close allies and friends ensured that he never walked forlorn and unaccompanied. Every time accolades were showered on him, he swiftly deflected them to all who walked along – to the collective and his manifold supporters. Mandela was acutely aware that nothing truly great is achieved by the sole exertion of one person.

For an unbroken period of two years shy of the sixty-seven years of Mandela's legendary voyage to freedom and well beyond, George Bizos was a loyal and very close friend and ally of Nelson Rolihlahla Mandela. In *65 Years of Friendship,* George Bizos renders an absorbing and heartfelt account of their enduring friendship founded on mutual abhorrence for injustice and reciprocal affection, respect and fidelity. The book narrates a riveting tale of how in the 1940s George Bizos and Nelson Mandela met at the University of the Witwatersrand. Then both pursued a post-graduate bachelor of laws degree with a view to qualifying as practising lawyers and both were outsiders to, if not foes of, the apartheid ruling elite. George Bizos was a Greek immigrant yet to be admitted to South African citizenship. Nelson Mandela was a denigrated citizen in his land of birth. Mandela's studies screeched to a halt because of racial profiling and his proclivity for robust political activism. In contrast, George Bizos qualified and joined the ranks of practising counsel. In that precast dichotomy, Nelson Mandela was to become the incessant political accused and trialist for charges related to the Defiance Campaign of 1952, followed by the Treason Trial of 1956 to 1961; later by the trial of 1962 and ultimately the Rivonia Trial, in which he and members of the African National Congress High Command were sentenced to life impris-onment. On the other hand, George Bizos was to become the dedicated and trustworthy counsel through the multiple trials of Nelson Mandela, but more importantly throughout his daunting decades of imprisonment. Over the twenty-seven years of imprisonment on Robben Island and later at Victor Verster prison, George Bizos visited Nelson Mandela and unfailingly provided support for his legal and familial needs. He also served as a trustworthy political envoy to Oliver Reginald Tambo and to other highly placed activists.

After the release of Nelson Mandela, up to his ascendancy to the presidency of the Republic, their tried-and-tested friendship flourished, albeit in a markedly different setting. Mandela's own tribute to the enduring bond between him and George Bizos appears in his affectionate foreword to Bizos' autobiography, *Odyssey to Freedom*. Their close com-panionship persisted for another twenty-three years, from the freeing of Mandela from prison to his passing on 5 December 2013.

I am grateful and privileged that George Bizos saw it proper to ask me to contribute this brief foreword. In his invitation he took time to remind me of the common friendship he and I have shared with Tata Mandela. For one thing, my ten years' imprisonment on Robben Island coincided with Tata's presence there and George Bizos' frequent visits to him. However, George and I met only after my release when I became an attorney and later a practising advocate and member of the Bar. We did a good few cases together. Together we successfully defended Dr Fabian Ribeiro facing charges of abetting terrorism. Together we defended a very young Ronnie Mamoepa, yet to become the renowned communicator and activist – may his soul rest in peace – and other ANC activists without success. We successfully appeared for Ingoapele Madingoane, the author of the anthology *Africa My Beginning*, charged for possessing his own banned publication. After his release Nelson Mandela asked Bizos, Pius Langa, who later became our Chief Justice, and me to defend his wife, Nomzamo Winifred Madikizela-Mandela. In time, I became a judge of the High Court, later a justice of the Constitutional Court and finally deputy chief justice. Every time George Bizos appeared before me as counsel in the Constitutional Court, I suffered the awkwardness of a mentee called upon to judge his seasoned don or master.

George continued to remind me in his note to me that like him – although not as long – I also became a close friend, if not more precisely a 'son', of Tata Mandela. For many years Tata Mandela sought advice from us. We advised him in relation to his litigation with his erstwhile attorney and sadly against two of his children and his wife Nomzamo. He appointed us as joint executors to his will and deceased estate. We are both trustees in his family trusts and obliged to look after his affairs and beneficiaries to the trusts. In a sense Tata joined us at the hip.

65 Years of Friendship at once enthrals and entertains as it records not only an enduring friendship between Mandela and Bizos marked by high fidelity and affection, but also another vista of Nelson Rolihlahla Mandela's long walk.

DIKGANG MOSENEKE
Tshwane, 14 August 2017

With Nelson at his house in Houghton, Johannesburg, 1995.

PROLOGUE

This is a short book about a long friendship.

My mother lived to almost ninety-nine and I met my wife, Arethe, the same year that I met Nelson. After them, my relationship with him is the longest of my life – beginning in 1948 when we were both students at the University of the Witwatersrand (Wits) and ending sixty-five years later with his death in 2013. From the start, the intrusive logic of apartheid infiltrated our association, cementing it as much on those things that we could not enjoy together as those we could. Still, we walked a long road, and over the decades Nelson was many things to me: my fellow student, my legal colleague, my client and my president.

He was also my friend.

When I asked Nelson to write the foreword to my autobiography, *Odyssey to Freedom*, which was first published in 2007, he did not hesitate.

'Of course, George, I would be delighted,' he replied, smiling mischievously. 'After all, who else is as good an authority on you?'

Typically, he did not ask for any further guidance and did not require any further prompting. Not a fortnight later, he was on the phone cheerfully reporting that it was written. His foreword inspired both the title and the logic of this book, and because of that I quote it here in full:

George Bizos and I have known each other well for close on sixty years. Over these years we have shared much and have grown to be close friends.

George came to South Africa with his brave, anti-Nazi father at the young age of thirteen – refugees, after a trying voyage of escape from the forces of fascism sweeping through their native Greece. We first met at the University of the Witwatersrand, and I am glad that what George records here includes his battle against the discrimination practised against black students at our alma mater.

George's identification with our struggle in defending victims of apartheid (often instructed by attorneys Mandela and Tambo), his acting for my former wife, Winnie, his general success in court became widely known, despite his status as a junior advocate. All of this assured me, early on, that George Bizos would continue to defend our people in their struggle for freedom with integrity, great dedication and complete commitment.

Perhaps it is George's tactical skills in matters of the law for which he is best known. It was this skill that led Bram Fischer, the leader of our defence team in the Rivonia Trial, to include George in that landmark event. Indeed it was George Bizos who warned us at our first consultation after the Rivonia arrests that Verwoerd's government was preparing the ground for the death penalty to be imposed on all of those arrested.

We were sentenced, instead, to life imprisonment and all of us appealed to George to continue defending our comrades and to assist our families, particularly by doing what he could to ensure that our children received a proper education during our incarceration.

While I was imprisoned on Robben Island and in other jails, George Bizos was one of my major lifelines. When I was hospitalised during my time at Pollsmoor Prison it was he, a wholly trusted confidant, whom I could send to assure Oliver Tambo in Lusaka of the preliminary negotiations I was conducting for the release of our comrades and plans to end apartheid.

Throughout my imprisonment, George unwaveringly shared our confidence that freedom for all and the dawning of democracy in our country was inevitable.

After my release from prison we were able to spend a great deal more time together. As a member of the ANC's Legal and Constitutional Committee, George played an important role in the writing of our country's Bill of Rights as well as in the shaping of its new constitution. He represented our government at the Constitutional Court to argue for the abolition of the death penalty and then represented us, too, when the country's new constitution was certified.

During my presidency of the Republic of South Africa, I often sought and received, always generously, George's counsel on many legal, constitutional and personal matters. He never once hesitated to assist where and how ever he was able and is considered a member of our family. Most of my children, grandchildren and great-grandchildren are rather partial, in fact, to their 'Uncle George'!

George's autobiography, *Odyssey to Freedom*, is not only a personal account of an extraordinary life but an invaluable addition to the historical record of our nation, captured here by a man whose contribution towards entrenching the human rights that lie at the heart of South Africa's constitutional values is impossible to overrate.[1]

This is my story of our friendship as I remember it. My friend and colleague, Arthur Chaskalson, the former chief justice, once said of me: 'George has such a good memory that he even remembers things that did not happen.' I will not take it as far as that, but recognise that there are things that I have forgotten, perhaps even some that I have muddled, and for that I apologise in advance.

With Nelson's death in December 2013, I lost a second close friend. Arthur Chaskalson had died the previous year. Within a year of Nelson, I lost Nadine Gordimer, author, Nobel Prize winner and good friend. In 2016, Jules Browde, a friend whose initiative led to my being granted South African citizenship thirty-one years after my arrival in the country, also passed away. And this year I lost my friend, Nelson's co-accused in the Rivonia Trial, Ahmed 'Kathy' Kathrada. In June, Joel Joffe, the instructing attorney in the trial, called me and told me that he was seriously ill but optimistic. I learnt of his death a week later.

On Saturday, 2 September, Arethe passed away peacefully in our family home.

I dream that the bell may soon toll for me.

GEORGE BIZOS
Legal Resources Centre, Johannesburg
September 2017

Further, such friendship requires time and familiarity; as the proverb says, men cannot know each other till they have 'eaten salt together'; nor can they admit each other to friendship or be friends till each has been found lovable and been trusted by each. Those who quickly show the marks of friendship to each other wish to be friends, but are not friends unless they both are lovable and know the fact; for a wish for friendship may arise quickly, but friendship does not.

This kind of friendship, then, is perfect both in respect of duration and in all other respects, and in it each gets from each in all respects the same as, or something like what, he gives; which is what ought to happen between friends.

Aristotle

Oh, those lovebirds! In our house, George was always, always right. If Madiba was not in a good mood and the phone rang and he cheered up, then I knew that it must be George on the line.

Graça Machel

TOP: Students' Representative Council, Wits, 1953. I am in the front row on the right.

RIGHT: Nelson (top row, second from left), the only African in the 1949 final year law class at Wits. H.R. Hahlo, head and dean of the law faculty, is in the centre of the front row.

Chapter 1

⁓

WITSIES

'Linksgesind en trots daarop'

I am eighty-nine years old. Each day I awake lightheaded and arrive after nine at my office on Albert Street in Marshalltown, the gritty commercial district alongside the M2 freeway in Johannesburg. The Legal Resources Centre (LRC) occupies the top two floors of Bram Fischer Towers, overshadowing the Department of Correctional Services on the bottom two. Bram would approve of this arrangement, I am sure. I leave the office at four-thirty each afternoon, often for an evening engagement. My job as senior counsel in the Constitutional Litigation Unit keeps me busy. So, still, does Nelson.

My long friendship with Nelson ended abruptly with his death in Houghton around nine o'clock on the evening of 5 December 2013. I cannot give as definite a date as to when it began. Enduring friendships are not in the habit of announcing their arrival with the same certainty as death and mine with Nelson was no exception. But this story of friendship has to begin somewhere and I think that that is most properly in Johannesburg in 1948. It was a most eventful year.

Nelson and I were both students at Wits University. It was considerably smaller than it is today. The Milner Park campus, edged by Jan Smuts Avenue and Empire Road, occupied what is now known as East Campus in Braamfontein, north-west of the city centre. As one of the two 'open' universities, Wits admitted a small number of African students from South Africa and the neighbouring countries of Basutoland (Lesotho), Mozambique and Bechuanaland (Botswana). There were then about two hundred black students among the more than three thousand white ones. The end of the Second World War had transformed the university as thousands of ex-volunteers, who had interrupted their studies to fight against fascism and Nazism, enrolled as mature students. Most of them returned home radicalised and committed to non-racism. Temporary wood and galvanised-iron huts were erected in the centre of campus to accommodate the influx.[2]

I was twenty-one years old and in my first year of a Bachelor of Arts (BA) degree, majoring in Greek and psychology. I had been provisionally admitted to the Faculty of Arts subject to the condition that I passed supplementary examinations in science and English and improved on my matric 'E' grades. I had only matriculated the year before, a foot taller and some three years older than my classmates. My English teacher at Athlone High School, Freda Greenberg, had decided that my poor results were not the fault of my four short years of English tuition, but of the school history master, a Scot who had spent much of his time telling us about Marxism and the Communist Manifesto of 1848. Ms Greenberg had cautioned me to avoid controversial matters.

Nelson was in what should have been the final year of his Bachelor of Laws degree. At thirty, he was nine years my senior, and repeating a number of subjects in his fifth year of part-time study at the university.

Neither of us presented much academic promise. We were both country boys who had arrived in the city seven years previously on trajectories that, at least in part, mitigated our rather dismal scholastic performances.

Johannesburg was unplanned, dynamic and surprising. The post-war economic boom had led to mass urban migration and the city was growing in a manner as disorderly as it was fast. With neither roots nor means, Nelson and I were both working hard to establish ourselves.

I was a refugee and lived alone in Jeppestown – my ground-floor bedroom looked onto a backyard and I shared a bathroom with others in the block. My father paid the five-pound monthly rental. He was my only family in the country, and worked as an assistant in a 'native' shop next to a compound in one of Pretoria's black residential locations. Every second weekend he would visit me.

Nelson had by then left the backyard room he had rented on Seventh Avenue in the 'dark city' that was Alexandra township and settled in Orlando West, the newly established township in the centre of what would later become South Western Township, or Soweto. He was living in the red-bricked matchbox on Vilakazi Street and working as an attorney's clerk to support his young family.

The year looked set to fulfil much of the promise that attended the aftermath of the war. The granting of independence to India, Ceylon and Burma had inspired hope that the rights to self-government and self-determination asserted in the Atlantic Charter would be realised in the remaining colonies. The end of the year would see the general assembly of the United Nations (UN) proclaim the 'equal and inalienable rights of all members of the human family' with the adoption of the Universal Declaration of Human Rights.

Amid the optimism of the times, the unexpected victory by the Afrikaner National Party in the May parliamentary elections was a tremendous shock. The general election had not attracted much interest on campus as it was widely anticipated that the United Party of General Jan Smuts would win. When, instead, the party that had refused to support the war effort came to power on an apartheid platform with a call for 'Die K—s en die Boesman op sy plek en die Koelie uit die land' (The K—s [Africans] and the Bushmen [Khoisan] in their place and the Coolies [Indians] out of the country), we were as surprised as we were horrified.

In his first speech to parliament, Prime Minister Daniel François Malan singled us out for attention when he denounced the presence of black students at the open universities as an 'intolerable state of affairs'.[3] He threatened to prohibit black students from white universities, to establish separate universities for black South Africans and to send all other black students back to their countries of origin.

The threats provoked an immediate reaction on campus. Almost half the student body, with the support of some of the academic staff, took part in a protest meeting. Ex-servicemen George Clayton and John Coaker took to the stage to condemn the government's policies and urge us to reject being governed by people who had opposed and sabotaged the war effort. On behalf of the student representative council (SRC), Sydney Brenner and Phillip Tobias extended their criticism to the principal of the university, the council and the senate for their failure to adopt a policy of non-discrimination against black students in all spheres of university life.

The majority of students on campus supported the United Party. Their student leader, Harry Schwarz, called for white unity and urged us to rally behind the party to ensure that the Nationalists were removed at the next poll. The United Party opposed the replacement of the segregationist status quo with codified racial discrimination, but they were not in favour of equal rights, conceding only reluctantly the need for some form of future qualified franchise for black people. Soon after the elections, Smuts confirmed to parliament that his party had always stood for segregation and the avoidance of racial mixture.

This was consistent with the university policy of 'academic non-segregation and social segregation'. Black students were at Wits for academic purposes only and their presence should not challenge 'the social customs of the country'.[4] African students could attend lectures, but they were not to swim in the swimming pool.

I was appalled by racism in any of its guises and strongly identified with the plight of black South Africans. For many years after my arrival in Durban harbour, I was haunted by my first sight of 'rickshaw boys' being treated like animals doing the work of beasts of burden. My own refugee status had, on occasion, singled me out as a target for discrimination, most memorably from my Afrikaans high-school teacher, Mr Scheepers, who, after asking me if I had seen recent press photographs of emaciated Greek children, told me that I looked well fed to him and asked whether I thought I was eating 'other people's food'. 'Not only do we feed you, but we have made you clever too,' he remarked.

My political home on campus was in the rather amorphous body loosely termed 'the left' – a coalition of members of religious and liberal groups as well as the Springbok Legion (the soldiers' trade union), the Labour Party and the Communist Party. Despite our differences, we were united in our opposition to apartheid, our belief in equal rights and our understanding that student politics could not be divorced from wider society. We were the most cohesive and well-organised section of the student body, enjoying a disproportionate majority representation on the SRC.

At a mass student meeting called in the Great Hall to respond to government plans to introduce a quota system to limit the number of black students in the medical and dental faculties, I stood up and, without prior consultation, proposed that an ultimatum be given to the university authorities: if they implemented the quota, we, the students, would go on strike. My proposal received enthusiastic applause, but was not put to the vote.

In parliament, a National Party member asked Prime Minister Malan what action would be taken to deal with the student protests. He replied that the university administration had reported that the trouble was being caused by a small, unrepresentative group of leftists and that normality would soon be restored by the level-headed student majority.

Back in the Great Hall the next day, I made an impromptu speech. I did not have a microphone but was told that I hit a high C when I declared to the assembled students, 'I want Prime Minister Malan to know that if advocating equal treatment for my fellow students makes me a leftist then I am proud to be one!' Scandalised, the daily Afrikaans newspaper, Die Transvaler, ran a banner headline on its front page the next morning: 'Links gesind en trots daarop' (Leftist and proud of it).

And so it was that a few days later, Nelson Mandela strode up to me on the steps of the Great Hall, smiling his wonderful smile. He did not have to introduce himself, although, of course, he did. Like most students on campus, I knew who he was. We had attended the same meetings and I had heard him speak at a small lunchtime gathering of the Transvaal

Indian Congress called to protest the remarks by a prominent cabinet minister that Indians did not belong in South Africa; they should be deprived of their immoveable property and restricted in their business activities or repatriated to India. Nelson had made a strong impression on me. He seemed to me to be a man of destiny, someone who knew that he had a role to play, yet he was no egotist. I noticed that he hardly ever said 'I' when discussing political matters – it was always 'we' or 'my organisation', or 'the liberation movement'.

Nelson was already a well-known political leader. At the time, he was a member of the executive committee of the Transvaal African National Congress (ANC) and the secretary of the ANC Youth League, which he, Oliver Tambo, Walter Sisulu, Ashby Mda and Anton Lembede were responsible for founding four years earlier. A popular figure among black students, he was considered a staunch African nationalist, suspicious of communists and cautious of political alliances with other race groups.

He was also the best-dressed student on campus; double-breasted suits, his polished shoes positively gleamed.

Nelson thanked me for my public stand and told me that it meant a lot to him and his colleagues. I expected that to be the end of the conversation, but Nelson was already possessed of that genuine interest in other people that so defined him. He wanted to know about me and how it was that I was prepared to make a public statement of that nature. I told him that I was Greek, a refugee from Nazi-occupied Greece. He wanted to know more. I told him how I had left my remote village on the Aegean Sea after my father discovered seven stranded New Zealand soldiers hidden in the bushes and resolved to take them to safety in Crete. I was the oldest of four children and did not want to remain behind without my father in a war that had already caused the closure of my school and the death of my beloved horse, Psaris. I had threatened to throw myself into the sea if he left without me. Somewhat to my surprise, my family agreed that I could accompany him. (I learnt only many years later that it was their concern that boys my age would meet the same fate under the German occupation as they did under the Turks, not my melodramatic ultimatum, which persuaded them.)

We did not reach Crete. The Germans invaded it the day we left the mainland and we were rescued from our small rowing boat after three stormy days at sea by the HMS *Kimberley*, an Allied destroyer. We were taken to Egypt and separated. My father was placed in a refugee camp in Cairo and I was sent to a Greek orphanage in Alexandria. After three months, with the Italians in Libya and Rommel approaching Cairo, the Middle East Command decided to evacuate refugees with children. We were given a choice of destination: India or South Africa. My father chose the latter on the strength of rumours that the streets were paved with gold.

We arrived in Johannesburg in August 1941, travelling by train from Durban. Our stop was diverted to avoid the crowds of white demonstrators protesting against Prime Minister Smuts allowing the vuilgoed (rubbish) of Europe into the country. Neither my father nor I could speak English. We shared a room in Victoria Mansion, a block of flats close to Park Station in the city centre. Philoptochos – Friends of the Poor – paid for our board and gave us a daily allowance for meals. I supplemented our income by working in downtown corner cafés and did not attend school until a teacher, Cecilia Feinstein, discovered me helping a customer at the cold-meat slicing machine in the Formain Café in 1943 and arranged for my enrolment at Malvern Junior High School.

I told Nelson that I hoped, like him, to become a lawyer. In this, our first proper conversation, I did the talking. The generosity of Nelson's interest, the sheer charisma of his concentration, rendered me utterly at ease. Apart from the extraordinary quality of his ability to listen, we parted with my knowing nothing new about him.

It was only later that we continued our conversation in earnest. In my third year, I started working as a clerk for the attorney Ruben Kahanowitz and was required to file documents at the Magistrates' Court on Fox Street. Nelson was then working for a downtown law firm and was often at court. We would meet up and, when possible, would take the time to chat, usually in the busy heat of the street or in the marbled corridors of the court. There were few places in the city that we were permitted to sit side-by-side, even less where we could share a meal. Unable to ride the tram together, we would occasionally take a walk.

In my short time in the country, I had not encountered any other African like Nelson. Certainly, none had addressed me with his confidence. He was proud and made no apologies for his blackness. He once described apartheid as a moral genocide – an attempt to exterminate an entire people's self-respect;[5] he was not prepared to bend his knee and I admired him for that.

I have since heard others describe Nelson as prickly, even oversensitive at the time, but I experienced him as a man of great personal warmth. He was, however, reluctant to talk about himself and it was only slowly that I learnt more about his personal circumstances.

I discovered that, more or less at the same time as I escaped the war, Nelson fled the confines of his life in rural Transkei. He was expelled from Fort Hare University in the second year of his undergraduate degree for refusing to accept a position on the SRC without the support of the majority of the students who had boycotted the elections in protest at the poor food. Back in the Transkei, his guardian, the Thembu regent Jongintaba Dalindyebo, insisted that he return to the university and informed him that he had arranged marriages for both Nelson and his own son, Justice. Neither Nelson nor Justice wanted to marry. They promptly stole two oxen, sold them to the local trader, and ran away to Johannesburg.

Nelson arrived in the city in April 1941 and worked briefly as a watchman on the mines before Walter Sisulu secured a job for him as a clerk in the law firm of Witkins, Sidelsky and Eidelman. He completed his BA by correspondence through the University of South Africa (Unisa) and registered for his LLB at Wits in 1943, attending evening lectures after work. By 1949, his final year at the university, he was married to Evelyn Ntoko Mase, and had a three-year-old son, Thembekile. Their nine-month-old daughter, Makaziwe, had died the previous year. I never visited their home in those days (it would have meant applying for a permit to do so legally), and consequently only met Evelyn on a few occasions. My impression was, however, that the marriage was troubled.

I was not yet married, but had already met my wife-to-be. I first saw Arethe on the red-and-white city tram that cheerfully rattled its way eastwards from the city centre along Main Street towards Bezuidenhout Valley. She was seated on the near-empty upper deck and, although there were plenty of other seats available, I took the one next to hers, prompting a charismatic blush that emphasised the sea-green of her eyes.

'How far are you going?' I asked to break the awkwardness of the moment.

'I have not yet decided whether I should get off at my father's shop – the Subway Café – or go straight home.'

'I know your father's café. You must also be Greek then.'

Yes, she was. Her full name was Arethe Ekatherine Daflos. She was in matric at St Mary's High School. I told her that I was Greek too, and briefly recounted how I had arrived in South Africa. In return, she told me that her father, Basil Daflos had, at my age, arrived in South Africa from his village on the north-western border of Greece and Albania to work for his uncle in his café in Stellenbosch. Her mother's family had come from the same part of Greece; her maternal grandfather, Vassiliou, was the first confectioner in Johannesburg, while her maternal grandmother, Arethe Botsaris (after whom she was named), was a descendant of the Greek national hero and freedom fighter Markos Botsaris.

So engrossed were we in our conversation that we both missed our stops. I got off with her at the stop nearest her home and walked her the half block up the hill to her gate on Dawe Street, where we continued our conversation.

In those days, I knew that no self-respecting Greek mother would allow her daughter out on a date in public with a young man, so I did not even ask. Instead, I began eating at the Subway Café and soon befriended Arethe's mother, Mary. It was not long before she was complaining to me about how little Greek her children knew and had invited me over for lunch on Sunday to speak Greek to them.

Arethe was the eldest of three children. She had a younger sister, Aspasia, and a brother, Niko. When I arrived for what would be the first of many extended Sunday lunches at the family home, she disguised her surprise, and with sweet complicity allowed her parents to introduce me to her.

Near the end of the year I got caught in one of those summer thunderstorms into which the heat of the day collapses on the Highveld. I arrived soaked at Dawe Street. Arethe pulled me into the carpeted hallway and, with a tenderness that I had never known, towelled my head and shoulders dry. When she had finished, we kissed. It was the end of eight years of loneliness and the beginning of a loving relationship that has lasted over half a century and produced three sons and six grandchildren.

I did not, however, share any of this with Nelson; the detail of our personal lives was not the stuff of our conversations. We wanted to talk politics. Nelson was eager to hear about what was happening on campus. In my second year, Harold Wolpe had invited me to a caucus meeting of the liberal–left alliance to select candidates for election to the SRC. I was given a slot on the ticket. Once elected, I became a 'front bencher' proposing and opposing motions as agreed upon by our group's caucus meetings. I was to serve three terms under three presidents – Sydney Brenner, Harold Wolpe and Godfrey Getz.

There was always something happening, and Nelson would listen to my reports in that deep, still way of his, asking questions at the end, but very rarely commenting.

For instance, when fellow student Eduardo Mondlane was served with a deportation permit, I was most upset. Mondlane, who went on to become the leader of the Mozambique Liberation Front (Frelimo), was a social-science student at Wits on a scholarship from the Christian Council of Mozambique. He spoke openly about the oppression of his people. Soon after the Nationalists came to power, the ubiquitous security police of the Portuguese dictator António Salazar requested that they expel Mondlane from South Africa. They obliged. Mondlane's permit to enter South Africa had been renewed regularly until mid-1949, when he was given a week to get out. Hundreds of students attended a campus meeting to protest the expulsion, denouncing it as part of a larger government strategy to exclude all black students from neighbouring African states. We knew that it could not have pleased the authorities that, even with the stringent immigration laws, the handful of students from the British protectorates still had little difficulty in entering and remaining in South Africa, where we still sang 'God Save the King' at the end of the bioscope shows. Sadly, neither our student protests nor appeals from other sources stopped the expulsion. Mondlane was sent home.

I confided in Nelson about how this had shaken me. My own refugee permit had expired when the war ended in 1945, and although I had been granted permanent residence in 1948, my application for South African citizenship was refused and would only be granted in 1972. The precariousness of my status instilled in me a fear of deportation that pervaded first my involvement in student politics and later much of my legal work. Each new political case that I took on carried an attendant dread that this would be the one to result in my expulsion from the country.

Nelson would listen impassively to my reports. Although he never said so, I suspect that the protracted dispute between Wits and the (Afrikaans) University of Pretoria (Tukkies) must have resonated with him much like the deportation of Mondlane did with me. The annual intervarsity rugby match between Wits and Tukkies was a highlight of the university sporting and social calendar. Black students were not allowed to play university sport and could not participate. They were, however, allowed to attend to cheer our sports teams on, as long as they did not sit with the rest of us while they did. The smaller stands in the south-eastern corner of Ellis Park Stadium and a separate portion of Loftus Versfeld in Pretoria were allocated to them. The Wits SRC challenged this and threatened to cancel the game if Tukkies would not allow the Wits supporters to sit together. The Wits All Sports Council proposed the appointment of a committee to meet with Tukkies to resolve the matter, and Ismail Mahomed, as the executive minute secretary, was elected as a member. Ismail Mahomed would later be recognised as one of the most outstanding constitutional and administrative law practitioners in southern Africa, and be appointed as chief justice in Namibia and South Africa. The Tukkies committee, however, objected to his presence on the Wits committee on the basis that he only represented black students, not the whole university. They refused to meet with the Wits committee if any of its members were black. We refused to remove him. Our negotiations were deadlocked and the game was not played that year. Eventually, the following year, Tukkies gave in and, to the indignation of parliament, allowed our black students to sit with us while we watched our team play.

Like his fellow black students, Nelson was no stranger to the discrimination on campus and braved many insults. As the only African student in the law department, he encountered routine prejudice. Certain of his fellow classmates were unequivocal in their objection to his presence in their classes and would emphatically vacate their chairs should he sit next to them in a lecture.

Overt racism was not the sole domain of the students. The head and dean of the law faculty, Professor H.R. Hahlo, was a German Jew who had assimilated to Christianity. He had drunk deep of the cup of apartheid and was outspoken in his belief that the law was a discipline for which Africans – and women – were not suited. Nelson was not spared the wisdom of his prejudice. Hahlo told him that he did not belong in the law faculty at Wits, and recommended that he continue his studies by correspondence at Unisa. 'Nelson, the advocates' profession is really only suitable for whites. It is simply beyond the ability of blacks. You should rather aim to be an attorney,' the professor counselled his student.

At the time, the university required students to pass all of their courses in the same academic year or fail the whole year of study and repeat them all. Provision was made for the writing of two supplementary examinations. When Nelson failed three of his final-year subjects, he wrote a letter to the dean in support of his request for permission to write all three supplementary examinations. He explained that he was not in a financial position to spend another year of study at the university to repeat the subjects, and wrote that:

I should also add that during the whole period I studied under very difficult and trying conditions. I was a part-time student and resided (as I still do) at Orlando Native Location in a noisy neighbourhood. In the absence of electric light I was compelled to study in the evenings with a paraffin lamp and sometimes with candlelight. I wasted a lot of time travelling between Orlando and city and returned home after 8pm feeling tired and hungry and unfit to concentrate on my studies. Even during the examinations I was compelled to work in order to maintain the only source of livelihood that I had. It is my candid opinion that if I could have done my work under more suitable conditions, I could have produced better results.[6]

Permission was refused and Nelson was unable to complete the LLB degree required to practise as an advocate in terms of the two-tiered South African legal system. He had set his sights on becoming the first black advocate at the Johannesburg Bar, but took the dean's advice and sat the attorney's admission exam at the end of 1951 instead.

H.R. Hahlo was a topic that Nelson and I returned to in our conversations when, perhaps inevitably, I too came into conflict with the good professor. In the first year of my LLB, Hahlo refused to allow the then eight black students in the law faculty to attend the annual dinner of the Law Students' Society. The dinner was to be held at the Ambassador Hotel in Hillbrow where blacks were prohibited because it was licensed to sell alcohol.

The SRC contributed 100 pounds to subsidise the dinner for non-paying invited guests, who included the attorney general and judges. Sydney Brenner had questioned this practice during his tenure as SRC president and had been told by the then faculty representative on the SRC that the tradition was necessary to expose students to the leaders of the legal profession and was an essential part of their training for a successful career at the Bar.

I could not resist the opportunity to expose this contradiction and the hypocrisy of the law faculty and sent a message to the dean notifying him that the SRC would withdraw its grant for the dinner if black students were not allowed to attend or if any pressure was put on them to withdraw. The following afternoon, at the end of Hahlo's lecture, mispronouncing my name and speaking in the third person, he called me to his office. He came straight to the point. He had nothing against black students, but the law prohibited them from attending the dinner. The law faculty could not break the law in the presence of the legal establishment, who would be uncomfortable if black students were present.

'Your first loyalty as a law student,' he admonished me, 'should be to the faculty and to the brotherhood of law. It is your duty to vote for the item on the SRC agenda and to persuade your friends to do the same.' I refused. When I then also refused his appeal to absent myself from the SRC meeting and to allow the elected law faculty representative to deal with the matter, I was promptly dismissed.

In the end, all eight black students attended the dinner. They undertook not to 'partake of intoxicating liquor', but this did not preclude some of the rest of us from discretely lacing their cool drinks. Smiling his characteristic smile, the acting judge president of the Transvaal, W.H. Ramsbottom, made plain his pleasure at their presence by speaking to each of them in turn. For the next two and a half years of my law degree, Hahlo refused to acknowledge me.

It was an indirect consequence of the law-dinner incident that I made another friend. When I was nominated for a further term as the law faculty's representative on the SRC, some in the faculty were determined to block my election and proposed a motion of no confidence in me. I was challenged on my lack of support for the faculty tradition of not involving itself in wider political issues and also for my role in the law dinner. At the end of the debate, a tall first-year student swung the vote in my favour with his persuasive intervention and I won by a narrow margin.

'Mr Chairman, we have for too long spoken about the university's tradition. Surely the question is not what the university policy is, nor what it has been, nor what it ought to be. The correct question to ask ourselves before we vote is a simple one: What is right and what is wrong?' The speaker was Arthur Chaskalson. And this, our first collaboration in what would become a lifetime of association, mutual support and friendship.

It is probably in the friendships that we formed at Wits that the university's most abiding influence on both Nelson and me can be found. The student left provided a rare opportunity for meaningful contact with people from other races. Through fellow students Ismail Meer, J.N. Singh and Ahmed Bhoola, Nelson began to appreciate the commitment of Indian South Africans to the struggle. His friendships with fellow students Joe Slovo, Ruth First, Harold Wolpe and Tony O'Dowd helped dispel his antagonism to white communists. The Afrikaner Bram Fischer, who was a lecturer in the law department, became one of his heroes.

For me, another of the cherished friendships of that time was with Duma Nokwe.

I first met Philemon Pearce Dumalisile Nokwe in the Wits law library. Most law lectures began in the afternoons to accommodate the many students who had jobs. Afterwards most of us would dash out for a quick meal before returning to the library for a few hours of study. One evening, on entering the seminar room adjoining the library, I noticed Duma, who was a year behind me, hurriedly hiding a packet of fish and chips. He froze when he realised that I had seen him. In that moment, it dawned on me that there was nowhere on or near campus for black students to have an evening meal. I approached him and introduced myself. We were soon in conversation.

After that I invited him to eat with me in the evenings in my room. I had by then moved to Kenlaw Mansions, two blocks from the university, where I had a larger room and the luxury of my own bathroom. Duma and I would order takeaways from the Cypriot owner of the Phineas Café downstairs, which we would eat on our laps. Duma lived in Soweto with his wife and young child – to get home in the evenings he would have to leave campus early, catch a train to New Canada and then walk some distance to his house in Orlando West. I offered him my couch for those nights he wanted to study late, and he would occasionally stay over.

Duma had been a mathematics teacher before he and his wife Tiny were dismissed by the Bantu education department for their participation in a stay-away. He was a member of the ANC Youth League, and friends with both Nelson and Walter Sisulu.

He was also an organiser of the Defiance Campaign of 1952. Inspired by Mahatma Gandhi's non violent campaigns in South Africa and India, the Defiance Campaign was an initiative of the ANC and its allies in the South African Indian Congress. A letter to the prime minister signed by the then ANC president, Dr James Moroka, but drafted by Nelson and Walter Sisulu, demanded that the government abolish six of the most oppressive apartheid laws or face a mass campaign of national civil disobedience.

Prime Minister Malan declined. His response, signed by his private secretary, explained that the differences between the races were permanent, not man-made, and represented the government's policies as a 'programme of goodwill to the bantu'.

The Defiance Campaign was launched in June. Over a period of five months, more than forty thousand volunteers across the country peacefully defied apartheid laws, ignored curfews and entered 'whites only' areas. About eight thousand were arrested.

A key aim of the campaign was to frustrate the administration of apartheid and to fill the jails to the limit. The protestors refused to pay bail or fines. As the campaign intensified, magistrates had to devise strategies to lessen the pressure on the prison system. They imposed corporal punishment on the younger accused. Others ordered that the pockets of those convicted were to be searched and that any money found on them was to be forcibly removed to pay their fines. Protestors easily countered this strategy, arriving penniless to court. In Mafikeng, the magistrate freed twenty protestors that he had just found guilty, as there was simply no space left in the jail.

Nelson was arrested for his role as the volunteer-in-chief in raids on the leaders of the campaign. In August, he and twenty others appeared in the Johannesburg Magistrates' Court on charges under the Suppression of Communism Act. Bram Fischer, Vernon Berrangé and George Lowen represented the accused, which included two Wits students, Diliza Mji and Nthato Motlana.

I joined a group of law students and attorneys' clerks led by Duma who went to court on the first day for the preparatory examination held to establish whether there was sufficient evidence for trial. With Duma, I was able to gain entrance into the packed courtroom. Harold Wolpe led another group from the university gates on Jan Smuts Avenue to Marshall Square. At least half of the marchers were white and many wore their university blazers. Students opposed to any public association of Wits with the campaign scuffled with the marchers at the start of the demonstration.[7]

The Magistrates' Court passages were soon filled with an exuberant crowd of supporters, at least a thousand of us. We demanded the withdrawal of the charges. Our protests were so loud that Magistrate Johannes interrupted the proceedings to request counsel to ask their clients to keep the noise down or disperse. Dr James Moroka and Dr Yusuf Dadoo appealed to us to keep quiet. We partly complied. The day turned into an extended protest meeting, with the large crowd singing songs and chanting freedom slogans. During the adjournment, I was part of the SRC delegation that approached Nelson to tell him that we were on his side and that we would call for the withdrawal of all charges against him and his co-accused.

The protests triggered a new round of Nationalist attacks on the university, with *Die Transvaler* contending in a lead article that the demonstration threw a spotlight on the undesirable fraternisation between white and black that was taking place at Wits.[8] The minister of posts and telegraphs, Tom Naudé, declared indignantly that there was no social segregation at Wits and that white girls went about with 'k—s'.[9]

The university authorities and our student opponents on campus were outraged by our behaviour. The only Nationalist on the SRC, one Wassenaar, proposed a motion to censure the Liberal Students' Association, of which Harold Wolpe was the leader, for the identification of Wits with the Defiance Campaign. I countered this with a motion noting that the president of the SRC, Godfrey Getz, had made it clear to the press that the Liberal Students' Association was responsible for the demonstration and that it was entitled, as an association, to do so. My motion was adopted by the SRC.

In Vernon Berrangé's closing address for the preparatory examination at the Magistrates' Court, he argued that there were no grounds for the charges under an Act 'which although supposedly intended to suppress communism, was now being used in an endeavour to suppress the legitimate aspirations of non-Europeans'. A visibly agitated Magistrate Johannes committed the accused for trial on the grounds that the campaign aimed at bringing about 'political, industrial, economic and social change by unlawful acts alternatively encouraging feelings of hostility between whites and blacks and in so doing, wrongfully and unlawfully advocated, defended, advised or encouraged the achievement of the aims of communism'.

Outside court, I watched as Nelson echoed the anti-Nazi German theologian Martin Niemöller. 'Today we are charged: tomorrow it may well be the parliamentary opposition – everybody who dares to criticise the Nationalists. The same thing happened in Nazi Germany. I am, however, convinced that the people have learned what they can do and no power can stop their forward march to freedom.'

The accused in the campaign trials would admit what they had done, but plead not guilty to the charges. I did not participate, but was kept up to date by Duma during our long evening discussions. The defence strategy was to turn the courts into a forum in which the denial of fundamental human rights, not those who defied apartheid laws, stood accused. It would lay the foundation for the defence for the next forty years of political trials.

I attended the Supreme Court trial of the campaign accused when I could. The scholarly Harold Hanson SC and Rex Welsh SC replaced the more flamboyant Vernon Berrangé and appeared for the accused before Judge Rumpff. Under their expert cross-examination, state witness after state witness confirmed that the ANC had never advocated violence at its meetings and that the campaign leaders had stressed co-operation between the races. The counsel for the accused did their best to persuade the court that, however wide the terms of the Suppression of Communism Act, they did not cover the conduct of their clients. The incongruity of this application of the Act was made apparent when, in response to a question posed by Judge Rumpff, the prosecution confirmed that 'a party of European ladies protesting jury rules by sitting down in the street would also be guilty of communism under the law'.

We hoped that examples like this would compel the court to acquit the accused. They did not. The twenty-one accused were convicted in December and sentenced to nine months' imprisonment with hard labour, suspended for two years. The judge stressed, however, that the accused were guilty of 'statutory communism', which he made clear was not the same thing as 'communism as it is commonly known'. An appeal before Judge Greenberg was dismissed. Following his conviction, Nelson was served with a banning order by the minister of justice, confining him to his city of residence and prohibiting him from attending any gatherings for two years.

The Defiance Campaign catapulted ANC membership from an estimated seven thousand at the start to about a hundred thousand. There was also a marked increase in international awareness and support for the organisation – including the establishment of a UN commission to investigate apartheid. The convictions were, however, a blow for peaceful opposition to apartheid. Few in the future would be prepared to risk a months-long jail sentence for sitting on a whites-only park bench. Just to make sure, however, parliament passed the draconian Criminal Law Amendment Act of 1953 that imposed three-year jail sentences and flogging for civil disobedience. Needless to say, none of this legislation would have passed muster in a constitutional democracy, but it did serve the intended purpose of criminalising non-violent protest and limiting what little space there was to express resistance to apartheid.

The campaign marked a turning point in Nelson's political shift from an Africanist to a non-racial democrat. His collaboration with people such as Dr Dadoo, the head of the Indian Congress, and Bram Fischer convinced him of the sacrifices that white, Indian and coloured South Africans were prepared to make in the fight for racial equality and freedom.

The following year, 1953, would see the National Party re-elected in the general election with a majority of the parliamentary seats. At the ANC's annual conference in Queenstown, Nelson would be a key mover behind the adoption of the proposal that would lead to the 1955 Congress of the People in Kliptown at which the Freedom Charter was adopted.

I would complete my final year of law, but not before inadvertently contributing to the end of the system that favoured the election of candidates of the organised liberal–left to the SRC. At a packed meeting calling for a vote of no confidence in the SRC, I provoked the ire of my colleagues when again, without any prior consultation, I said that I did not want to continue serving on the body unless we enjoyed the confidence of a substantial majority of students. I then proposed a referendum to decide the matter. We lost the referendum, but in the elections that followed in May 1953, the SRC under Godfrey Getz was re-elected almost to a man. This time, however, the council included a woman, Irma Lief, and two new black members, one of whom was Ismail Mahomed. Complaints were raised against the university electoral system, and as the senior law faculty representative I was called on to chair a commission to investigate. The commission found that some of the criticisms were valid and the university changed to a system of proportional representation.

I graduated with my law degree at the end of 1953. Nelson would obtain his from Unisa thirty-six years later in 1989, a year before his release from prison. In 1991, Wits would award him an honorary doctorate of laws.

When Professor Bruce Murray was writing a history of Wits, he found the original letter sent by Nelson to Professor Hahlo. He sent a copy to Nelson in prison and asked for his comment. When he received no reply, he approached me to ask Nelson if he had received it. Nelson confirmed that he had, but told me that as he now believed that Wits was doing such a good job he did not think it would be helpful to revive the matter. He asked me to apologise and explain his reasons to Professor Murray.

Nelson would later write that he met both generosity and animosity at Wits, and although he formed friendships with sympathetic white people of his own age, most of them were neither liberal nor colour blind.[10] Typically, he expressed no bitterness nor bore grudges. Fifty years later, as the president of South Africa, Nelson invited his Wits law class to a reunion, greeting each one of the nineteen attendees by name. He told them: 'I am what I am both as a result of people who respected me and helped me, and of those who did not respect me and treated me badly.'[11] He also expressed his gratitude to Dean Hahlo for one thing – making it easier for him to decide what to study in prison.

In his will, Nelson bequeathed R100 000 to the university. Hahlo had long since emigrated to Canada, citing apartheid as the reason he could no longer bear to remain in the country.

TOP: Arethe and I on our wedding day.

BOTTOM: Nelson (on the far left) next to Evelyn Mase on the wedding day of Walter and Albertina Sisulu, 1944.

TOP: At the graduation for my Bachelor of Arts degree in 1950.

RIGHT: Nelson in the offices of Mandela and Tambo, Johannesburg.

Chapter 2

⁓

MANDELA AND TAMBO

'Hey you, I told you to sit down!'

Somewhat like Nelson before me, I was forced to make another plan for my legal career when I discovered in my final year at university that I could not register as an articled clerk because I was not a South African citizen. On graduation, my only option was to join the Bar as an advocate and not work for a firm of attorneys as I had intended.

I was anxious that my application for admission might encounter difficulties. It was not clear whether a Greek national could take an oath of allegiance to the queen. I discussed my concerns with Joe Slovo, who had been successfully admitted despite his own statelessness. Joe was happy to represent me in court in my application for admission, however, he cautioned, 'It might not be entirely strategic for a stateless, Lithuanian Jew, and a communist at that, to submit before a Waspish judge that there is nothing equivocal about a Greek refugee taking an oath of allegiance to her majesty the queen.'

Joe referred me instead to the appropriately named Rex Welsh, who assured me that unless we struck a judge more royalist in outlook than the queen, there should be no objections from the bench. Rex prepared the papers, but was not available on the day of the application and so arranged for H.C. Nicholas QC, an equally prominent member of the Bar, to appear on my behalf. Nicholas was delighted when he saw on the court roll that judges Lucas Steyn and Frans Rumpff were to hear the matter. Our painstaking preparations in anticipation of a robust legal debate proved unnecessary. Both judges were Afrikaner Nationalists who likely believed that if they could take an oath of allegiance to the queen, then anyone could. Steyn's clerk, a young Johann Kriegler, administered my oath and no questions were asked.

I was admitted in 1954 and almost immediately started receiving briefs from the law firm of Mandela and Tambo, the attorney's practice that Nelson and Oliver Tambo, assisted by Mendi Msimang, Godfrey Pitje and Ruth Mompati, had established two years earlier. One of the first all-African law firms in the country, the practice occupied the second floor of the unassuming Chancellor House across the road from the Johannesburg Magistrates' Court. In large letters on the window, the firm gaily announced its defiance of the Group Areas Act, further antagonising those conservative members of the legal fraternity already irritated by the mere fact of its existence.

As the firm of choice for black South Africans, Mandela and Tambo was busy. Clients crowded into the waiting rooms and overflowed into the corridors, seeking help with the typical, grinding issues of black South Africans of the time: farm evictions, pass arrests, labour matters. In his autobiography, Nelson later wrote of the practice:

> Africans were desperate for help: in government buildings it was a crime to walk through a Whites Only door, a crime to ride a Whites Only bus, a crime to use a Whites Only drinking fountain, a crime to walk on a Whites Only beach, a crime to be on the streets after 11pm, a crime not to have a passbook and a crime to have the wrong signature in that book, a crime to be unemployed and a crime to be employed in the wrong place, a crime to live in certain places and a crime to have no place to live. Every week we interviewed old men from the countryside who told us that generation after generation of their family had worked a scraggly piece of land from which they were now being evicted. Every week we interviewed old women who brewed African

45

beer as a way to supplement their tiny incomes, who now faced jail terms and fines they could not afford to pay. Every week we interviewed people who had lived in the same house for decades only to find that it was now declared a white area and they had to leave without any recompense at all...Every day we heard and saw the thousands of humiliations that ordinary Africans confronted every day of their lives.[17]

The firm seemed to take on any work that came in and had to brief newly qualified junior advocates just to manage the caseload. This was costly and clients who could not afford their legal fees were not turned away. Despite the activity, the business was financially strapped. It had also hardly been established when Nelson was charged under the Suppression of Communism Act for his role as the volunteer-in-chief of the Defiance Campaign. Following his conviction, the Law Society of the Transvaal applied to the Supreme Court for him to be struck off the roll of accredited attorneys. He received offers of support from a number of well-known Afrikaner lawyers, many of whom were supporters of the National Party, and was represented at the hearing by two leading members of the Bar, Walter Pollak QC and Blen Franklin. They argued on his behalf that his conviction for participation in the Defiance Campaign was not a crime of moral turpitude and should not lead to his disbarment. Judge Ramsbottom agreed and ruled that Nelson had a right to campaign for his political beliefs. He noted that, while an attorney may be expected to observe the laws more strictly than other people, the fact that an attorney had deliberately disobeyed the law did not necessarily disqualify him from practising his profession or justify his removal from the roll by the court.

Nelson was encouraged by this experience. The response of his colleagues at the Bar showed that even in racist South Africa professional solidarity could transcend colour. He had great respect for the giants at the Bar at the time – Bram Fischer, Isie Maisels, Sydney Kentridge, Ernie Wentzel and Vernon Berrangé, all of whom would end up defending him in court.

There was always something of the aristocrat about Nelson. At six foot two, he cut a dashing figure and he had a weakness for fine clothing. I was once sent as a clerk to the prestigious Johannesburg tailor Alfred Kahn to collect a list of customers in default on their accounts. Kahn was the tailor to Johannesburg's elite; his clientele was drawn from the wealthy members of the Rand Club on Loveday Street and included billionaire mining-magnate Harry Oppenheimer. When I arrived, I was amused to find a couple of Kahn's society customers disconcertedly watching him on his knees at Nelson's feet measuring the length of his trouser leg for the final fitting of a suit.

Impeccably dressed, physically imposing, Nelson commanded authority in the courtroom. He had a flamboyant, rather theatrical style. He made his presence felt and soon earned a reputation among the magistrates as 'uppity'.

By his own admission, Nelson did not act as though he were a black man in a white man's court, but rather as if everyone else was a guest in his. An anecdote in Anthony Sampson's biography is typical of his approach: 'Mandela, walking boldly through the "whites only" entrance to a courtroom, was stopped by a young white clerk with a dark complexion who told him "This is for whites". Mandela immediately responded: "Then what are you doing here?"'[13]

In court, he would turn racial tension to his own advantage. In a case in which he was defending an African domestic worker accused of stealing her 'madam's' clothes, he approached the madam in the witness stand, balancing a pair of ladies' panties on the tip of his pencil, and asked her if they were hers. Too embarrassed to answer in the affirmative, she said no, and the magistrate dismissed the case.

By the mid-1950s Nelson had gained a certain celebrity in Johannesburg. As one of the more prominent leaders of the ANC, he was a likely successor to Chief Albert Luthuli, the then president general. He appeared regularly in the press and was the most well-known black lawyer in the city. It was likely this renown that provoked the ire of Magistrate Willem Dormehl.

Nelson first consulted me about his problems with the Kempton Park magistrate on a Sunday afternoon. I was housesitting the home of a former employer who had two young daughters. The children did not conceal their surprise at the sight of a black man pulling up in his Oldsmobile to the driveway of their leafy northern-suburbs home and being invited in the front door as a guest. I was embarrassed. Sensing this, Nelson was concerned to put me at ease. 'My children show the same curiosity when whites come to our house,' he remarked with a conspiratorial laugh as we sat down at the large mahogany dining table.

Once we were settled, he recounted his story.

Nelson had appeared before Magistrate Dormehl on behalf of Elliot Setoaba, a government clerk who was charged with accepting a bribe. When the accused was called to plead, Nelson stood to put himself on record as his attorney, but before he could continue the magistrate asked him whether he was entitled to appear. When Nelson confirmed that he was an admitted attorney, the magistrate instructed him to produce his certificate of admission as proof. It is neither standard practice for attorneys to carry their certificates with them nor for magistrates to request them, and Nelson did not have his. The magistrate instructed him to obtain it and promptly adjourned the court. In those pre-technology days, the only way that Nelson could produce a copy of his certificate was to drive from Kempton Park, then no more than a dorp near the airport, to his office in downtown Johannesburg to collect it himself. It was impossible for him to do so and return in time for the afternoon session. When court resumed after lunch, Nelson explained this self-evident difficulty to the magistrate and undertook to produce his certificate at the next hearing of the matter.

The magistrate refused to proceed with the trial without Nelson's certificate. He requested the prosecutor to suggest a date for the remand of the case. Nelson informed the court that he was unavailable on the first date suggested by the prosecutor due to a court appearance in another matter. Declaring 'I am not interested in you', the magistrate remanded the case to the date suggested by the prosecutor. *Sotto voce*, Nelson asked the prosecutor if they could postpone instead to one day later. The prosecutor agreed, as is common court etiquette, and recommended the postponement to the alternative date, causing the magistrate to shake his head rudely.

Nelson then stood up and requested that the reason for the remand together with his offer to produce his certificate at a later date be recorded. The magistrate ordered him to sit down. Still on his feet, Nelson repeated his request. Incensed, the magistrate threatened to throw him out of court and lock him up if he did not sit down by the count of three. As Nelson slowly sat, the magistrate warned him to be very careful or he would get him into trouble. He adjourned the case. Nelson picked up his file and, without the customary bow, left the courtroom. The magistrate pursued him into the corridor to warn him that he would go to jail if he were impertinent to the court. 'You will find it very difficult to do that,' Nelson retorted, striding off.

Two weeks later, on the agreed date, Nelson returned to the Kempton Park Magistrates' Court with his certificate, and the trial began. The complainant, Elias Songwane, testified for the prosecution that the accused had extorted six pounds from him for a work permit. Nelson began his cross-examination by asking Songwane how exactly the accused had forced him to pay the money. Immediately, the magistrate interrupted the proceedings to disallow the question and warn Nelson not to put any irrelevant questions to the complainant. Nelson attempted to justify the question, but the magistrate cut him short. 'I warned you not to ask irrelevant questions and I won't have any nonsense from you. Proceed. Ask your next question!' When Nelson hesitated, the magistrate actually shouted, 'Ask your next question!'

Instead, Nelson calmly requested that his original question, together with the ruling that it was inadmissible, be recorded.

'I do not take any instructions from you,' Dormehl snapped back.

'Your Worship makes it very difficult for me to proceed if I am not allowed to put questions and you refuse to record the questions asked and the rulings given.'

49

'If you are going to take this attitude,' the magistrate threatened, 'I shall record every question you put and every answer to show how irrelevant your questions are.'

Nelson replied that this would suit him fine and agreed to proceed on this basis.

He had hardly restarted his cross-examination when the magistrate again interrupted him to declare his question irrelevant. Once more, Nelson argued the merits of the question and insisted that it be recorded. Once more, the magistrate told him that he did not take orders from him and instructed him to sit down. Nelson said that he would not sit down until he had finished his cross-examination, provoking a very un-magisterial: 'Hey you, I told you to sit down!' Turning to the court orderly, the magistrate commanded, 'Get this man to sit down.' Even more slowly this time, Nelson sat.

When Dormehl wanted to know if Nelson had any more questions for the witness, Nelson only asked that his earlier questions be recorded. Dormehl shouted, 'I am giving you a final warning. If you don't listen you will get into trouble.'

Nelson repeated his earlier question: how did the accused force the complainant to pay the money?

At this, Dormehl threatened to discharge the witness if Nelson persisted with 'these irrelevant questions'. When Nelson insisted that the question should be allowed, Dormehl said, 'Hey you, I have warned you before not to ask these irrelevant questions and if you persist I will have you thrown out of this court. Do you hear?' With that he adjourned the court.

After the adjournment, Nelson asked the witness the same question again. The magistrate lost all remaining composure. Leaping up from his bench he yelled at Nelson, 'Hey you, sit down!' To the witness he said, 'You! Go.' Nelson objected and pointed out that it was irregular for the court to dismiss a witness before counsel had completed the cross-examination. Dormehl would not listen. 'Hey you, I told you to sit down. Will you sit down? I will count up to three and if you are still standing when I have counted three I will call the orderly to eject you from the court. One. Two. Three. Get this man out!' This time Nelson waited until the orderly was a hair's breadth away before, with the speed and agility of an amateur boxer, he sat.

When the magistrate called the next witness, Nelson addressed the court. 'In view of Your Worship's attitude, I find it impossible to proceed with the case for the following reasons—' At which the magistrate interrupted to ask if he was withdrawing from the case. Before Nelson could provide the reasons why he felt that he had no other course but to withdraw, he was again instructed to sit down. The magistrate then turned to Nelson's client, Elliot Setoaba, and asked him if he wanted the case to proceed or if he wished for an adjournment to find another lawyer. When Setoaba insisted that he did not want to change his attorney, he was given short shrift by the magistrate. 'You must get another attorney.'

Dormehl was about to adjourn the matter when Nelson again stood up and asked that the reasons why he could not proceed be recorded. Again he was forced to sit down or be thrown out of court, and the matter was remanded.

Displaying none of the hot indignation that his account elicited in me, Nelson calmly asked my opinion on how best to take the matter forward. We discussed a number of options, including approaching the press or reporting the magistrate to the Department of Justice. In the end, Nelson agreed to my suggestion that his client petition the Supreme Court for the recusal of the magistrate for racist behaviour and for the proceedings to be set aside.

A few days later, Setoaba signed the petition. He contended that the magistrate had objected to his being represented by a black attorney, but that he did not want to be defended by anyone other than Nelson Mandela. He asked that the magistrate be replaced, the proceedings set aside and that Dormehl pay the costs of the application.

In his affidavit in support of the petition, Nelson wrote: 'Magistrate Dormehl must find it offensive to mention my name because during the proceedings he preferred to use the word "you" or more often, "Hey, you" in order to draw attention to what [he] was saying. I say further that it is most unlikely that [he] did not know that I was practising as an attorney as my name had often appeared in the press and in the law reports. [His] requests that I should produce my authority was, in my respectful submission, made solely for the purpose of embarrassing me and not for the purpose of satisfying himself about the appearance of unqualified persons.'

The petition was served on the magistrate and the attorney general, as first and second respondents respectively. The attorney general was quick to indicate that he would abide by the decision of the court. Not so Dormehl, who opposed the petition, denying all the allegations. He submitted that the sole reason he had refused to record Nelson's arguments was because he had not been accepted as the attorney of record. He tendered a number of affidavits from the court orderly, the prosecutor and other witnesses present on the day, some of which claimed that 'die naturel' (the 'native') had his hands in his pockets on occasion in court – apparent proof that Nelson had not shown any respect for the magistrate.

These additional affidavits were served on us on the day before the hearing and meant that we would have to seek a postponement in order to reply to them. We sent a colleague in Pretoria to attend to these formalities. Judge Quartus de Wet presided in the Pretoria Motion Court. He had an abrupt, no-nonsense approach and was known for his intolerance of peremptory behaviour by officials. Nine years later, he would sentence Nelson to life imprisonment. On this occasion, he defended his dignity.

The judge called the parties into his chambers. He addressed our counsel first to ask why the matter was improperly on the Motion Court roll when it had to be heard before two judges. Our correspondent's lack of a ready answer was of no matter because the judge had already impatiently turned to Dormehl's advocate, a Mr Myburgh from the Pretoria Bar. 'What is your client up to?' Without so much as a glance at the affidavits that Myburgh handed him, De Wet stuck them back in the file and demanded, 'Tell me, Myburgh, why did he [Dormehl] ask Mandela to produce his certificate? I would have thought that everyone knows that Mandela is an attorney?' Myburgh dutifully relayed his instructions that the magistrate simply could not believe that Nelson was an attorney as he had come into the court in 'such an arrogant manner'. The judge would have none of it. 'I do not think that many of my brother judges will believe him, Myburgh. You'll know what to tell the magistrate. The matter is not properly before me. It should be before two judges. I do not want it mentioned in court. This is the sort of thing that brings the administration of justice in our country into disrepute. Myburgh, tell your client that the quicker he recuses himself from this case, the better for all concerned.'

And that was the end of the matter.

A few days later, we received notice from the state attorney that Dormehl would recuse himself and that the trial would start anew with another magistrate. Nelson did not attend court to witness the recusal. He briefed me to represent Setoaba in the new trial. The man's guilt or innocence remains undecided as he was killed in a railway accident before the trial could be concluded. Magistrate Dormehl stayed on in his court and no doubt continued presiding with prejudice.

Nelson and I gave our small victory the nod by sharing a mincemeat curry at the rose-tinted, fairy-light-strewn Kapitan's restaurant on Kort Street, around the corner from his office.

After this, I became the junior counsel of choice for Nelson.

It was a sign of the times that my briefs were not limited to the firm's clients but that I would represent both of Nelson's clerks, Godfrey Pitje and Douglas Lukele, in similar racist incidents in the Magistrates' Courts.

Godfrey had been the principal of a school before resigning in protest at the Bantu education system. Although he was just a clerk, he was my senior in years, and a seasoned activist. He was not easily intimidated. Oliver Tambo had asked Godfrey to stand in for him in a remanded matter before a Boksburg magistrate, a Mr F.A.H. Johl. At the first appearance, the magistrate had instructed Oliver to sit at a small table in his court reserved for 'non-European' lawyers. Oliver objected and applied for the magistrate to recuse himself on the grounds of racial bias. The magistrate refused and Oliver approached me to launch an application similar to that against Dormehl. We were unable to get the consent of the client, one Stefaans Niekerk, before the next hearing and so Godfrey appeared on his behalf. In the courtroom, the interpreter asked Godfrey to sit at the special table. Godfrey ignored him and took his place at the well-worn table used by 'European' lawyers.

When the magistrate saw Godfrey at the wrong table, he instructed him to move. Godfrey asked why.

'I say sit there,' ordered Johl. 'This is my court and I am not going to argue.'

'Is that an order of court?' asked Godfrey.

'Yes, this is an order of the court.'

'But surely, sir, I am entitled to an explanation.'

'If you persist I shall fine you five pounds for contempt of court.'

'Will you please note my protest, sir?'

'I shall not listen to you as long as you are standing there.' Johl pointed at the large table.

'Then I have no option but to withdraw from this case,' Godfrey replied.

'You may do so if you please,' Johl retorted.

Godfrey asked to be excused and then left the courtroom. In the corridor, the court orderly caught up with him and demanded payment of the five-pound fine. Godfrey disputed that a fine had been imposed – as far as he was concerned, he had only been warned. He was promptly arrested and taken to the cells for contempt of court. Although he was prepared to spend five days in jail in protest at his treatment, the fine was paid on his behalf and he was released.

Godfrey and Oliver consulted with me and we resolved to appeal the conviction and fine. In his affidavit, Godfrey explained that he wanted only to address the magistrate from the table at which all legal practitioners sat:

My intentions in attempting to ascertain from the magistrate the reason I was to be confined to what is referred to as a small table was because I had good reason to believe that the special treatment meted out to me was because I am an African. If the magistrate had told me that that was the reason, it was my intention to tell the magistrate that neither I nor my client would feel that he had been defended in his best possible interests if he was to be defended by me, and for that reason I was going to withdraw. I intended also to say that I was not aware of any statutory provision, or any other law, which entitled the magistrate to order me to take a specific place or compel me to assume such a place.

In his affidavit, Magistrate Johl argued that '[t]he table I asked Mr Pitje to occupy is a brand new heavy kiaat table, clean and clear...an exact replica of the larger table in a smaller size. The chair is a padded chair...' He went on to lament that Mr Pitje had refused to comply with an order of court and surely this was a wilful refusal and must of necessity bring the presiding magistrate into disrepute. Johl continued:

> Had Mr Pitje occupied the smaller table at my initial request nothing would have been said and to me it is indifferent whether the defending attorney is a European or a non-European. Both are accorded a deferential hearing...This being a special case it seems to me natural that Mr Tambo, when he instructed his junior Mr Pitje to appear, must have warned him what to expect and advised him on his course of action...His protestations etc must have been preconceived and in consequence his disobedience was most certainly wilful.

Judges Piet Cillié and Wes Boshoff, early Nationalist appointees to the bench, presided over the appeal to the Transvaal Provincial Division. The attorney general of the Transvaal, Rudolf Rein QC, who rarely entered a courtroom, appeared for the Crown. Despite these warning signs, we were fairly confident the appeal would be allowed and the conviction set aside. We argued that Godfrey had not had a proper hearing on two grounds: the failure to allow him to explain why he was not prepared to move to the smaller table and the fact that the order was incompetent because it was based on racial discrimination. For this I relied on precedents in the Court of Appeal that supported the submission that it was unreasonable to deal unequally with practitioners equally entitled to practise in the courts. Judge Boshoff immediately challenged both arguments.

'But there is no evidence that the table set aside for the appellant was in any way inferior to the table set aside for European practitioners,' he said.

'But, M'Lord, we are surely not concerned with the quality of the wood,' I replied. 'We are surely concerned with the feelings, the perceptions of our colleagues and their clients who are parties to the litigation. They must surely feel offended by being treated differently.'

'Differently, but equally, Mr Bizos. Surely there is nothing wrong with that?'

'But, M'Lord, there is good authority that separate cannot be equal.'

'Authorities in our courts, Mr Bizos? I'd like to be referred to them.'

'No, M'Lord, not in our courts, but in *Brown* v *Board of Education of Topeka*—'

'Well, if it's not in our courts then it's no authority, Mr Bizos. The dicta that you rely on from Rasool and Abdurahman were made in 1934 and 1950. Has what was said in those courts any application now that our Legislature, in its wisdom, has passed the Separate Amenities Act?'

'M'Lord, there is no suggestion that the magistrate acted in terms of the Separate Amenities Act. In terms of that Act notices have got to be put up. It can hardly be argued that powers given to local authorities and other public bodies to segregate parks and toilets should be used in a courtroom.'

'No, you don't seem to understand my point, Mr Bizos. The question is whether this was a reasonable order or not which had to be obeyed, or was so unreasonable an order that it could be defied. The fact that a democratically elected Legislature passed an Act authorising segregation is surely more than adequate evidence of the reasonableness of separating people on the grounds of colour?'

I decided that this was not the time to debate with his Lordship the meaning of the term 'democratic'.

The attorney general noted his regret that the appellant sought to politicise a matter that was 'nothing more than a convenient arrangement of the courtroom to comply with government policy and the general practises of the community'.

Our appeal was dismissed. The court accepted the magistrate's version of events and held that his request was not unreasonable. Godfrey's conduct was 'calculated to bring the administration of justice into disrepute and indicated his contempt of the order'. He was guilty of misbehaviour, which entitled the court to sentence him for contempt.

Judge Boshoff, together with Judge Lammie Snyman, granted our application for leave to appeal to the Appellate Division in Bloemfontein. The appeal was presided over by Chief Justice Lucas Steyn, together with Judges Hoexter, Van Blerk, Ogilvie-Thompson and Botha. I tried to advance our argument by deracialising it. I submitted that a woman advocate would be entitled to object to separate tables for women lawyers. Chief Justice Steyn remarked that he would see nothing wrong with a ruling like this. Judge Hoexter chastised me: 'Mr Bizos, similes are for poets. Let's go down to the facts of the case.'

Six days after the hearing, the chief justice delivered a unanimous judgment finding Godfrey guilty of contempt.

A magistrate like other judicial functionaries is in control of his courtroom and of the proceedings therein. Matters incidental to such proceedings if they are not regulated by law are largely within his discretion. The only ground on which the exercise of that discretion and the legal competence of the order might in this instance be called in question, would be unreasonableness arising from alleged inequality in the treatment of practitioners equally entitled to practise in the Magistrates' Court... From the record it is clear that a practitioner would in every way be as well seated at the one table as at the other and that he could not possibly have been hampered in the slightest in the conduct of his case by having to use a particular table. Although I accept that no action was taken under the 1953 Act, the fact that such action could have been taken is not entirely irrelevant. It shows that the distinction drawn by provision of separate tables in this Magistrates' Court is of a nature sanctioned by the Legislature and makes it more difficult to attack the validity of the magistrate's order on the grounds of unreasonableness. The order was, I think, a competent order...

The legal fraternity was silent in response to this condonation of avant-garde apartheid by the highest court in the land. Despite the ruling, however, this form of petty apartheid was not followed in most courts in the country. Administrative directions must have been issued cautioning magistrates not to follow Magistrate Johl's example.

Godfrey eventually became the president of the Black Lawyers Association. Some thirty years later, in 1987, he was called upon to thank the American Bar Association (ABA) for inviting members of the South African judiciary and the Bar to their annual conference. In his address, he alluded to the discrimination still experienced by black lawyers: 'We want to thank the ABA for inviting us to its conference. It gave us an opportunity to meet some of our judges.'

Douglas Lukele, the other clerk at Mandela and Tambo, also qualified as an attorney. His objection to racial discrimination by a presiding officer had more serious consequences. In a Bethlehem Magistrates' Court he was ordered to sit at a separate table reserved for 'non-white' lawyers. He refused and was forcibly removed from the court. He briefed me and we issued summonses against both the magistrate and the court orderly. Douglas, a Swazi citizen, was promptly arrested, detained and then deported from South Africa.

There was an occasion, however, when we did not object. One Saturday, I went with Nelson's partner, the gentlemanly Oliver Tambo, to the home of Judge Tos Bekker to apply for a stay of execution on behalf of the family of a young man who was due to be hanged on the Monday. While I shared crumpets and tea with the judge, the attorney general's representative and the secretary of justice in the warmth of the family home, Oliver sat alone outside. Concerned not to endanger the success of our application, we said nothing in protest at the casual racism of our colleagues. Oliver simply waited in the car until I emerged and gave him the thumbs-up; whereupon, without any trace of bitterness, he jumped out to embrace me.

When I was not fighting for the right of the lawyers at Mandela and Tambo to discharge their professional responsibilities, I was kept busy with their clients. Much of our work was aimed at resisting the neurotic reach of the extensive apartheid laws introduced by the enthusiastic minister of native affairs, Hendrik Verwoerd. Those charged would rarely pay an admission-of-guilt fine. Instead, Mandela and Tambo would be called and a brief would be directed to His Majesty's Building, where the advocates were housed.

Our cases involving the cultural clubs were a good example. Prior to the introduction of the Bantu Education Act 47 of 1953, the vast majority of African schools in the country were state-aided mission schools. The Act transferred control of African education to the Bantu education department, made it an offence punishable by a fine or imprisonment to run any Bantu or native school without proper authority, and empowered the minister of native affairs to close down any school he deemed not in the 'interests of the Bantu people'. Minister Verwoerd elaborated on these interests. It was not in the interests of the Bantu to 'participate in a school system which drew him away from his own country and misled him by showing him the green pastures of European society in which he was not allowed to graze' or 'to be taught to expect to live his adult life under a policy of equal rights as there was no place for him in the European community above the levels of certain forms of labour'.

By 1955, the Nationalist government had exclusive control of African education. A school boycott resulted in the expulsion of more than seven thousand students and the firing of more than a hundred teachers. The African Education Movement was formed to resolve the crisis. It established 'cultural clubs', carefully designed to avoid prosecution while offering an imperfect alternative to the limited Bantu education curriculum of basic literacy and numeracy. The clubs were frequently raided and any teachers present would be arrested and charged with unlawfully conducting an unregistered school. Merely conveying information was, however, not (yet) a crime and the convenors of the clubs devised strategies, often largely semantic, to ensure that the clubs fell outside of the ambit of the Act. Members were not taught, but rather 'participated' in cultural activities with club leaders, and there was no syllabus, no textbooks and no blackboards.

My first case with Nelson under the Act was on behalf of a cultural club in Alexandra township. The courtroom was packed with international press gathered to report on the extraordinary spectacle of a government sending a teacher to prison for keeping children off the streets while imparting knowledge to them. Nelson, Oliver and I, together with the attorney Shulamith Muller, researched dictionaries and cases that dealt with the proper legal meanings of terms like 'school' and 'education'. The *Oxford Dictionary* definition of a 'school' as an 'establishment in which boys or girls receive instruction' was of help.

The witness for the prosecution, an Afrikaans policeman, described what he had seen under a tree in the veld on the outskirts of the township. Under cross-examination he confirmed the absence of any educational aids. We argued that this did not meet the criteria for either an 'establishment' or a 'school'. The accused was found not guilty and discharged. Pending prosecutions in Benoni, Soweto, Nelspruit and Kliptown were dropped.

The testimony of an eighteen-year-old police 'plant' in a Benoni court several months later marked the beginning of the end for the clubs. The policeman, who had joined the club undercover as a student, recounted details of the furtively distributed worksheets and handed in a number of exhibits. When a school inspector testified for the prosecution that the contents of a geography lesson on Egypt titled 'The Pharaoh and his daughter' were of such a high standard that he intended to recommend the introduction of some of the material into the Bantu education curriculum, we were in little doubt of the outcome. The accused was convicted and fined, and given a warning by the magistrate that next time he would be imprisoned. One after the other, the cultural clubs closed.

The Native Administration Act of 1927 provided for the administration of black affairs by proclamation. I was instructed by Mandela and Tambo to appeal the conviction of five of their clients – Tanci and four others – in terms of a notice under the Act prohibiting gatherings at which more than ten black people were present. Our clients had organised a meeting to protest the Peri-Urban Areas Board taking over the administration of Alexandra and had not applied for permission. There were more than ten people present.

Our first ground of appeal failed. Judges Galgut and Theron dismissed our argument that the government notice that granted absolute discretion to a native commissioner or magistrate to ban a meeting was an invalid delegation of authority. They found that the official's discretion was sufficiently limited as the regulation specified the prohibition of a very limited type of gathering.

Our second succeeded. We argued that, while the Native Administration Act of 1927 prohibited gatherings of natives, the notice under which our clients had been convicted prohibited gatherings at which more than ten natives were present. Properly construed, the notice prohibited any meeting, including a meeting of white people, at which more than ten natives were in attendance. The judges agreed that the Act was clearly intended to refer to meetings only attended by natives – the fact that the notice could affect meetings of whites as well meant that it exceeded the scope of the powers conferred on it. The conviction of Tanci and the others was overturned.

Timothy Fefo Rampai was an ANC activist in Germiston. The local authority served him with an eviction notice from his home in terms of the Blacks (Urban Areas) Consolidation Act 25 of 1945 for his political

activities. Two weeks later, he was sentenced to three weeks' imprisonment with hard labour and ordered to leave the area on his release. Nelson was concerned about the implications of this case for both his client
and the future of local ANC committees and grassroots organisations.
In response to his request for the council to furnish the details of his
client's wrongdoing, he was simply advised that Rampai had shown
opposition to the law and organised a campaign to defy legislation.

Nelson briefed me in the matter. We requested the minutes of the
special meeting convened by the local authority to banish our client from
his home. The minutes reflected that the council had been split down the
middle – with the five National Party members for and the five United
Party members against his expulsion. The mayor had cast the deciding
vote. They also revealed that the councillors had failed to conduct a
proper investigation to determine whether Rampai's presence in the area
was detrimental to the peace, or to afford him an opportunity to reply to
any allegations. We argued that the council had not acted in terms of
the provisions of the Act and had not had sufficient information to properly consider or decide the merits of the case. The magistrate rejected
our argument and upheld the decision of the local authority.

We lodged an appeal. The magistrate was required to give written
reasons for his decision. He phoned me and asked if I would repeat our
argument very slowly. He transcribed what I said word for word and
simply appended his written reasons as 'There is no substance whatever
in this argument'.

On appeal, Judge Bekker, together with Judge Steyn, set aside Rampai's
conviction on the grounds that the local authority misunderstood the
legislation it was administering and therefore its decision was invalid.
Rampai was allowed to return to his home, and to Nelson's great relief
the provision was rarely invoked in the future.

I was often impressed by the resourcefulness of our clients. A good
example of this was a quick-witted community leader we defended.

As the supreme chief of all the African people in South Africa, the
governor general could make laws without consulting either his subjects

or parliament. Under these powers he passed a law banning meetings of more than ten natives in a reserved area without prior permission from the native commissioner. The only exceptions to this prohibition were meetings presided over by the government-appointed chief and religious gatherings.

I was briefed in one such matter in which there was irrefutable evidence of both a meeting of more than ten people and the absence of the chief. Our client had only one possible defence.

'But what made it a religious meeting?' I asked him. 'Did you have a Bible with you? Did you read from it?'

'It was not necessary to read from it. Everyone knew chapter five of the Lamentations of Jeremiah by heart,' he replied wryly and quoted:

> Remember, O Lord, what is come upon us: consider, and behold our
>   reproach.
> Our inheritance is turned to strangers, our houses to aliens.
> We are orphans and fatherless, our mothers are as widows.
> We have drunken our water for money; our wood is sold unto us.
> Our necks are under persecution: we labour and have no rest...

Our defence failed. The magistrate did not indicate in his judgment whether it was the evidence that the meeting called for a minimum wage of one pound a day or protested the extension of pass laws to women that decided him. I suspect it may have been the shouts of 'Africa Mayibuye' (Bring back Africa) at the meeting that did it.

Creative problem-solving was not the sole preserve of Nelson's political clients.

Vark and Banda were two criminal clients of Mandela and Tambo. Their striking appearances – Vark (Pig) bore an unfortunate resemblance to the farm animal of the same name, while Banda was uncannily similar to the then president of Malawi, Hastings Banda – rendered them rather conspicuous partners in crime. When a concession store on a mine was robbed by two armed young black men, Detective Warrant Officer van der Linde immediately ordered his detective constable: 'Go and get Vark and Banda.' They arrived handcuffed to one another. Van der Linde, a large, lanky man, did not beat about the bush. 'Where's the money?' he demanded and banged their heads together. A search of their pockets revealed a receipt for fifty pounds from the law offices of Mandela and Tambo. The policeman threatened to break their necks if they did not disclose the location of the money. He placed them in separate cells and assaulted Vark, but to no avail. After just a few blows, Banda confessed to the policeman that the money and the gun were hidden at Mandela's offices. He agreed to sign a sworn statement to the effect that, in keeping with the policy of the firm, the money and the gun were stored for safe-keeping in a small room at Mandela and Tambo.

Van der Linde was thrilled. Without further delay, he took Banda and his statement to the offices of Mandela and Tambo. Depositing his prisoner in the crowded reception room, he barged into Nelson's office, triumphantly waving the statement and demanding that he produce the money and the gun. From the reception room, Banda called for Nelson. Nelson pushed past the preening policeman to find his client most apologetic. He was terribly sorry for involving Mr Mandela as he had, but it was the only way he thought he could stop the police from torturing him and his friend. Nelson returned with Banda to his office and ordered Van der Linde to leave. 'I will send a doctor to examine the two suspects. They had better appear in court in the next forty-eight hours,' he told the deflated detective. Nelson was still chuckling when he called me on the phone and briefed me.

Because of his particular interest in the matter, Nelson assisted me in the trial. Percy Yutar was the prosecutor. This was the first time that the three of us were to meet in court. The next would be when Yutar was calling for the death sentence to be imposed on Nelson at the Rivonia Trial. This initial encounter would serve Nelson and me well.

Yutar had a doctorate in law and referred to himself, as did many judges, as 'Dr' Yutar. His less experienced juniors, including me, held him in awe for his quick wit, irony and attention to detail. He was known as

zealous and hardworking, but I now discovered that he was also obse-
quious with a tendency to over-elaboration. More importantly for later
purposes, it was my first experience of his vanity and political fervour.

I called Banda as my first witness. When he testified about his ruse to
get the police to take him to see Mandela I noticed the shadow of a smile
cross Judge Joseph Francis Ludorf's face. Nevertheless, he interrupted my
questions relating to the assaults by the police and determined that the
evidence was not relevant to the case as no confessions had been extracted.

This was not enough for Yutar. He, too, objected to the evidence: 'I
trust that his Lordship will not allow the court to be used to besmirch
the good name of a fine officer who had so competently, so efficiently
and so fairly conducted this investigation.'

Outside court, Yutar turned on Nelson and me. 'Why do the two of
you want to introduce this sort of irrelevant matter into this case?' he
demanded. 'I warn you there may be serious consequences if you persist in playing to the gallery and the newspapers by making false and
unfounded allegations against the police.'

In the end, Judge Ludorf found Vark and Banda guilty and they were
sentenced to comparatively short sentences of six years' imprisonment.
Nelson and I had mixed feelings about our clients, but entertained no
ambivalence about either Yutar or Judge Ludorf, both of whom we were
to meet again.

My briefs from Mandela and Tambo, as well as those from the attorney Shulamith Muller, sent me to remote Magistrates' Courts across the
country. The rural courts were strictly segregated: two entrances, two
witness boxes and two public galleries. The black galleries would usually
be packed with neatly dressed middle-aged men, while the white side
would remain almost empty. It was the practice to dispense of the cases
involving whites first, so by mid-morning there would be no one sitting
on the one side of the court, while those who could not fit into the black
side would be forced outside. These courts were usually presided over by
magistrates whose English was as rudimentary as their legal training.
My command of Afrikaans was of little assistance and often served only

to widen the divide between my rural fraternity and me. Lawyers from Johannesburg were often as unpopular as their clients. My colleagues would not greet me and the local traffic police would regularly find cause to fine me for minor traffic infractions, such as not parking my Morris Minor dead centre in a parking space or having mud on my number plate.

Occasionally, Arethe would accompany me and sit silently sketching in the back of the courtroom. Usually, however, I went on my own. On return from my trips into the hinterland, I would often meet Nelson for a meal. We were opportune companions – Nelson, restricted to the Johannesburg area since 1953, was hungry for news from the countryside, while I, newly returned from the solitude of my small-town alienation, was eager to talk about my cases. Our meals were convivial and extended.

Apartheid Johannesburg offered us only two choices of venue – upstairs at Kapitan's or downstairs in the Little Swallow on Commissioner Street. Thankfully they were both good. Nelson was a habitué of the festive Kapitan's, the city's oldest Indian restaurant. Across the road from the central police headquarters on Commissioner Street, the Little Swallow was reputed to be the oldest Chinese restaurant in Johannesburg. Its Cantonese owners turned a blind eye to our breach of the law prohibiting blacks and whites from eating together. The policemen who from time to time wandered in extended us the same courtesy.

Nelson was particularly interested in my cases with the Bafurutse in North West (then the Western Transvaal) and in Sekhukhuneland in Limpopo (then the Northern Transvaal). These mostly involved revolts by the communities against the extension of passes to women and the removal or banishment of their chiefs by the Bantu authorities for supporting the resistance of their people.

The first was in Lichtenburg in the then Western Transvaal at the initiative of Ruth First, at the time a journalist for the *New Age*. In their wisdom, leading ethnologists and native commissioners had identified Setswana-speaking women in the 'tranquil' rural areas as the most docile in the land and recommended to the government that it start the implementation of the extension of passes to women there. They were mistaken.

Angry protests erupted and four men were killed and a number of women were injured when police baton-charged and shot at an anti-pass march. Eighteen men were arrested and charged with public violence. Ruth was convinced that the charges were trumped up and that the police action was cold-blooded murder.

When I told him about this case, Nelson could not conceal his gentle amusement at my concern about my unwitting contravention of the section of the Prisons Act that prohibited introducing drugs, dagga or tobacco into a prison. At the end of my first consultation with the accused, I had left them my still-full packet of fifty cigarettes. At my next visit, they reported to me that the cigarettes had been confiscated. Not long afterwards, the honorary secretary of the Bar Council, Chris Plewman, told me that the attorney general had notified him that I was guilty of an offence. The attorney general had elected not to prosecute, but asked the Bar Council to warn its members that a more serious view would be taken if the offence were repeated. Nelson dismissed the matter as absurd, but I was more concerned, and although I continued offering cigarettes to my clients until I stopped smoking some ten years later, I never again left a box without the consent of their jailers.

In the Lichtenburg case, my clients protested their innocence. At the preparatory examination, more than a dozen policemen testified and described in near-identical terms how they had been compelled to open fire in self-defence after the 'murderous' crowd attacked them. Cross-examination revealed that none of the policemen had been injured. The police officers were as unanimous in denying that their captain had threatened the crowd with violence of any kind. This was somewhat contradicted by the captain who testified last and could not explain why none of his men had heard him loudly and clearly warn the crowd to disperse or violence would be used to break up the demonstration as required by the provisions of the Riotous Assemblies Act.

Nelson had a dry sense of humour. He was not one to laugh in a hearty manner, but he would let out an abrupt 'ha' at times, particularly at his own jokes. My story of the evidence of a surprise witness – the

Afrikaans bus owner and driver who transported the people to and from the township – elicited such a 'ha'. The elderly witness testified that he was as fluent in Setswana as he was in Afrikaans and easily confirmed the identity of most of the accused, particularly Accused Number 1, a certain Solomon Moseshe. He told the court that he had heard him shout 'A re ye, a re ye, re ilo lolaya mapolesa' (Come, come, let's go and kill the police) just prior to the attack.

The matter was remitted to a magistrate for trial. Moseshe insisted that the bus driver did not speak Setswana. During my cross-examination, I asked the bus driver to read from a Tswana bible. He could not, he explained, because he only *spoke* Setswana, he could not read it. When the interpreter read the verse, the bus driver was unable to say what it meant. I passed the interpreter a piece of paper with two sentences to read out to the court. 'A re ye, a re ye, mapolesa a tlilo re bolaya' (Come, come, the police are going to kill us), and 'A re ye, a re ye, re ilo lolaya mapolesa' (Come, come, let's go and kill the police).

The witness said that they meant the same thing.

The accused were also not very satisfactory witnesses, but the magistrate found them not guilty and discharged them. Significantly, he held that the evidence of the police had been contradictory, improbable and unreliable. This was unusual. At the time, and for a long time to come, few magistrates would disbelieve or question the credibility of a police witness.

Soon after this case ended, Shulamith Muller briefed me to represent twenty-five men and women in Zeerust. When the Bafurutse chief, Abram Moiloa, was deposed and banished by the native commissioner for his defiance of orders to issue passes to women, the tribe convened a kgotla and sentenced four men to death for treason. Twenty-five members of the tribe were charged with incitement to murder, public violence, inciting persons to burn their pass books and, most unusually, *crimen laesae majestatis*, for usurping the function of the state and establishing a court. The newly admitted Ismail Mahomed appeared with me on behalf of the accused. The *crimen laesae majestatis* charge was eventually dropped and in the end only five of the accused were convicted and sentenced to relatively lenient sentences. I believe that this was, to some extent, because of the evidence given in mitigation by the local Anglican priest, Father Charles Hooper, who had taught me English at Wits.

In our subsequent trials, most of the women charged with burning their pass books were acquitted – usually because of the inexperience of the prosecutor, the sloppiness of the police work or the lack of sophistication of the magistrate, rather than my forensic skills.

To deal with the situation, a senior magistrate was brought from Pretoria and a prosecutor from Johannesburg. The prosecution team had what they thought was a watertight case that would put an end to pass burning. I represented Gertrude Mpekwa and two others charged on nine counts of contravening the sections of the Criminal Law Amendment Act promulgated in 1953 in response to the Defiance Campaign. They faced up to three years' imprisonment on each count 'committed...by way of protest against the law or in support of any campaign against any law'. When I first met the magistrate, I responded to his Afrikaans greeting in English. During the trial, he refused my request to conduct the debate in English, and insisted on questioning me in Afrikaans. He convicted the accused and imposed heavy jail sentences, which were all set aside on appeal before Judge de Wet and Judge Trollip.

Protests against passes spread to other Bafurutse villages. The government appointed a one-man commission of inquiry into the origin of the troubles, headed by Harry Balk, a native divorce-court judge. Shulamith and I arrived at the small office of the native commissioner in Zeerust where the semi-private hearing was to take place, accompanied by the hundreds of men and women that we represented. We demanded a public hearing, forcing the inquiry to move outside onto the veranda and into the dusty courtyard. The native commissioner was the first witness. He claimed that ANC agitators from Johannesburg had incited women not to carry their passes and had disrupted the tranquillity of the area. He blamed Father Hooper for allowing his rectory to become a gathering place to defy the law. He then pronounced Shulamith and me guilty as well for our roles in coming from Johannesburg to secure the acquittal of the accused and for encouraging others to disrespect the law. My angry response on the duty of lawyers was widely published in the media, but I was not given the opportunity to cross-examine the witness – the chairman ruled that I could not do so as we had not made it clear whom we represented or how the evidence could affect them. As there was no useful purpose in our remaining at the hearing, we left, declaring that we would return to lead our own witnesses.

At the next scheduled date for the hearing, the police, army and air force had taken to the roads and skies. Roadblocks were set up and those without passes were arrested. Others were turned back. It was clear that neither our clients nor our representations were welcome, and we abandoned the effort.

I discussed all of these cases with Nelson. He and the ANC were concerned about the levels of violence in the rural areas, where, far from the scrutiny of the media, people were arrested, beaten, tortured and even murdered. And yet still they resisted at great personal cost.

When Abram Moiloa's successor, Chief Boas Moiloa, invited me to become an honorary member of the Bafurutse, I was reminded of Jim and told Nelson my story about him. Jim was the black driver of my erstwhile Greek employer, George Caratasis, who had changed his name to Caradas. I had worked as a shop assistant at his Parkgate Café, laying the table for breakfast and handing up loaves of bread and milk to the customers. I never knew Jim's surname, and although he was already a grown man, he was referred to only as the shop 'boy'. Like me, Jim stayed in a small room at the back of the shop – somehow his was even smaller than my own tiny one. Unlike me, Jim was not permitted to make use of the upstairs communal shower, so he washed in a galvanised-iron bathtub outside.

Jim accompanied Mr Caradas on his daily trips from one shop to the other to deliver goods and take orders. In the large sedan motorcar, Caradas would sing Greek freedom songs. In his deep baritone, Jim would hum and, eventually, sing along. He soon knew most of the words. During our evenings together in the café backyard, he and I would sing the same songs. One evening, I translated them for him. 'Hey, this man wrote for us as well!' he exclaimed in wonder.

Nelson and I had both been influenced by stories of conquest from our childhood and were emboldened by our ancestral mythologies. Although Nelson was never in line for succession to the Thembu throne, his father was the great-grandson of King Ngubengcuka, and considered his a royal family under an occupying force, as their powers had been circumscribed since 1832; first by the British government, then after 1910 by the new Union of South Africa.[14]

The province of Messenia in Greece where I was born had been colonised by Sparta. The Messenians were considered serfs or helots, the Greek word for slaves. I learnt in primary school about revolts against the Spartans and the escape from persecution of a million Greeks in Asia Minor in 1922. My family folklore was rich with stories of personal sacrifice and speaking truth to power. I was very close to my grandfather, who was a staunch supporter of the liberal democratic prime minister Eleftherios Venizelos. Although he lost his first son, my namesake George, to the First World War, my grandfather never regretted Greece's participation in the conflict.

Nelson and I were both sons of fathers that had been deposed from positions of authority when we were young: my father was forced to resign his position as mayor of our village after the dictator General Metaxas toppled Venizelos in the 1936 coup, while Nelson's father was removed as chief of his village by a local white magistrate.

Their influence in our lives was, however, as mythological as it was real. Nelson's father died when he was still a child and my relationship with my own father was strained. He had refused to intervene when a group of leaders from the Greek community complained to him about my public political positions while I was at university, but he remained disappointed with my choice of law over medicine. When I left the Hellenic Community annual ball held at the Johannesburg City Hall without dancing with a young woman to whom he had introduced me, he did not talk to me for a long while. After we reconciled, he still sat separate from Arethe at my graduation and would attend neither my engagement party nor my wedding. This would change after the birth of our eldest son, Kimon Anthony, when he became a loving grandfather, and would join us for evening strolls around Emmarentia Dam, proudly pushing his first grandson's pram.

My alienation from my father was particularly painful as ours was a family divided. It was only after the war that we heard any news from home. It came one afternoon in the form of a letter in an envelope addressed simply to 'Antonio Bizos, Johannesburg, South Africa', delivered in person to my inner-city lodgings. The conscientious postal official who brought it described how he had taken the letter from one city corner shop to another until he had been directed to me. Written in a child-like handwriting on a page torn from a ruled exercise book, my illiterate mother's note to her husband was short: 'We are well. We learnt from the Red Cross letter we received more than a year ago that you too are well. Your father died last year, happy to have heard that you had survived your journey and that you are well. Your loving wife, children and mother'.

The end of the Second World War had not ended the suffering in Greece. In fact, more people were killed in the 1946 to 1949 civil war that followed than in the war itself. Our village and extended family had been rent apart. My mother's anti-Nazi brother, my uncle Vasili Tomaras, was detained without trial for many years on Makronisos, the Greek equivalent of Robben Island, while my father's sister was married to Vongeli Christopoulos, a Nazi collaborator whose name, together with thirty others killed by the partisans, is commemorated on a memorial plaque in the church square of our village. To this day members of my family refuse to speak to one another.

Civil war was a matter that concerned both Nelson and me, and we frequently discussed its ramifications. Some commentators have claimed that Nelson's commitment to forgiveness and reconciliation was something that he mellowed into in prison, but that is not my understanding. From the very early days of our acquaintance, he was clear that black racism in retaliation for white racism would tear South Africa apart and not result in a country that was free. He believed that the challenge we confronted was to find a way for all races to live together in harmony in order to normalise our society. 'There are no winners after annihilation like that in Greece. How do we avert such a bloodbath here?' he would remark somewhat rhetorically.

It was a question we often considered over our chicken chow mein. In this, our mutual love of the classics was of some assistance.

In my opinion, Thucydides is the best historian of antiquity. He is most famous for his writings on the civil war between Sparta and Athens in the fifth century. I related to Nelson Thucydides' account of what is known as the Mytilenian debate in his *History of the Peloponnesian War*.

In 431 BC, the Spartans invaded Attica, sparking a twenty-seven-year civil war between Sparta and Athens. As revenge, the Athenian assembly passed a resolution to send the navy to Sparta-allied Mytilene on the island of Lesbos to kill all the men and sell the women and children into slavery. A trireme was dispatched to Mytilene to implement the decision.

But Diodotus called for a new gathering of the assembly to reconsider the decision and a second debate was held the next day. Diodotus was a vocal opponent of the death penalty and he called for the revocation of the harsh and inhumane punishment imposed on the Mytilenians. Warning that 'haste and anger are the two greatest obstacles to wise counsel', he argued that the issue before parliament was not whether Mytilene was guilty, or whether Athens should seek vengeance; rather it was a question of what was in Athens' best interests. He challenged the notion that the death penalty was a means of deterrence from revolt and suggested instead that the proper basis for security was good administration, not fear of legal penalties. He urged the assembly to rather do what was right and spare the Mytilenians in an effort to create an alliance. He persuaded the assembly to rescind the resolution and a ship was urgently dispatched to stop the navy.

Thucydides has Pericles commenting:

Indeed it is true that in these acts of revenge on others men take it upon themselves to begin the process of repealing these general laws of humanity which are here to give a hope of salvation to all who are in distress, instead of leaving those laws in existence, remembering that there may come a time when they too will be in danger and need their protection.

In our lawyerly quest for an understanding of the notions of justice, Nelson and I found the notion of the laws of humanity – those laws that exist for everyone's protection and require the strong to recognise that they, too, may one day be in distress and seek to rely on their universal acceptance – compelling.

I had done a course on classical life and thought for my BA degree and could recite Pericles' famous funeral oration by heart. Pericles, credited for the golden age of Greece, was also famously modest: when praised for his achievements, he said that he did what his wife told him to do and she did what her daughter told her, so it 'was a young girl that ruled Athens'.

I recited his funeral oration for Nelson:

> We are lovers of beauty without extravagance, and lovers of wisdom without effeminacy. Wealth to us is not mere material for vainglory but an opportunity for achievement; and we think poverty nothing to be ashamed of unless one makes no effort to overcome it. Our citizens attend both to public and private duties and do not allow absorption in their own affairs to diminish their knowledge of the City's business. We differ from other states in regarding the man who keeps aloof from public life not as 'private' but as useless; we decide or debate, carefully and in person, all matters of policy, and we hold, not that words and deeds go ill together, but that acts are foredoomed to failure when undertaken undiscussed. For we are noted for being at once most adventurous in action and most reflective beforehand. Other men are bold in ignorance, while reflection will stop their going forward. But the bravest

are surely those who have the clearest vision of what lies before them, glory and danger alike – and yet go forth to meet it.

When I had finished, Nelson grinned. 'That sounds just like what is needed here.'

Our mutual enthusiasm for the classical historians strengthened our friendship. Of our many shared interests this was perhaps the one that led to our most animated exchanges. We would return to the conversations that we started in the downtown dining room of the Little Swallow on many occasions over the years, and the debates of the philosophers of Ancient Greece would permeate not only our discussions, but also our decisions on legal strategy in the future. The stoics in particular had a significant influence on the development of Nelson's political views.

Our collegial lunches were short-lived as Nelson and I only had the chance to work together for a few years. The political demands on its partners probably meant that Mandela and Tambo never stood much chance of success. There was only a short four years between Nelson's conviction in the Defiance Campaign trial and the arrest of both partners for treason in 1956. The Treason Trial would take up most of the next five. In the end, Hymie Davidoff was appointed to wind up the practice. In 1960, the offices of Mandela and Tambo were closed. Soon afterwards, Nelson went underground and Oliver left the country to lead the ANC from exile.

Nelson's incapacity to practice law from prison was apparently still not enough for some members of his profession. Some ten years after the first attempt to remove him from the roll of attorneys, the Law Society filed a second application citing his conviction for sabotage and life imprisonment. From Robben Island, Nelson responded that he would need two weeks in the Pretoria court to oppose the application. He asked the commanding officer of the prison to arrange for his transfer and notified him that he would need access to the prison library. The Law Society did not proceed any further and the matter was never set down for hearing.

In a speech to the Law Society in 1993, Nelson remarked:

I was pleased to receive your invitation to open the general meeting of my chosen profession. Mind you, this was at least the third time the Law Society thought of me. The two previous invitations were delivered by the sheriff. Here I am with my name still on the roll even though I have not yet got around to applying for a fidelity certificate to go into competition with you.[15]

No longer my colleague, Nelson would become my client, a role he would perform as well as any other instructing attorney who briefed me.

TOP: Duma Nokwe.

BOTTOM: Nelson
and Winnie on their
wedding day,
June 1958.

This photo of the original one hundred and fifty-six accused in the
Treason Trial still hangs in my office.

Chapter 3

⁓

BLACK MAN
IN A WHITE MAN'S COURT
'George, I have married trouble'

In 1956, Duma Nokwe fulfilled the dream that Nelson had been forced to abandon and became the first African member of the Johannesburg Bar. At the initiative of Isie Maisels, he was invited to join our group. Nelson and I were delighted. Nelson assured him that he would not be short of briefs from Mandela and Tambo, while I invited him to hang his robes and put his few books in my chambers. Counsel chambers were located over five floors of His Majesty's Building on Commissioner Street in the city centre. There were not enough offices, so many junior members shared rooms. I belonged to a group led by Walter Pollak QC and was fortunate enough to have occupied my own offices for about eighteen months when Duma joined me.

Duma's admission as an advocate attracted the attention of the Department of Foreign Affairs. It recognised the media opportunity and published a story with a photograph of him in his gowns. *Die Transvaler* followed with a report of how some members of the Bar were unhappy to have a 'native' member of the Society of Advocates and asked whether the Native Urban Areas Act permitted Duma to rent chambers with the other advocates in the city centre. The publicity around Duma alarmed the Bar, which was accustomed to conducting its affairs quietly.

Duma had hardly settled in when a group of advocates led by Lammie Snyman and George Munnik protested against his use of the common room, the Bar library and the counsel's robing room on the grounds that it was a criminal offence under the Group Areas Act. They threatened to lay a charge against him if he continued. The Bar Council appointed a commission to hear the objections of the protestors and I appeared before it to explain my relationship with Duma. The commission recommended that Duma be regarded as a fully-fledged member of the Bar, entitled to chambers and to the full use of the library. It remained non-committal on his other rights, finding that, in light of the threats of criminal prosecution, he should use his own discretion as to whether he would make use of the common room.

We were upset by this equivocation and met with Nelson, Oliver and Walter Sisulu to discuss how Duma should respond. After a long discussion we agreed that, as distasteful as the qualifications were, the right to occupy premises and practise at the Bar were too important to forego. Ever the wise old man of the struggle, Walter summed up the issue: 'Are we to lose an opportunity to break the barrier for a cup of tea?'

A general meeting of the Bar was called to discuss the commission's recommendations. Isie Maisels QC presided and reported that the owners of the building had agreed that Duma could take office once the authorities granted the requisite permission. Balthazar John Vorster (the future prime minister) had recently left his attorney's practice in Brakpan to join the Bar. He warned that permission would not be granted for Duma to occupy chambers in a white area and recommended that he seek assistance from the Department of Native Affairs for office space in a black location. He was proved right and Duma's application for a permit was refused. Nonetheless, I put his name beneath mine on the door and he continued to share my chambers.

In December that year, at the end of a day-long court session in Klerksdorp, the presiding judge, Joseph Francis Ludorf, called me to his chambers. The *Rand Daily Mail* was leading with a story on early-morning arrests for treason. Nelson, Duma and Oliver were rumoured to be among those arrested. The judge wanted to know what my friends were up to and what evidence there was of a plan to overthrow the government by force. I knew nothing. I had been away from Johannesburg and could only shrug my shoulders.

Treason trials are a time-honoured South African tradition. Since the 1815 trial of Dutch frontiersmen revolting against British rule, charges of treason have been prosecuted against African chiefs, Boer War rebels, striking white miners and Nazi sympathisers. Judge Ludorf himself had defended Robey Leibbrandt, who was sentenced to death in 1943 for a plot to assassinate Prime Minister Smuts. The judge reminded me that Leibbrandt had refused representation in court so that he could speak his mind freely. Having said that, Ludorf stopped short and said that he should not say anything further as he might be appointed for the trial. He was right. In 1958, when the trial proper finally began, Judge Rumpff, who had been another of Leibbrandt's counsel, appointed Ludorf as an additional judge to sit on the special court constituted for the case. The bench was selected by the minister.

When I returned to chambers that evening, I discovered that one hundred and forty-four leaders from the Congress Alliance, including Nelson and Duma, had been arrested. It would be a hundred and fifty-six by the end of the week. The accused comprised the leadership of forty-eight organisations. These co-conspirators, some of whom had not met each other, included one hundred and five Africans, twenty-three whites, twenty-one Indians and seven coloureds from towns and cities across the country. The 'non-white' accused were detained at the Johannesburg prison – the Fort – for two weeks before bail was granted. Now the site of the Constitutional Court, the Fort was built by the Boers to defend Johannesburg from the British. With these arrests it became a very crowded jail. Nelson referred to their time there as 'the largest and longest unbanned meeting of the Congress Alliance in years'. During his stay in the Fort he enjoyed a freedom of association that had been denied him for some time. Typically, he would insist on wearing his suit and tie all day, and when he was not in political meetings, would consult the common-law prisoners on their cases.

The one hundred and fifty-six were charged with high treason and potentially faced the death penalty. The basis of the charge had been their involvement in the adoption of the Freedom Charter by the Congress of the People in Kliptown, outside Johannesburg, on 25 and 26 June 1955.

The proposal for a charter for South Africa akin to the Universal Declaration of Human Rights was first made to a Cape regional ANC conference in 1953 by Professor Z.K. Matthews, an academic and devout Methodist who had just returned from a visit to the United States. The proposal was taken forward by the National Action Council for the Congress Alliance, a body comprising delegates from the ANC, the South African Congress of Trade Unions, the South African Congress of Democrats, the South African Indian Congress and the South African Coloured People's Congress. A call for 'freedom demands' was made in a series of public meetings and a pamphlet titled 'Let us Speak of Freedom' was widely distributed. Proposals for the charter were written on scraps of paper, even scribbled on cigarette packs, by people across the country and collected by volunteers. These were compiled into a document by Lionel 'Rusty' Bernstein. It was called the Freedom Charter and began with the assertion: 'We, the People of South Africa, declare for all our country and the world to know: that South Africa belongs to all who live in it, black and white, and that no government can justly claim authority unless it is based on the will of all the people.'

Everyone was invited to attend the Congress of the People, the national convention called to consider the charter. The banned ANC president, Chief Albert Luthuli, unable to attend in person, sent a message of support:

> Why will this assembly be significant and unique? Its size, I hope, will make it unique. But above all its multi-racial nature and its noble objectives will make it unique because it will be the first time in the history of our multi-racial nation that its people from all walks of life will meet as equals, irrespective of race, colour and creed, to formulate a Freedom Charter for all people in the country.

Needless to say, none of the white parliamentary parties, all of whom were invited, came. Nelson, in flimsy disguise, defied his banning restrictions to watch at a distance as the three thousand delegates adopted the Freedom Charter. It became the statement of core principles of the Congress Alliance.

The government declared the charter a communist document that necessitated the violent overthrow of the state if its aims were to be achieved. All those considered responsible were charged with treason.

I attended the preparatory examination held to determine whether the accused should stand trial before the Supreme Court. It was held in the Drill Hall of the army headquarters in the centre of Johannesburg with the chief magistrate of Bloemfontein, F.C.A. Wessel, presiding. At their first appearance, a giant metal grille specially constructed for the purpose framed and enclosed the accused, who appeared in the makeshift court as if on display. Someone had attached a small handwritten sign to the cage: 'Do Not Feed'. The arrangement meant that the accused could neither see nor hear one another, nor could they follow the proceedings. Defence counsel, which included Isie Maisels, Vernon Berrangé, Bram Fischer and Sydney Kentridge, were all present when Maurice Franks stood up to address the court. Regarded as one of the most effective cross-examiners of the time, Maurice was known for his gentle and softly spoken manner. On this occasion, he could not conceal his outrage:

> Your Worship confronts this unprecedented scene which we see before us today: the accused caged, as Your Worship sees. Caged, one almost said – I am most anxious not to allow my indignation to get the better of the language I use but I think I am justified in submitting to Your Worship that they appear before the court caged – like wild beasts. I state on behalf of every member of the Bar and Side Bar engaged in the defence in this case, that if these are the conditions upon which it is proposed to hold the preparatory examination, then the whole body of us propose to leave this court, and take no further part in the proceedings.

The cage was removed and a more effective loudspeaker system installed. Outside court, thousands of supporters clashed with police. Stones were thrown and the police opened fire before order was restored. Eighteen people were injured. Inside court, bail was granted to the accused and the matter remanded until January 1957.

Although I was not briefed for the defence, the Treason Trial would turn out to occupy much of my personal and professional life over the next five years. At the time of Nelson's arrest, Arethe and I were married and living in an apartment in Emmarentia, with my youngest brother Yianni, newly arrived from Greece. By the time the trial had ended we had three sons – Kimon, Damon and Alexi – and had moved into the narrow, three-bedroomed house designed by Arethe on a plot in Parktown North in 1958. It is still our home.

Political trials of the time were conducted on a shoestring, with sympathetic counsel or counsel committed to the principle of a fair trial who provided their services at reduced or no fees. Along with other members of the Bar, I volunteered to help with the legal preparation for the case.

I was close to Vernon Berrangé and John Coaker who were counsel for the defence in the preparatory examination. They asked me to examine those documents that had been seized by the security police but which had not been tendered as evidence by the prosecution and identify those that contradicted the state's case. They also briefed David Soggot and me to find examples of provisions in democratic constitutions across the world similar to those in the charter. These were not difficult to find and our research on the constitutions of social democracies like Canada and France, together with the post-war constitutions of the Nordic countries and Germany, was put to good use by the defence to show that 'the ideas and beliefs which are expressed in this charter are shared by the overwhelming majority of mankind of all races and colours, and also by the overwhelming majority of the citizens of this country'.

Duma and the other accused lawyers served on the defence committee that liaised between the clients and the lawyers appearing on their behalf. Their families had lost their breadwinners and needed support. I assisted them where I could, as did other leading members of the Bar. Walter Pollak would regularly hand me a sealed envelope containing his personal cheque as an anonymous donation for the Nokwe family.

The complexity of the issues, the number of the accused and the length of the trial required substantial resources. Christian Action in London took responsibility for fundraising and the Treason Trial Defence Fund was set up in South Africa to ensure that a proper trial could be conducted. It received contributions from the church and eminent citizens, including a former judge of the Court of Appeal and the archbishop of Cape Town. The American Committee on Africa, the British Labour Party, Holland and some of the other Nordic countries later reinforced these efforts.

With both Nelson and Oliver accused, the management of their practice fell to their law clerks Godfrey and Douglas. I stepped in to offer them what support I could. I was still sharing chambers with Duma and so I took responsibility for his desk. Walter Pollak, the guardian of professional ethics, advised that I do so by relying on the precedent of the wartime practice of holding briefs for attorneys away on active service, but unlike the wartime protocol of making a statement in court, I say nothing formally.

I was also asked by the Treason Trial attorneys to monitor the criminal trial of two white policemen who had stopped Duma one evening in his two-stroke Auto Union motorcar and beat him up when he addressed them as 'Meneer' (sir) instead of 'Baas' (master). The two constables were convicted of assault and fined, and we won a small civil claim for damages.

Once the accused were released on bail, Duma came to chambers before court in the mornings and after court in the evenings, and we would discuss the case late into the night. Our office soon became the unofficial after-hours meeting place for the ANC – both Nelson, then leader of the Transvaal ANC, and Chief Albert Luthuli would hold meetings there,

debating the political and legal strategy for the defence. I would leave
when there were sensitive matters to be discussed. Their meetings would
sometimes spill over into the library or the offices of my fellow advocates, and I was once severely reprimanded by Advocate Viera SC, who
returned unexpectedly to his office one evening to find it occupied.

In the busyness of the Treason Trial years, particularly after the start
of the trial proper in August 1958, it was really only in his evening visits
to our chambers that Nelson and I had the chance to talk – the court
was as hustling as it was noisy, and the demands on his time were pun-
ishing. He was never harried, always warm and friendly; and would
take the time to ask after my family and my work, thank me for the
support I was giving the clerks at Mandela and Tambo, and give a short,
often humorous account of the goings on in court that day. Never did
his calm composure betray the stresses he confronted, or the fact that,
technically at least, he faced the death penalty. His equanimity seemed
to stem from a rare sense of confidence, even certainty, about who he
was and what he wanted in life, and what he wanted for his people.
And he was prepared to lead by example to get it.

The preparatory examination would last the year. It took eighteen
hours for J.C. van Niekerk QC to outline the case for the prosecution. The
accused were alleged to be intent on the 'incitement and preparation
for the overthrow of the existing state by revolutionary methods involving violence and the establishment of a so-called People's democracy'.

The state had spent months preparing and submitted some twelve
thousand documentary exhibits. Nothing, it appeared, was irrelevant –
including posters for 'Soup with meat' and 'Soup without meat' seized
at the Congress of the People. The prosecution called over one hundred
witnesses, most of whom would readily concede under cross-examination
that the speakers at the Congress of the People stressed non-violence
and that the call was for a non-racial democracy. Those who did not were
given short shrift by Vernon Berrangé.

'You say a speaker said, "It is time to shoot Malan"?' he asked one
witness.

'Yes.'

'How do you spell "shoot"?'

'S-H-O-O-T.'

'Now read the letters you have written down in your notes. Is it not C-H-E-C-K?'

'Yes.'

'Does that spell "shoot"?'

'No.'

'In fact your notes show that the speaker said, "It is time to check Malan."'

'Yes.'

'Then why did you say "shoot"?'

'It was a mistake,' the witness conceded.

Professor Andrew Howson Murray of the University of Cape Town's philosophy department testified as an expert witness for the state. He claimed that his expertise extended to being able to easily distinguish documents calling for communism and the violent overthrow of the state from those that advocated peaceful democratic change. His credibility as an expert was somewhat damaged when, under cross-examination by Vernon, he identified some of his own earlier writing as 'communism straight from the hip'. He was forced to acknowledge that a proper understanding of a text required the context of the author. Nonetheless, the state was determined to use his evidence and would call him again as a witness in the Supreme Court trial.

After nine months, in September 1957, the state closed its case. Three months later, A.J. McKenzie, the attorney general of the Transvaal, announced that charges against sixty-one of the accused, including Chief Albert Luthuli and Oliver Tambo, would be withdrawn as there was no case against them. This proved to be a grave tactical error on the part of the prosecution, as it would be almost impossible to prove an organisational conspiracy without the involvement of top leadership.

In January 1958, the semi-retired Oswald Pirow QC was appointed to lead the prosecution team. As minister of justice in the 1920s and early 1930s he was responsible for introducing the Riotous Assemblies Act, often regarded as the first piece of anti-communist legislation in South Africa. He was also a public supporter of Hitler, who he had visited in 1933. He appeared infrequently in court and died before the end of the trial, leaving behind a prosecution team of mixed ability.

On one of his rare appearances at the Drill Hall, he clarified the case for the prosecution:

> The Crown case was based on the Freedom Charter whose objects were intended to achieve the setting up of a communist state by other than peaceful and legal means. All the accused subscribed to the Freedom Charter and were pledged to carry it out. They were all communist or communist sympathisers.

None of the accused was alleged to have committed an act of violence. In the failed application for the dismissal of the charges, the defence argued that 'the Crown has established nothing more than a desire to put an end to any form of effective opposition to the government of this country'. The court disagreed and decided that there was a case to answer against the remaining ninety-five, who were committed to trial before the Supreme Court of the Transvaal.

During an adjournment in the preparatory examination in 1957, Nelson, then thirty-nine years old and a separated father of three children (his second son Makgatho was born in 1950, his daughter Makaziwe in 1954) had met twenty-two-year-old Nomzamo Winifred Madikizela (Winnie). He was captivated from the time he first saw her and said that he knew immediately that he wanted her for his wife. They were married in June 1958 in a large traditional ceremony in the Eastern Cape, which Nelson had to obtain special permission to attend and at which he could not speak in terms of his banning order. His sister Constance delivered the bridegroom's speech on his behalf. Sadly, I was unable to attend because of distance, my work and the fact that I was waiting for the imminent birth of my second son.

At the time of the marriage, both Nelson and his firm were in financial difficulties. Nelson had no savings and Oliver confided his concern to me that Nelson had spent much more money than the partnership could afford on the wedding. In turn, Winnie's father had told her that Nelson was married to the struggle and that marriage to him would be 'no bed of roses'. Nevertheless, the couple was very happy. Nelson sung the praises of his beautiful wife and looked forward to a new and happy life.

I had not yet met Winnie when, soon after the wedding, I received a call from Nelson. His voice was upbeat, even proud, as he proclaimed, 'George, I have married trouble.'

He needed my help. His new wife had been arrested and charged for assaulting a police officer and he wanted me to defend her.

The following evening, Winnie arrived at my chambers. Elegantly dressed, she was as striking as she appeared in the wedding photographs that I had seen. She was too shy to address me by my first name – and has never done so in the many years since. I was instead always 'Uncle George'.

Winnie recounted how she was woken early one morning by the police arriving to arrest her for her role in a meeting protesting the extension of passes to women. She was alone in the house on Vilakazi Street that she and Nelson now shared and asked the police to wait while she dressed. Without knocking, one of the policemen, a Detective Sergeant Fourie, opened the door to her bedroom and grabbed her aggressively by the wrist, pulling her forward. She resisted and pushed him away.

Somehow her elbow struck him on the chin, and he lost his balance and fell, pulling the dressing table down on top of himself and fracturing his neck in the process. He managed to get up and quickly handcuff her before taking her to the police vehicle waiting in the street.

On the day of the hearing, I met Winnie outside the courtroom. She appeared relaxed and laughed when I told her that she should enter the courtroom like a lady and not like an Amazon.

She stepped confidently into the dock and to the charges against her, translated into Xhosa by the court interpreter, pleaded 'not guilty Your Worship' in perfect English.

The injured police officer was called to the witness box and gave his evidence in Afrikaans. The interpreter started translating it into Xhosa for Winnie's benefit, but she interrupted him politely and asked him to please continue in English. I cross-examined Detective Sergeant Fourie in English, but he was not nearly as fluent as Winnie. He was also a poor witness, half-heartedly denying Winnie's version of events. I was sympathetic to his predicament – there was no easy compromise between the competing prerogatives of preserving his superiority as a white male and securing Winnie's conviction by detailing how he was floored by an unarmed, half-naked black woman.

Winnie testified in confident English and did not falter in her account of how she had acted in self-defence against the unprovoked aggression of the policeman. The prosecutor did not argue for her conviction with much enthusiasm. My own argument was brief. The magistrate gave an *ex-tempore* judgment: 'The accused is found not guilty.' Winnie and I bowed and walked out of court. She giggled when I congratulated her on her ladylike deportment.

Nelson had deliberately not come to court, but was waiting for us in his offices across the road. 'Not guilty,' Winnie exclaimed triumphantly as we entered. With a large laugh, Nelson embraced us both in his arms. It was obvious that he was mad about her.

I would go on to represent Winnie in court on more than twenty occasions over the next thirty-five years. She was repeatedly acquitted for many minor transgressions and some serious offences. She was rarely convicted. Always, however, she endured her trials with a stoicism that never failed to impress me.

The Treason Trial proper began in August 1958. Far from the accused's supporters in Johannesburg, a special court was established in the Old Jewish Synagogue in Pretoria, with judges Rumpff, Ludorf and Kennedy presiding.

The attorney Michael Parkington instructed the defence team of eight counsel under the leadership of Isie Maisels. It included Bram Fischer, H.C. Nicholas, Rex Welsh, Vernon Berrangé, Tony O'Dowd and Sydney Kentridge. The defence applied for the recusal of both judges Rumpff and Ludorf. The application against Judge Ludorf for the prejudice inherent in his representation of the police and minister of justice against an application to exclude them from a conference called to plan the Congress of the People, succeeded. That against Judge Rumpff for usurping the minister of justice and appointing Judge Ludorf, failed. I believe that the appointment of the thorough and enquiring Judge Tos Bekker to replace Judge Ludorf made a vital difference to the outcome of the trial.

The Treason Trial was the second in a trilogy that began with the Defiance Campaign trial and would end with the Rivonia Trial. It would be the last of the political trials in which some of the normal legal procedural safeguards to ensure a fair trial were observed. After this the rules were changed and acquittals made even more difficult.

For the next three years, the state tried to convict a progressively diminishing number of accused. The defence successfully chipped away at the indictment and certain of the charges under the Suppression of Communism Act were withdrawn. The state was also forced to concede that the failure to prove a conspiracy would result in no case against the accused. At one stage, all the charges were temporarily suspended to allow the state to prepare a fresh indictment.

In the end, there were thirty accused, but after Wilton Mkwayi skipped the country and Elias Moretsele died, only twenty-eight remained in the dock when the verdict was delivered. These included Nelson, Walter and Helen Joseph. Professor Tom Karis, who followed the trial closely, wrote rather aptly that 'all that distinguished the thirty [accused] was the more violent tone of their rhetoric'.

More than one hundred and fifty police witnesses were called and over four thousand documents entered as evidence. Professor Murray was demolished as a witness and forced to admit that not only was he not an expert on the policy of the Soviet Union, but also that the Freedom Charter was not a communist document. Under cross-examination by

Isie Maisels he eventually conceded that the Freedom Charter was, in fact, similar to many religious and political documents produced over the centuries and could be considered 'a natural reaction of oppressed people to prevailing conditions'. Maisels' cross-examination of Murray was so convincing that Duma remarked to me afterwards that, although himself a victim of government policy, he had not realised quite how bad things were until he heard Maisels.

I attended the proceedings as often as I could. My legal practice comprised mainly appeals that would be dealt with very speedily in the morning, after which I would go to listen at court, often staying past the lunch hour. In our conversations, Nelson and Oliver acknowledged the financial burden and personal hardship of the trial, but there was much that pleased them. The failure of the state to put together a proper indictment raised doubts about the government's damning assertions against the ANC, and the propaganda campaign against the liberation movement suffered. A majority at the UN voted to condemn apartheid. Significantly, too, the lengthy trial had not crippled the various organisations, and campaigns were being waged in protest against passes for women, rural communities were resisting the Bantu authorities, and the trade-union movement was strengthening.

The trial demanded most of Nelson's time. His days were spent in court, his evenings in meetings, often until late into the night. He was in court during the birth of his and Winnie's eldest daughter, Zenani (Zeni), at Baragwanath Hospital (now the Chris Hani Baragwanath Hospital) in Soweto on 5 February 1959. The trial was still on when their second daughter, Zindziswa (Zindzi), was born at the Bridgman Memorial Hospital in Mayfair (now the Garden City Clinic) on 23 December the following year. Court was in recess, but Nelson was in the Eastern Cape with his second son, Makgatho, from his first marriage to Evelyn.

It was not only his personal life that was strained by the trial. Nelson was not as available as he would have wished when it came to internal disputes within the ANC, particularly the opposition to the multi-racial Congress Alliance by the Africanists in the organisation. In mid-1958, the growing dissent split the ANC, and Robert Sobukwe led a breakaway group to form the Pan Africanist Congress (PAC). Duma and Sobukwe had been close friends in the early days of the ANC Youth League. Sobukwe was a teacher who had been temporarily suspended for speaking out in favour of the Defiance Campaign in 1952. He was soon reinstated, however, when he decided not to participate in the campaign after all. As a result, he was not invited to the Congress of the People and aligned himself with an Africanist faction within the ANC. Duma believed that it was partly Sobukwe's desire to purge his own failure eight years earlier that caused him to call for a mass defiance campaign against the pass laws.

On 21 March 1960, Chief Albert Luthuli was called as a defence witness in the Treason Trial. He was giving a systematic account of the history and policies of the ANC, with Nelson and the remaining accused listening in the dock, when news of the Sharpeville massacre interrupted his evidence. Sixty-nine people participating in an anti-pass demonstration in the steel-mining town south of Johannesburg had been shot dead by the police.

The government declared a state of emergency. Habeas corpus was suspended and there were mass detentions. Many of the Treason Trial accused were woken at dawn and taken to Pretoria Central Prison; the others were arrested as they arrived at court.

Not two weeks later, on 8 April 1960, the ANC and PAC were banned. The ban would stay in place for the next thirty years. Many, including Oliver Tambo and Ruth First, went into exile. Robert Sobukwe was sentenced to three years' imprisonment.

Kept in solitary confinement on Robben Island, Sobukwe's sentence was prolonged without trial in terms of the Sobukwe Clause, which allowed the minister of justice to extend a prison sentence indefinitely. It was only ever used against him.

The defence team submitted that the conditions imposed by the state of emergency rendered the proper defence of their clients impossible and they withdrew from the trial. Duma took over the defence and the accused began calling each other as witnesses. The defence team returned when the emergency regulations were amended.

When Nelson, led by Sydney Kentridge, finally testified, he was impeccably prepared. His evidence summarised the development of African nationalism in the 1940s and the formation of the Youth League. He explained his acceptance of the non-racialism of the Defiance Campaign and the principles of the Freedom Charter, and described the rationale for the M-Plan network of underground cells for organisation on a street basis. Much of this evidence would be condensed and incorporated into his statement from the dock at the Rivonia Trial a few years later.

The accused were acquitted on 29 March 1961. Judge Bekker delivered the most comprehensive of the three judgments and ruled that the Crown had not disproved the denial by the accused of a conspiracy to overthrow the state by violence. 'On all the evidence presented to this court and on our findings of fact,' he said, 'it is impossible for this court to come to the conclusion that the African National Congress has acquired or adopted a policy to overthrow the state by violence, that is, in the sense that the masses had to be prepared or conditioned to commit direct acts of violence against the state.'

After the acquittal, the party at the home of Joe Slovo and Ruth First carried on until late into the night, the guests reflecting the non-racial unity that the trial had only served to strengthen. Members of the legal team, who had been carried from court on the shoulders of the accused, were among the revellers, much to the disapproval of many of our colleagues at the Bar, who did not think it proper for members of the profession to celebrate with people accused of treason, even if they had been acquitted.

The ubiquitous security police were of course also there. A posse raided the party in search of evidence that the hosts were selling or providing intoxicating liquor to 'natives' in contravention of the apartheid liquor laws. There was no evidence to prove this. Within seconds of their arrival, glasses were downed and every drop had vanished.

The party would be the last occasion that I saw Nelson until his trial in 1962. Soon after his acquittal, he left home to lead the ANC from underground. It was too risky for me to see him during this period, so I relied on Duma for occasional reports, although he was always careful not to compromise me or anyone else. Duma shared responsibility for finding safe houses and arranging Nelson's meetings, and would confide his exasperation at how Nelson exposed himself constantly to risk by meeting with people all over the country.

Nelson's first task from underground was to organise a three-day strike. Threats of dismissal and media disapproval conspired with the government's show of force to turn it into a failure. It was clear to the ANC leadership that it was time for a change in strategy.

And then Duma had a nasty encounter with one Detective Carl Johannes Dirker, a thuggish member of the security branch, well known to us all. What he lacked in intelligence he made up for in zeal and tenacity. One afternoon, Duma left chambers only to return not fifteen minutes later in obvious distress. Dirker had stopped him, searched him and found a document headed 'The time has come for V to be met with V'. The meaning was pretty clear and Dirker kept the note. Duma told me that he had been on his way to a meeting to discuss the strategic sabotage for which certain of the leadership, particularly the more militant youth, were campaigning in the face of resistance from the older leaders steeped in the non-violent tradition of the ANC. In broad hypothetical terms, we discussed potential charges against him and the legal implications of a move away from non-violence. Would members of an unlawful organisation be liable for the acts of violence committed by others? What would be the consequences for the leadership of an organisation with a political wing and an armed wing if some of the members became involved in acts of selective violence? Despite his fears, however, Duma was not arrested.

On 16 December 1961, the manifesto of Umkhonto we Sizwe (MK) was published and the first acts of sabotage were committed against symbols of apartheid. The manifesto declared:

The time comes in the life of any nation when there remain only two choices; submit or fight. The time has now come for South Africa. We shall not submit and we have no choice but to hit back by all means within our power in defence of our people, our future and our freedom. The government has interpreted the peacefulness of the movement as weakness; the people's nonviolent policies have been taken as a green light for government violence.

The government policy of force, repression and violence will no longer be met with non-violent resistance only! The choice is not ours; it has been made by the Nationalist government which has rejected every peaceable demand by the people for rights and freedom and answered such demand with force and yet more force!

We of Umkhonto we Sizwe have always sought – as the liberation movement has sought – to achieve liberation without bloodshed and civil clash. We do so still. We hope – even at this late hour – that our first actions will awaken everyone to a realisation of the disastrous situation to which the Nationalist policy is leading.

MK was led by a National High Command, with Nelson as commander-in-chief, and had about two hundred and fifty members organised into about a hundred units. Although the ANC, particularly Bram as I would later learn, was careful to insist on a separation between the ANC and MK as two different and distinct organisations, the government would respond by promulgating a proclamation to the effect that the one organisation included the other and declaring that the ANC had finally shown its true colours as the violent revolutionary organisation it had always been.

On 11 January 1962, Nelson, who had earned himself the title 'the Black Pimpernel' for his activities, left the country. He led the ANC delegation to the conference of the Pan-African Freedom Movement of East and Central Africa in Addis Ababa and travelled to the African countries of Tanzania, Libya, Tunisia, Morocco, Nigeria, Egypt, Mali, French Guinea, Sierra Leone, Liberia, Ghana, Senegal and Botswana. He met African leaders to canvass their support and confront their concerns about the influence of the Congress Alliance and the communists, in particular, within the ANC.

The Sharpeville massacre had catapulted Sobukwe and the PAC to the forefront of the struggle, and Nelson worked hard to persuade African leaders that the ANC was still the primary resistance movement in South Africa. Nelson would receive military training before travelling to London to meet with Oliver Tambo and the leaders of the Labour and Liberal parties.

Nelson returned to South Africa in July 1962, where he remained in hiding. It was even riskier for me to see him then and even Duma's reports stopped. I relied on unreliable newspaper reports and gossip for my news of Nelson.

On 5 August 1962, Nelson was returning from a visit to Chief Albert Luthuli, who was under house arrest in Natal, when, outside Howick, a Ford full of white men sped past the black Austin Westminster in which he was driving with the theatre producer Cecil Williams. The Ford stopped ahead of them and another two cars came up from the rear. After almost seventeen months on the run, Nelson, dressed as a chauffeur, was caught.

Nelson was charged with inciting workers to strike illegally and with leaving the country without a passport. There was no defence to the charges and no doubt that he would be convicted. He briefed Bob Hepple as his legal advisor, but decided to conduct his own defence. 'This case is a trial of the aspirations of the African people,' he would explain to the court. He would speak for himself without the constraints imposed on counsel.

I attended his first court appearance before Regional Magistrate W.A. van Helsdingen at the Old Synagogue in Pretoria on 15 October. Nelson arrived magnificent in full traditional Xhosa dress, including a jackal-skin kaross and a beaded necklace in the black, green and gold colours of the ANC.

From the public gallery, Winnie complemented him in a beaded head-dress and ankle-length Thembu skirt. There was no ambivalence in the symbolism. Nelson asked for the recusal of the magistrate. He knew him from legal practise and took pains to emphasise to him that he held him in high esteem. When the trial proper began on 22 October, Nelson addressed the court:

> The point I wish to raise in my argument is based not on personal considerations, but on important questions that go beyond the scope of this present trial. I might also mention that in the course of this application I am frequently going to refer to the white man and the white people. I want at once to make it clear that I am no racialist, and I detest racialism, because I regard it as a barbaric thing, whether it comes from a black man or from a white man. The terminology that I am going to employ will be compelled on me by the nature of the application I am making [...]
>
> In a political trial such as this one, which involves a clash of the aspirations of the African people and those of whites, the country's courts, as presently constituted, cannot be impartial and fair.
>
> In such cases, whites are interested parties. To have a white judicial officer presiding, however high his esteem, and however strong his sense of fairness and justice, is to make whites judges in their own case. It is improper and against the elementary principles of justice to entrust whites with cases involving the denial by them of basic human rights to the African people. What sort of justice is this that enables the aggrieved to sit in judgement over those against whom they have laid a charge? A judiciary controlled entirely by whites and enforcing laws enacted by a white parliament in which Africans have no representation – laws which in most cases are passed in the face of unanimous opposition from Africans [...] cannot be regarded as an impartial tribunal in a political trial where an African stands as an accused.
>
> The Universal Declaration of Human Rights provides that all men are equal before the law, and are entitled without any discrimination to equal protection of the law. In May 1951, Dr DF Malan, then Prime Minister, told the Union parliament that this provision of the Declaration applies

in this country. Similar statements have been made on numerous occasions in the past by prominent whites in this country, including judges and magistrates. But the real truth is that there is in fact no equality before the law whatsoever as far as our people are concerned, and statements to the contrary are definitely incorrect and misleading.

It is true that an African who is charged in a court of law enjoys, on the surface, the same rights and privileges as an accused who is white in so far as the conduct of this trial is concerned. He is governed by the same rules of procedure and evidence as apply to a white accused. But it would be grossly inaccurate to conclude from this fact that an African consequently enjoys equality before the law.

In its proper meaning equality before the law means the right to participate in the making of the laws by which one is governed, a constitution which guarantees democratic rights to all sections of the population, the right to approach the court for protection or relief in the case of the violation of rights guaranteed in the constitution, and the right to take part in the administration of justice as judges, magistrates, attorneys-general, law advisers and similar positions.

In the absence of these safeguards the phrase 'equality before the law', in so far as it is intended to apply to us, is meaningless and misleading. All the rights and privileges to which I have referred are monopolised by whites, and we enjoy none of them. The white man makes all the laws, he drags us before his courts and accuses us, and he sits in judgement over us.

It is fit and proper to raise the question sharply, what is this rigid colour-bar in the administration of justice? Why is it that in this courtroom I am facing a white magistrate, am confronted by a white prosecutor, and escorted into the dock by a white orderly? Can anyone honestly and seriously suggest that in this type of atmosphere the scales of justice are evenly balanced? Why is it that no African in the history of this country has ever had the honour of being tried by his kith and kin, by his own flesh and blood?

I will tell Your Worship why; the real purpose of this rigid colour-bar is to ensure that justice dispensed by the courts should conform to the policy of the country, however much that policy may be in conflict with the norms of justice accepted in judiciaries throughout the civilised world.

I feel oppressed by the atmosphere of white domination that lurks all around in this courtroom. Somehow this atmosphere calls to mind the inhuman injustices caused to my people outside this courtroom by this same white domination.

It reminds me that I am voteless because there is a parliament in this country that is white-controlled. I am without land because the white minority has taken a lion's share of my country and forced me to occupy poverty-stricken Reserves, over-populated and over-stocked. We are ravaged by starvation and disease [...]

Your Worship, I hate race discrimination most intensely and in all its manifestations. I have fought it all during my life. I fight it now, and I will do so until the end of my days. Even although I now happen to be tried by one whose opinion I hold in high esteem, I detest most intensely the setup that surrounds me here. It makes me feel that I am a black man in a white man's court. This should not be. I should feel perfectly at ease and at home with the assurance that I am being tried by a fellow South African who does not regard me as inferior, entitled to a special type of justice. This is not the type of atmosphere most conducive to feelings of security and confidence in the impartiality of a court [...]

In their relationship with us, South African whites regard it as fair and just to pursue policies which have outraged the conscience of mankind and of honest and upright men throughout the civilised world. They suppress our aspirations, bar our way to freedom, and deny us opportunities to promote our moral and material progress, to secure ourselves from fear and want. All the good things of life are reserved for the white folk and we blacks are expected to be content to nourish our bodies with such pieces of food as drop from the tables of men with white skins. This is the white man's standard of justice and fairness.

Herein lies his conceptions of ethics. Whatever he himself may say in his defence, the white man's moral standards in this country must be judged by the extent to which he has condemned the vast majority of its inhabitants to serfdom and inferiority.

We, on the other hand, regard the struggle against colour discrimination and for the pursuit of freedom and happiness as the highest aspiration of all men. Through bitter experience, we have learnt to regard the white man as a harsh and merciless type of human being whose contempt for our rights, and whose utter indifference to the promotion of our welfare, makes his assurances to us absolutely meaningless and hypocritical [...]

The recusal application was dismissed. There were no legal grounds for it to succeed. Nelson was asked to plead, evidence was led and over a hundred state witnesses were called. Nelson cross-examined them himself. He called no witnesses.

On 7 November, Nelson was convicted and sentenced to the maximum five years' imprisonment. His closing speech prefigured his later statement from the dock. Restrictions on quoting banned persons meant that most of his hour-long address to the court in mitigation of sentence was not published.

I hate the practice of race discrimination, and in doing so, in my hatred I am sustained by the fact that the overwhelming majority of mankind hate it equally. I hate the systematic inculcation of children with colour prejudice and I am sustained in that hatred by the fact that the overwhelming majority of mankind, here and abroad, are with me in that. I hate the racial arrogance which decrees that the good things of life shall be retained as the exclusive right of a minority of the population, and which reduces the majority of the population to a position of subservience and inferiority, and maintains them as voteless chattels to work where they are told and behave as they are told by the ruling minority.

Nothing that this court can do to me will change in any way that hatred in me, which can only be removed by the removal of the injustice and inhumanity which I have sought to remove from the political, social and economic life of this country.

Whatever sentence Your Worship sees fit to impose upon me for the crime for which I have been convicted before this court, may it rest assured that when my sentence has been completed I will still be moved, as men are always moved, by their conscience; I will still be moved by my dislike of the race discrimination against my people when I come out from serving my sentence, to take up again, as best I can, the struggle for the removal of those injustices until they are finally abolished once and for all [...]

I have done my duty to my people and to South Africa. I have no doubt that posterity will pronounce that I was innocent and that the criminals that should have been brought before this court are the members of the Verwoerd government.

I managed to speak to Nelson during the adjournment. He was composed, almost formal, and unsmiling. He was also brief: 'George, look after my family.'

Nelson began serving his sentence in Pretoria Central Prison. He spent his long days sewing mailbags before he was transferred to Robben Island, where he was held in solitary confinement, before being returned, abruptly, to Pretoria Central.

Winnie was banned under the Suppression of Communism Act and restricted to Johannesburg. She could not attend any gatherings, communicate with other banned persons or join any political organisations. Her restrictions undermined her capacity to manage the family's affairs, including those of Nelson's three children from his first marriage, while he was serving his prison sentence.

Soon after Nelson's imprisonment, Duma arrived at chambers in a pair of sandals and gestured to me to leave the office with him. At the end of the passage, he told me that he was going into exile. His family would have to remain behind and he asked me to help them. We embraced and said goodbye. Fear stopped us from ever communicating with each other again. Duma went to Zambia. His family joined him eventually, but he died prematurely in exile. Fear, again, stopped me from writing a letter of condolence to his family.

'We stand by our leaders': a scene during the Treason Trial.

Chapter 4

⟨~⟩

LIFE

'...if needs be'

I heard the coin drop into the tickey-box before I heard the voice. It was early in the afternoon of 11 July 1963 and I was in my chambers. Harold Wolpe was on the phone. 'Meet me on the corner of Commissioner and Loveday streets,' he said, and hung up.

I found Harold outside the CNA. He did not turn to greet me. Instead, we stood side-by-side on the pavement gazing at the window display, our backs to the passers-by. 'The ANC leadership has been arrested at their secret Rivonia headquarters,' he told me. 'I am going into hiding. Please excuse me from court and tell James [Kantor, his partner and brother-in-law] what has happened.' He handed me a case file and was gone. It would be thirty years before I saw him again.

Harold's news was soon confirmed in triumphant media reports. Walter Sisulu, Govan Mbeki, Ahmed 'Kathy' Kathrada, Raymond Mhlaba, Denis Goldberg, Rusty Bernstein and Bob Hepple had all been arrested in a surprise raid at Liliesleaf, a smallholding in the opulent northern suburbs of Johannesburg. On a winter-dry Highveld afternoon, in a neighbourhood more easily associated with thoroughbred horses than African revolutionaries, sixteen policemen and a dog called Cheetah sprang out of a dry-cleaning van to interrupt what was intended to be the very last meeting on the premises.

Harold Wolpe's first escape bid was unsuccessful and he was arrested on the border of Bechuanaland in heavy disguise. His second succeeded. A month into their detention at the police headquarters in Marshall Square, he and Arthur Goldreich bribed a young policeman and walked out of their cell. They emerged onto the empty downtown street in the early hours of the morning later than planned to find that their getaway car had already left. Quite by chance the playwright Barney Simon happened upon them, picked them up and drove them to safety. In retaliation for Harold's escape, the police arrested his brother-in-law, the apolitical James Kantor, and kept him as a de facto hostage.

For three months, there was no word of or from the others. They were detained in isolation and interrogated without access to lawyers. Section 17 of the General Law Amendment Act 37 of 1963 had been enacted only two months previously by the then minister of justice, my old colleague B.J. Vorster, a Nazi sympathiser who had himself been detained without trial on suspicion of high treason during the war. His new law was aimed at interrogating suspects under conditions that would induce them to speak, depriving them of internationally accepted procedural safeguards such as habeas corpus. It constituted legalised torture and not two months later would claim its first victim: Looksmart Solwandle Ngudle, who was found hanging in his cell in Pretoria North police station on 5 September 1963.

With the accused disappeared into unchecked months of solitary confinement, the authorities broke all protocol relating to trials and the rules of *sub judice*. They ran a scandalous media campaign, hinting at treason charges and death penalties, and predicting the end of terrorism. There were rumours that Nelson was to be charged along with the others and that there was incriminating evidence, including his own diaries, that proved that he was the leader of MK and had received military training abroad.

Rusty Bernstein's wife, Hilda, approached Bram Fischer for help on behalf of the families. He called Arthur Chaskalson, Joel Joffe and me to a meeting in Arthur's chambers. Bram assumed that his own were bugged. He asked us to form part of the defence team. Joel, who had taken over James Kantor's practice, was instructed as the attorney and had to delay his imminent immigration to Australia. Vernon Berrangé, then abroad, would return to complete the team.

Joel, Arthur and I assumed that Bram would lead the defence. There was no doubt that he was the best man for the job. An outstanding lawyer, he had represented the accused in both the 1952 Defiance Campaign trial and the 1956 to 1961 Treason Trial. Instead, without offering any explanation, he told us that he was not available. Arthur challenged him. As the Afrikaans son of the judge president of the Orange Free State and the grandson of a president of the former Orange River Republic, Bram was the only member of the Bar who could persuade the court and the world at large that the people in the dock were no different to Afrikaner patriots charged with treason in the past. Arthur cited the example of General Christiaan de Wet, the Anglo-Boer War hero who, in 1914, led a rebel force against the government's decision to enter the First World War. A few hundred people died in the uprising and he was convicted of treason, yet was only sentenced to a short prison term.

At the time, we could not understand Bram's reticence, as we had no idea of the insecurity of his position. We would learn only much later that Bram was the leader of the banned South African Communist Party (SACP) and a frequent visitor to Liliesleaf. While we were in chambers discussing the defence, our detained clients were being interrogated by members of the security branch on Bram's role in the underground and taunted by their warnings that they knew exactly what he was up to. Bram understood that he might at any time be arrested and charged with the others, or be identified in the course of the trial by a witness. He confronted the bitter choice between trying to save his comrades lives by offering them the best possible defence and risking his exposure as a co-conspirator in breach of the ethical rule prohibiting legal counsel from appearing in a case in which they were involved. Ultimately Arthur prevailed and Bram agreed to lead us.

We knew nothing about the case beyond what was published in the press, as our enquiries to the authorities went unanswered. We were not sure who the defendants were or what charges they faced. Joel called the head of the prosecution team, Deputy Attorney General Percy Yutar, towards the end of the ninety-day detention period to verify media rumours that the detainees were due to appear in court. Yutar confirmed that they were – in fact, their appearance just happened to be scheduled for the very next day in the Palace of Justice (the Supreme Court) in Pretoria. He offered no apology for not notifying us.

Joel, Arthur and I arrived in Pretoria the following morning to find Chief Criminal Court C in darkness. Yutar was nowhere to be found and the court registrar knew nothing about the case. The attorney general, Rudolf Rein QC, was in his office. He did not disguise his contempt for his deputy when we explained the purpose of our visit. He advised us that the matter had been delayed (we would later discover that this was to allow Yutar time to draw up a new indictment after Rein rejected his first one). In our presence, an irritated Rein telephoned Yutar, had an abrupt conversation with him and reported to us that we could visit the accused in the local jail.

We drove the three kilometres to Pretoria Central Prison in search of our clients. We still did not know who they all were and so, in fear of leaving someone out, we wrote simply on the requisition sheet 'Walter Sisulu and those charged with him'. A senior warder arrived to tell us that it was contrary to prison policy for us to consult our black and white clients together. We objected and appealed to the commissioner of prisons, who granted us special permission to hold a joint consultation.

In the dank staleness that suffocates every jail I have ever visited, we waited in silence in the prison interview room for our still unknown clients to appear. I smoked cigarette after cigarette, lighting a new one from the butt of the old. This was as much to dull the stench of the prison as to calm my anticipation.

The white accused came first: Denis Goldberg, Rusty Bernstein, Bob Hepple and James Kantor. They were followed soon afterwards by Water Sisulu, Govan Mbeki, Raymond Mhlaba, Ahmed Kathrada,

Andrew Mlangeni and Elias Motsoaledi. And then, sometime later, Nelson Mandela, in his prison shorts and sandals, looking thin. A year in prison had shrunk him, but his exuberance was undiminished.

Nelson was elated to see us. He had not been told why he was being transferred from Robben Island, and although this surprise reunion did not augur well for him and his colleagues, he could not conceal his delight at seeing everyone. His joy was intoxicating and the mood of the meeting was euphoric, if bewildered. After months of isolation, the accused were as men emerging into the sunlight from the dark. In turn, our relief at finally meeting with our clients and having the opportunity to consult was burdened by what lay ahead of us all. We hugged one another, even those who had not yet met. I did not know Denis, Andrew and Elias, while they and some of the others did not know Joel and Arthur. Such was the emotion of the occasion that the formal introductions followed the embraces.

First, our clients wanted news of their families. Are they safe? Are they supported? How are they surviving with their breadwinners in jail? Next, they wanted to know what they should expect. What are the charges? What is the evidence against us? What sentences are we facing? We did not have much to tell them, and what we did was not good. 'The media hype points towards a sensational show trial. The likelihood is that you are facing charges of sabotage or treason for plotting to overthrow the state by violent revolution,' I told them, before adding, gently, 'The state is preparing the world for death sentences.'

A short, sober silence acknowledged my warning. When the consultation resumed, the mood shift was as distinct as it was phlegmatic. Our clients instructed us that we were to conduct a common defence for all of them except James Kantor, who was not involved and would seek alternative counsel. Denis Goldberg told us that he had implicated himself in a statement under interrogation and had no possible defence. He offered to plead guilty and take whatever blame might secure the acquittal of the others. Bob Hepple stunned us into silence. He had been offered indemnity if he gave evidence for the prosecution and he was considering taking this option. We could not discuss the defence any further with him present and waited for him to leave, before moving on to more practical issues.

Newspapers had reported that Ruth First was among the accused. When I had asked Yutar if she was, he had answered, 'George, why would you think she might be? Should she be?' And so, after our consultation with the men, we went deeper into the prison to look for her in the women's section. The matron denied us access. Her orders were clear: no one was to see her.

The next morning, 9 October 1963, the accused arrived at the elaborate Renaissance-styled Palace of Justice in a commotion of sirens and flaring blue lights. The two kilometres between the prison and the court resembled a warzone: the armoured vehicles that barricaded the streets buttressed by combat-ready policemen. The distance from Johannesburg had not deterred the trialists' supporters, who lined the streets to cheer the arrival of their Black Maria.

It was the press, not the prosecution, that had confirmed the accused's appearance in court and a preening Yutar, who had already distributed the indictment to the media under embargo, dominated the front pages of most of the country's newspapers. We arrived at court without having seen a charge sheet.

In the half-dark of the poorly lit cell underneath the court, our clients welcomed a robed Bram with emotion before watching him lead his defence team up the stairs into the courtroom. The police, self-appointed court ushers, had separated the spectators according to skin colour – an unusual practice in the superior courts. The black gallery was crowded with the families and supporters of the accused; the white side contained as many security police as friends. At least fifteen policemen stood guard between the specially constructed large dock and the public galleries, forcing the families of the accused to stand on tiptoes to see their relatives as the eleven men were led into court. Winnie, still under a banning order, was at first refused permission to attend. Ironically for a government so obsessed with tribal identity, the minister of justice would eventually grant her permission on condition that she did not wear the traditional dress that she had so effectively donned at Nelson's 1962 trial.

Just before ten, Percy Yutar (or 'Percy Cutor', as we came to call him) flourished into court surrounded by his large entourage. He distributed bound copies of the fresh indictment to the assembled press, before, in the manner of an afterthought, handing one copy to the four of us.

As anticipated, the judge president of the Transvaal Provincial Division, Judge Quartus de Wet, presided. The last appointee of the United Party administration, he was no government lackey, but he was tough. We knew that we could have done worse. The absence of assessors sparked a feeble hope that he might not impose the death penalty.

Yutar, shrill in his distinctive high falsetto, called the case of the state against 'the National High Command and others'. Bram stood to put the defence team on record. Yutar instructed the registrar to put the charges to the accused and declared that the trial should commence immediately. Bram requested a postponement: our clients had been detained incommunicado in solitary confinement for three months. The charge sheet had just been presented in court and our clients had not yet seen it. They needed time to prepare their case in response. Yutar was soon up on his feet again, strongly objecting to any postponement, as he feared for the safety of the state witnesses. Nonetheless, the judge granted a three-week postponement and the accused were hurried back to their cells without the chance to greet their relatives.

Outside the court, supporters of the trialists held placards proclaiming, 'We Stand By Our Leaders'. Apart and to the side, a small group of white protestors held their own unequivocal one: 'Laat hulle vrek' (Let them die like animals). And in Church Square, overshadowing them all, the imposing statue of the Boer leader Paul Kruger declared:

> Met vertrouwen leggen wij onze zaak open voor gehele wereld.
> Hetzij wij overwinnen, hetzij wij sterven:
> de vrijheid zal in Afrika reizen als de zon uit de morgenwolken.
> [With confidence we lay our case open before the whole world.

Whether we conquer or whether we die:

freedom shall rise in Africa like the sun from the morning clouds.]

After the adjournment, James Kantor, represented by H.C. Nicholas QC, applied for bail. The eminent silk argued that Kantor's arrest was an act of persecution. He almost guaranteed Kantor's innocence to the court before taking the unusual step of handing in Kantor's statement extracted under interrogation. It was clear from the statement that Kantor himself was of no interest to the security police and that they were concerned only with what Kantor knew of the activities of Harold Wolpe. In what would be the first of many brazen misrepresentations in the course of the trial, Yutar confidently assured the judge that there was more than adequate evidence to prove that Kantor was fully involved in the sabotage. Bail was refused. A second application would be dismissed some time later.

There was no case against James Kantor. He had no knowledge of the crimes with which he was charged. He was eventually released on bail, and once it became apparent that he would be acquitted, Yutar tried to persuade him to testify for the state in exchange for the withdrawal of all charges against him. When he refused, the state had his bail withdrawn and he was forced to return to prison. He was eventually acquitted, but the damage had been done. His practice collapsed during the trial, and he would die young ten years later in exile.

The accused were charged with offences under the Sabotage Act that were quicker and easier for the state to prove than treason. The Sabotage Act also carried the death penalty, but did not require a lengthy preparatory examination and shifted much of the burden of proof from the prosecution to the defence.

The principal offence for which the accused were charged was the planning of a conspiracy with a military basis and hostile intent for violent revolution, and an armed invasion of the country. The indictment, a curious, rambling document, listed two hundred and thirty-five offences under the Sabotage Act, including recruiting numerous named and unnamed co-conspirators for military training, performing acts of sabotage, training people in the preparation, manufacture and use of explosives, guerrilla warfare, and raising funds to finance the conspiracy. Bizarrely, the National High Command was Accused Number 1. Nelson was Accused Number 2.

The indictment was what is known in law as 'vague and embarrassing'. The charges had no specificity. It was unclear who was implicated in what. Arthur was tasked with analysing the document, drawing attention to ambiguities and inconsistencies. He suggested that we request further particulars to find out the specific acts of which our clients were accused. Joel and I were tasked with taking instructions on the evidence and spent the three short weeks of the postponement consulting with our clients. It was clear from the start that this would be no ordinary trial. Our clients were the political representatives of their organisations before they were accused. Their defence was to be conducted in a manner that made it clear that they were not the criminals, the apartheid government was, and the court was to be used as a forum to put their accusers on trial before the world. They would plead the justness of their cause and the illegitimacy of the prosecution, but they would also insist on their rights to a fair trial and due process. They would not deny their political affiliations, their activities or their beliefs, but they wanted to set the record straight and challenge the distortions of the apartheid state. They insisted that our cross-examination only expose lies and inaccuracies – the truth, no matter how damaging, was not to be challenged.

In the dingy little room we assumed to be bugged, our progress was slow. Much of our communication was done in silence – key words were written on bits of paper, shrugs and gestures used for emphasis or nuance. We would burn our notes in a tin ashtray at the end of each session. After a few days, the wooden door to our consultation room was replaced with an iron grille and locked while we worked. Chief Warder Breedt, whose office was opposite, would occasionally glance in. The brutal Colonel Aucamp, chief of security for political prisoners, and the notorious interrogator 'Rooi Rus' Swanepoel would lurk in the corridor outside to observe us from time to time. On one such occasion, Govan Mbeki wrote something on a piece of paper and passed it to Nelson. Nelson studied the note, gave his fellow accused a long meaningful look, and began whispering to them with almost theatrical urgency. He was reaching to burn the note when Swanepoel rushed into the room, muttered stupidly that he had left his ashtray behind, and grabbed the tin with the still intact note inside. No doubt extremely pleased with himself, he disappeared down the hall. The note read, 'Isn't Swanepoel a fine-looking chap?' It was a while before he appeared outside our door again.

The police had seized extensive documentation in their raid on Liliesleaf. Key to the case for the prosecution was a document scheduled for discussion at the unfinished 11 July meeting titled 'Operation Mayibuye'. A proposal for guerrilla warfare, the status of this document would prove critical to the outcome of the trial.

Nelson had spent time at Liliesleaf before his arrest, and personal diaries, writings and books that he had instructed be destroyed were not and were among the documents seized. They alone proved his liability and were among the reasons we decided that he should not testify. His meetings with heads of state to solicit financial and material support for people who left the country for military training were also an impediment. It would have been embarrassing to have the prosecutor put to him, 'You met president so and so in Africa...' After his objection to being a black man in a white man's court in his trial the previous year, he was also a reluctant witness.

And so instead of giving evidence, Nelson would deliver an apologia in the true sense of the word; that is, not a request for forgiveness, but a justification of his actions. In a statement from the dock, he would explain what the liberation movement stood for and the reasons why it had shifted from non-violence. We believed that this would convey his views much more effectively than interrupted testimony and cross-examination.

Nelson asked for a transcript of his evidence at the Treason Trial and his statement from the 1962 trial, and spent most of his time in preparation. He told us that it was challenging to write on the small rickety table in his cell. When next Aucamp crept up to the grille door of our consulting room, Nelson approached him to ask in Afrikaans if his table could be replaced with a more stable one suitable for the homework that his lawyers had assigned him.

'Mandela, you forget that you are a prisoner and not a lawyer. I am in charge here and will decide what you get.'

'Have you finished, Colonel?' Nelson asked politely.

'Yes.'

'Thank you, Colonel.' Said even more politely and with a military about-turn, Nelson sat down again. On his return to his cell that evening he found a recently varnished, sturdy new table.

With Nelson working on his statement, Joel and I consulted extensively with the others who we assumed would all give evidence. I resolved to pass my other work on to colleagues and did not accept new briefs. Friends and family helped where they could, as the local and international press wanted details of the accused and their families. The author Nadine Gordimer edited their autobiographical notes, which were duplicated and distributed.

Waiting for our clients to be brought to the consulting room each morning, I would look from the window onto the deserted courtyard outside. Bram had pointed out to me the spot where the Boer rebel Jopie Fourie was executed by firing squad in December 1914. This corner of the courtyard and the gallows, not a kilometre away, were both daily reminders of the life-and-death struggle that confronted us. In the afternoon, I would drive the long road home to Johannesburg alone or with Joel, both of us numbed into silence by the gravity of the predicament. I recall a late afternoon under a large tree in the Fischers' garden when Bram, Arthur and I admitted grimly to one another that it seemed that most of our clients had no defence.

Soon after the adjournment, I was working in the cool of the dawn in my vegetable garden when I heard the familiar stammer of the Fischers' VW Beetle in the driveway. Bram, *Rand Daily Mail* in hand, approached excitedly. 'Look! Look!' He directed my attention to the front page. In a vote of one hundred and six votes to one, the United Nations general assembly had demanded the abandonment of the Rivonia Trial. He thrust the newspaper into my hands. 'Take this to them and tell them that they will not dare to hang them after this!' He refused my offer of a cup of coffee. The resolution required an active campaign, and he had work to do. With that he rushed off. I bought a number of cop ies of the newspaper and laid them out on the table in the consulting room for our clients to see as they arrived. Their initial joy dissipated into concern that the decision might prove counterproductive – the regime was known to dismiss the UN as a talk-shop.

Joel and I would take meals for our clients to eat while we consulted. Prison regulations prohibited food being brought to convicted prisoners from outside, and at first Nelson refused to eat with us. Technically a convicted prisoner himself, Walter had no such compunction. One day, contemplating the home-grown salad, fruit, cheese, cold-cuts and loaves of bread spread out on the table before him, Nelson asked Chief Warder Breedt, 'Meneer Breedt, wat doen 'n man wanneer hy honger is, en daar is kos op die tafel?'(Mr Breedt, what does a hungry man do when there is food on the table?) Breedt, half turning his back as if to avoid witnessing any impropriety, responded gently, 'Hy eet, Mandela.' (He eats, Mandela.)

Colonel Aucamp was not cut from the same cloth as Breedt. When he saw me arrive one morning with a bag of ripe peaches freshly picked from my garden, he called me into Breedt's office and asked me why I was bringing food. 'As a lawyer the well-being of the clients I represent is part of my work,' I replied. Aucamp, puce faced, grabbed a peach in each hand and squeezed them hard. 'Is this part of your work?' he demanded as he threw the two crushed peaches into the wastepaper basket.

While Joel and I were consulting our clients, Bram and Arthur were working on the indictment. They had requested further particulars from the prosecution and believed that if they were not answered, the charges would have to be dropped. In his eagerness, Yutar was as sloppy as he was arrogant. His vague answers did not disclose what each accused was alleged to have done, or which organisation they represented. Indifferent to established principles of criminal procedure, he replied to our questions with general statements such as 'the facts were known to the accused' or were 'blatant and peculiarly within the knowledge of the accused'. Bram and Arthur drafted a notice of exception and we resolved to move for the dismissal of the indictment when court resumed.

We returned to court on 29 October 1963. Nelson, now suited, was the first to enter the dock. He cut a dramatic figure as he turned defiantly to the packed gallery and threw up his fist. 'Amandla!' he shouted. Power! 'Ngawethu!' the gallery roared. To the people! It was a sign of the times that even these small gestures of solidarity were risky: the security branch took the names and addresses of the spectators and photographed them as they left the courtroom.

Bram stood to address the court. He had a gentle charm and in his laconic address there was no hint that he was fighting for the lives of his close friends and comrades. He delivered a devastatingly clinical attack on the indictment and further particulars. He drew the court's attention to the numerous glaring non-sequiturs and inconsistencies: all one hundred and fifty-six acts of sabotage with which Nelson was charged had been committed while he was in jail. George Lowen SC followed Bram on behalf of James Kantor. At the end of his neatly forensic attack on the indictment, he directed the judge to an answer provided by the prosecution. It consisted of 'three dashes and an exclamation mark'. We were encouraged by the judge's hint of a smile as he pointed out, 'In my copy, there are four dashes, Mr Lowen.'

When the judge turned to Bob Hepple and asked him if he would like to add anything about the indictment, Yutar again got to his feet to announce that he was withdrawing all charges against Accused Number 11, as he would be the first prosecution witness against the accused. We were prepared for this, but there was an audible sigh of disbelief from the gallery as Hepple was escorted back down the steps.

Bob Hepple had been placed under immense pressure in detention. Yutar – 'Daardie kwaai Jew boy' (That angry Jew boy), as the interrogator

Swanepoel referred to him – was a proud and public member of the National Party. He wanted to rehabilitate the reputation of the Jewish community, which he believed was sullied by the large number of Jewish accused. He was determined to use Hepple as an example to show that not all Jews were communists. He visited him in detention and implored him 'as a Jew' to 'save himself, his family and all the Jews in South Africa' by testifying against the accused. When he did not get his way, Yutar left Hepple with the threat: 'I am going to prosecute you. All of you can expect to be sentenced to death.' Hepple's revenge would come later when he was finally released on bail as a witness. Leaving his two tiny children behind with his parents, he and his wife fled across the border into Botswana before he could be called to testify. Yutar blamed his escape on his terror of the ANC, but Hepple sent a message to the court from Dar es Salaam clarifying that he had never been threatened by the accused, only by the police. He had made his statement under duress and had never intended to testify. He still identified with the struggle. He eventually settled in England with his family.

Yutar did not respond to the substance of Bram's objections to the indictment. Instead, he questioned the integrity of the accused and attempted to hand in his neatly bound opening address, which he assured the court contained all the necessary detail on the charges. Before Bram could object, the judge did. Time and again, an increasingly agitated Yutar persisted with his unorthodox address: listing documents that he would hand in and experts that he would call; proffering summaries of evidence and alluding to proof that Nelson was planning to escape from jail. Time and again, the judge reminded him that he was in a court of law, not a political meeting, and admonished him to submit his allegations in the proper manner. Eventually, an overwrought, almost tearful Yutar begged the judge not to 'squash' (instead of 'quash', that is, reject) the indictment and undertook to comply with any order made by the court as to how the indictment should be amplified. 'It is not the function of the court to guide the prosecution as to how to draw an indictment,' retorted De Wet, before ruling that '[t]he accused are assumed to be innocent until they are proved to be guilty. And it is most improper in my opinion when the accused ask for particulars in regard to an offence which is alleged to have been committed, to say to them: "This is a matter which you know all about." That presupposes he is guilty and he will not be told anything about the offence.' With that the judge threw out the indictment.

The accused were technically free to go, but remained where they were as Swanepoel clasped each of them in turn on their shoulder, and with a curt 'I am arresting you on charges of sabotage', led them back downstairs to the cells.

A further bail application on behalf of Kantor and a new one on behalf of Rusty Bernstein, against whom there was no cogent evidence, were quashed on the basis of a 'top-secret document' detailing a plot to spirit any accused released on bail out of the country. With stage-managed drama, this was passed to Yutar by a senior police officer who had arrived in court specifically for that purpose. Yutar objected that he had overhead our colleague, Dennis Kuny, remarking that the authorities would do anything, including commit perjury, to keep the accused behind bars. The usually restrained Dennis denied saying this, but added to the rest of us as he sat down: 'But I should have.'

Two days later, our clients were taken to court and, contrary to practice, remanded to a date not arranged with us. A second indictment was served shortly before the next court appearance. This time the National High Command and Bob Hepple were removed from the list of accused and Nelson was Accused Number 1. Still there was no indication of what each accused was alleged to have done, and Bram and Arthur made further detailed submissions to challenge the new indictment. This time, the judge was not interested in our objections and not even the eloquence of Harold Hanson, appearing on behalf of Kantor, could persuade him.

'My Lord, look at the seven alleged acts set out in the particulars against Kantor. Not one of them supports the allegation that he is guilty of conspiracy.'

'Mr Hanson, even though each one of the individual allegations might not amount to much, the cumulative effect may be sufficient.'

'My Lord, the cumulative effect of seven noughts is still nought.'

'You will have great difficulty in convincing me that this indictment does not implicate Kantor.'

'I have yet to hear, My Lord, that an indictment is made good by implication.'

At our next appearance, the judge entered the court before the accused, an unusual move clearly aimed at avoiding a repeat of the previous exchanges between the accused and their supporters. Even more unusually, microphones were installed on the desks of the attorney general and the prosecution team. For the first time in South African history, the opening address was to be broadcast over the radio by the state-controlled South African Broadcasting Corporation (SABC). There were no microphones in front of our clients or us.

The court registrar stood and read the charge. 'Accused Number 1, Nelson Mandela, how do you plead to the indictment served upon you?'

'The government should be in the dock, not me. I plead not guilty.'

The judge objected and ruled that he did not want any political speeches. In defiance of his order, each of the accused repeated this plea, except James Kantor, who simply pleaded not guilty.

Yutar handed up a bound and ribboned copy of his opening address to the judge and a stapled one to us, before switching on his microphone. Before he could begin, Bram stood up to enquire politely on whose authority the radio transmission had been arranged and whether an undertaking would be given that the defence team would also be permitted to read their opening address over the air. A visibly embarrassed De Wet replied quickly that, in light of the defence's objection, he withdrew his permission for the broadcast and instructed the SABC to remove their equipment.

Yutar's opening address was as melodramatic in its content as he was in its delivery. If the startling allegations were to be proved, there was no doubt that the accused would be sentenced to death.

The accused deliberately and maliciously plotted and engineered the commission of acts of violence and destruction throughout the country; directed against the offices and homes of municipal officials as well as against all lines and manners of communication. The planned purpose thereof was to bring about in the Republic of South Africa chaos, disorder and turmoil which would be aggravated, according to their plan, by the operation of thousands of trained guerrilla warfare units deployed throughout the country in various vantage points. These would be joined in various areas by local inhabitants as well as specially selected men posted to such areas. Their combined operations were planned to lead to confusion, violent insurrection and rebellion followed at the appropriate juncture by armed invasion of the country by military units of foreign powers. In the midst of the resulting chaos, turmoil and disorder, it was planned by the accused to set up a provisional revolutionary government to take over the administration and control of this country [...] The documents and witnesses will reveal to the court that the accused together with other persons and associations named in the indictment had so planned their campaign that the present year, 1963, was to be the year of their liberation from the so-called yoke of the white man's domination.

Back in the cells, the accused confirmed their instructions that all sabotage actions were planned to avoid loss of life and that there had been discussion, but never any agreement, to embark on guerrilla warfare. There was definitely no consideration of inviting military units from other countries to fight in South Africa. And most certainly no one among the accused had ever believed that liberation would come that year.

A date in November was set for the trial proper. This would be difficult for us: Vernon was still overseas and Bram was appearing before the Privy Council in London.

The judge would not consider our requests for more time – the trial would commence without our lead counsel. When, however, court resumed to the news that the state's star witness, Bob Hepple, had escaped to Tanzania, the judge immediately granted Yutar his request for a further postponement for a week.

Still, neither Bram nor Vernon was available when the prosecution began leading its case in early December. Arthur and I were both relative juniors and we were apprehensive. As we drove up to Pretoria together, we anticipated eventualities and agreed that we would not betray our fears to our clients. We did not need to take this precaution. When we entered the cells below court, stiff in our starched collars and junior-counsel robes, Nelson came between us, put his arms over our shoulders, and smilingly reassured us that he and his colleagues had the utmost confidence in us.

The first witnesses for the prosecution were the staff at Liliesleaf. There was little in their evidence that we disputed. Nelson conceded that he had lived on the farm before his arrest along with some of the other accused. Joseph, the young son of Thomas Mashefane, the groundsman, testified that he had seen Rusty Bernstein setting up a broadcast for Walter's 26 June speech on the farm, confusing him with another red-headed technician who had made a brief experimental broadcast before that date. Walter was adamant that his evidence be challenged. When I pointed out that this would make no difference to the verdict, as he was not denying that he had done the broadcast, only where he had done it, Walter said firmly, 'No, it must be challenged. I am not so interested in the legal aspects but politically it is very important for the ANC. Many of our people know that the police can trace where a broadcast is taking place. Our people will ask what sort of leaders we have who broadcast from their regular hiding place. It could be very damaging to us.'

In the cells at the end of our long first day in court, Nelson put his arm around me and said, 'Ingadinwa nangomso' (Don't get tired even tomorrow). He explained that it was an expression that meant thank you for a job well done. I was encouraged.

The main purpose of our cross-examination was to establish the reason for witnesses being detained in solitary confinement. Yutar objected to this line of questioning and clarified for the court that it was 'protective custody', not detention. When Mashefane completed his evidence, he requested permission to speak. 'Did the police have the right to assault me if I have done no wrong?' he asked. More confident and experienced counsel than Arthur and I would have taken this up, as would a more concerned judge, but De Wet dismissed the witness with a simple instruction to Yutar to investigate the complaint. The press interest was whetted, but Yutar later put out an assurance that the matter had been investigated thoroughly and he was confident that the allegation was without substance.

In the short period before the Christmas adjournment, Yutar called minor witnesses whose evidence was not seriously in dispute. Bram's absence from court was noticed and reported on. There was widespread and persistent speculation that he had not appeared in court for fear of being identified by the staff as a frequent visitor to the property.

We took no holiday that year, working the full two months of the Christmas adjournment. There were reams of documents to examine. Nelson worked on his speech from the dock and we asked the others to write comprehensive statements. Walter quipped that the reason there was so little evidence against him was because he understood the dangers of putting pen to paper. He would be our first witness to give evidence under cross-examination. For more than a month he and I worked on his statement. We would perform mock trial cross-examinations in front of the others, me doing my shrill Yutar impersonation.

Govan Mbeki wrote his own statement, but he was bored by the exercise. He asked for a copy of Tolstoy's *War and Peace*. I dropped it off with Chief Warder Breedt who immediately handed it over to the security police. I informed the investigating officer that it was a classic novel, not a manual for guerrilla warfare. I asked if he would like me to produce a certificate from a professor of literature to that effect and he nodded in the affirmative. 'In that case, could I give the professor your full name for the purposes of the certificate?' I asked. He understood the innuendo and quickly promised to get the book to Govan.

The defence took issue with the prosecution on four points. Firstly, we denied that Denis Goldberg, Ahmed Kathrada, Rusty Bernstein and Raymond Mhlaba were members of either the National High Command or MK. Secondly, we disputed that membership of the ANC automatically meant membership of MK – they were distinct and independent organisations. Thirdly, we challenged the portrayal of the ANC as a mere tool of the SACP and not the broad-based national democratic organisation that it was. Fourth and finally, we denied that either MK or the national liberation movement had adopted Operation Mayibuye, or that there was any intention of embarking on guerrilla warfare in 1963 or the foreseeable future.

We knew that, even if we proved our version, most of the accused would not escape legal liability. The chief purpose of the defence was not to secure an acquittal. For the accused, it was to present a case in which the grievances of the disenfranchised people of South Africa were articulated by their leaders. For the lawyers, it was to avoid the death sentence. Forlorn as our hope was, we mapped out what we hoped to achieve.

Ours was not a popular case among our colleagues at the Bar and in the white community in which we lived. It was not only the police and the prosecution who blurred the distinction between the lawyers and the accused. I played a weekly social bridge game at the home of my friend Dimitri Roussos, but stopped due to the pressure of work. One evening Dimitri asked me to be his partner at the home of a well-known society lady, Evang. The wife of one of the other players pulled me aside at teatime.

'George, I was worried about you, seeing your picture and name in this big case. I was so worried about you that I phoned Evang and asked her, "Is George a Red?" She told me not to be silly, "George will do anything for money." And I said to Evang, "Oh, I am so relieved."'

On the day the trial resumed, both Vernon and Bram were in court. Vernon lost no time in making his feelings for Yutar known. On entering the court to find Yutar complaining to me about our clients' lack of co-operation with the police guarding them in the cell below, Vernon exclaimed loudly for all to hear: 'George, why do you allow this silly little man to talk to you in that way?' 'Did you hear that? Did you hear that?' squealed Yutar to no one in particular.

The court had been rearranged in our absence. The witness box had been moved to the side of the prosecution, facing the jury box with its back to the press. The witness would now stand flanked by the prosecution team and the security branch. The jury box was empty save for the imposing Detective Sergeant van Rensburg of the security branch, a notoriously brutal interrogator. Yutar asked the judge to clear the court to allow his first substantial witness to testify in secret, because he faced mortal danger if his identity became known. His reason was spurious – like us, the prosecutor well knew that those who had agreed to give evidence after months of isolation would often refuse to testify once they saw their friends and family in court. A closed court prolonged the fear their interrogators had instilled in them. In turn, Vernon directed the judge's attention to the intimidating arrangement of the court. The judge cleared the courtroom of the public and the jury box of its solitary occupant.

Vernon was a master of the art of cross-examination, but he was sharply constrained by our clients' firm instructions to leave much of the evidence unchallenged and contest only those portions that constituted lies and slander. It is an extremely difficult task for any cross-examiner to accord credibility to a witness by accepting most of his or her evidence and then challenge the small, but vital, portions that are untrue.

Bruno Mtolo was 'Mr X', the star witness for the prosecution. He was a member of MK who had committed several acts of sabotage on the instructions of the Natal Regional Command. He was the first witness to implicate Nelson by describing a meeting of the National High Command that he had attended. Nelson admitted that he was there, but denied portions of Mtolo's evidence as to what was said. He insisted that we challenge Mtolo on his claim that Nelson was a communist and that he had instructed others to deny that they were. Mtolo testified for three days, at the end of which Vernon managed to extract the important concession that Nelson's instructions to avoid loss of life had not changed prior to his arrest. This was key to establishing that guerrilla warfare had not been endorsed.

Vernon cross-examined a number of witnesses who had made statements while in ninety-day detention. One after the other they eventually conceded that they had only given a statement after the effects of the detention had worn them down and in dread of any more time under interrogation. Vernon's expert techniques were to be adapted and used by many of us in successive political trials over the next twenty-five years.

The danger of placing too much reliance on the evidence of witnesses trying too hard to please their police captors was vividly illustrated when a less sophisticated witness, who had participated at a camp run by Denis Goldberg in the Cape, was asked to identify the leader of the camp. Without any hesitation, he pointed his finger directly at me, causing even the surly judge to laugh. For my part, I did not consider it an accusation that needed denying.

Dozens of security police were cross-examined. Arthur had researched their evidence and found that most of it was hearsay and inadmissible. Vernon would establish this in court after only a few questions.

In the course of evidence, the state produced an incriminating document. A handwriting expert identified Harold Wolpe as the author. The prosecutor passed the document to Bram in court, who looked at it calmly and passed it on to the rest of us. We were stunned to see that it had actually been written by Bram. It would later become clear that the prosecution team knew the extent of Bram's involvement in the underground movement. We can only speculate on their probable motives for not making it public. Perhaps the branding of the accused as dangerous terrorists would not have been as easy if it was revealed in court that a prominent and respected Afrikaner had made common cause with them. Perhaps they wanted to avoid the predictable international outcry that would have followed the arrest of the lead defence lawyer.

It was not only the courtroom that had been re-arranged. We returned to find our consulting room customised to render our laborious consultations even more difficult. A long, partitioned counter now divided our conference room in two. Perched on high chairs, the nine accused stretched in a long row facing the five lawyers, which meant we had to shout to be heard by everyone at once. The first time we were ushered in the accused were already seated. Nelson alighted from his stool to ask cheerfully: 'What will it be today, gentlemen? Chocolate or ice-cream soda?' As our consulting room was elongated, our consulting hours were shortened, ostensibly to allow for a two-hour lunch break from twelve to two. We would leave Johannesburg at six-thirty every morning to arrive at nine for three hours of consultation before being forced to break for lunch. Without offices in Pretoria, we would wait around in restaurants for two hours, consult for two more, and then return to our chambers in Johannesburg to continue working.

Under these conditions, we prepared our clients for their evidence. Bram and I worked with Nelson on his statement and prepared Walter, Govan, Denis, Andrew and Elias. Vernon worked with Rusty, Raymond and Kathy Kathrada. Arthur analysed the documentary evidence. Joel coordinated the work, liaised with the families and prepared for mitigation of sentence.

We kept the fact that Nelson was not going to testify in the witness box a secret from the prosecution. Any suspicions they might have had would have been dispelled when we took piles of the hundred-volume Treason Trial record to the chief warder for Nelson to prepare his case in his cell. The co-operation between the prison authorities and the prosecutors sometimes worked to our advantage. Within days similar copies were seen on Yutar's desk – no doubt for his preparation for the cross-examination he anticipated.

Nelson's statement was to be substantially similar to his speech from the dock in his 1962 trial. In the evenings, at the now steady desk in his cell, he would work on his drafts. He would bring them to me for review and discussion during our consultations, and then return to his cell and re-work them. As the end of the prosecution's case neared, Nelson produced the first complete draft. His closing words chilled me:

I have cherished the ideal of a democratic and free society in which all persons live together in harmony and with equal opportunities. It is an ideal which I hope to live for and to achieve. It is an ideal for which I am prepared to die.

After yet another fretful night of little sleep, I visited Nelson to express my concerns. I was worried about the implicit challenge in the assertion that he was prepared to die. The government and the prosecution, if not the judge, would surely find this too provocative to resist. During the trial, Nelson had developed a broad support base around the world. I feared that the militancy of this declaration would alienate some of his supporters. I thought he should end with an affirmation of what he wanted to accomplish, not an assertion that he was prepared to die.

He was not convinced. In an effort to dissuade him, I relied on our earlier conversations about the classics, his admiration for the stoics in particular. I explained to him that my hesitation about the final line was influenced by the argument that Socrates might have saved his own life had he not challenged the Athenian jury in so resolute a manner. I reminded Nelson of how the philosopher had accepted his conviction and death sentence and refused an offer by his pupils to help him escape. His rationale had been that they lived in a constitutional state and that he had been convicted by a majority of his peers in a public trial. I thought that Socrates had made a serious mistake after his conviction when he was asked what punishment he expected. Instead of asking to be ostracised – which would have meant leaving Athens for a period of ten years – he said, 'I have done no wrong. I have wisely tried to persuade you to obey the laws. You should not punish me. You must honour me like you honour Olympic champions: you feed them at the city hall and that is what you must do with me.' While a majority of the five hundred jurors of the assembly had convicted him, an even greater majority voted for the death sentence. I told Nelson that this was an example of the foolhardiness of daring the court.

Nelson was unshakeable. Arthur agreed with him. Walter was also cautiously supportive and reminded us that during the Defiance Campaign he and others had said that they were prepared to sacrifice their lives. It would be wrong to say anything that might sound like a retraction of his earlier position or a plea for mercy. Bram was ambivalent. As a compromise, I proposed a small amendment. The inclusion of 'if needs be' to qualify the declaration that he was prepared to die. It was a minor adjustment that rendered the statement less challenging. Nelson and my colleagues agreed to the change.

With Nelson's permission, I took a copy of his statement to Nadine Gordimer. Anthony Sampson was staying with her. He had an international reputation as a writer and a journalist, and, as the editor of *Drum* magazine in the early 1950s, he knew Nelson well. I asked him to look at the statement and suggest any improvements. He withdrew to Nadine's study for what felt like hours while I waited in the lounge with the family's Impressionist art collection. Anthony was visibly moved when he returned. He rightly predicted how important a historical document it was. He suggested the rearrangement of certain paragraphs for maximum impact, because journalists, forever on deadline, would hurriedly scan the first few lines. He renumbered the paragraphs so that those dealing with the nature of the struggle, the ANC's democratic traditions and its independence were set out at the start. He was pleased with the concluding paragraph.

By then none of the lawyers was sleeping through the night. I sought the comfort of my vegetable garden earlier and earlier each day and it was a rare morning that I was not there sometime before dawn.

Court was adjourned after the prosecution closed its case and we finalised our preparations for the defence. And then, almost on the eve of the trial's resumption, Joel called an urgent meeting. In the fading light of the Fischers' garden in Beaumont Street, he argued that it was too risky to call all the accused as witnesses as it would only worsen the case against them. He warned that Yutar's cross-examination would seek to establish that the loss of life had been foreseen and that there was no difference between MK, the ANC and the Communist Party. If Yutar

obtained an admission of membership from any of the accused that would
be sufficient to convict all of them, including Raymond, Rusty and Kathy,
who might still be acquitted. Certain of them should not testify as there
was little they could say to prove that a plan for guerrilla warfare had
not been adopted that could not just as easily be established by counsel
and documents. Arthur was in tentative agreement. There were large
gaps in the documentary evidence that the accused might fill in under
cross-examination to the disadvantage of the three.

I disagreed. I predicted that Yutar would not conduct the forensic cross-
examination envisioned by Joel. Yutar's concern was more political than
technical, his case more a justification of the government's apartheid
policies than a legal case for the prosecution. I was sure that he was more
concerned with discrediting the trialists' political beliefs than proving
the elements of the crimes with which they were charged. He would
want to engage Walter and Govan on their beliefs, to challenge their
credibility, and our clients would be more than a match for him. I was
so confident I was prepared to bet on it.

'If we do not give evidence denying that guerrilla warfare had been
agreed upon as an option then the judge could draw an adverse infer-
ence,' I argued. 'If, however, he wanted a reason not to impose the death
penalty then this evidence would influence him in our favour.' I reminded
my colleagues that, like most white South Africans, the judge had never
had any meaningful contact with African people except at the level of
master and servant. I was convinced that our clients' courage and intelligence, their deeply felt grievances and the justness of their cause would
become clear to the judge if they testified. This is what would encourage
him to spare their lives. I knew that I was speaking for our clients when
I argued that, with their organisations banned and their freedom of
expression denied, they could not miss this opportunity to speak to the
people of South Africa and the world.

In the end I persuaded my team that our clients must be heard in open
court. Despite the dangers, the accused would speak for themselves.

On the resumption of the trial, we were ready to present the case for the defence. Bram stood and outlined in broad terms what would be admitted. He made it clear that an agreed policy of guerrilla warfare would be denied. Although preparations had been made from 1962, no plan was ever adopted and it was hoped that such a step could be avoided.

Bram called our first witness. 'The defence case, M'Lord, will commence with a statement by Nelson Mandela, who personally took part in the establishment of Umkhonto, and who will be able to inform the court of the beginnings of that organisation and its history up to August 1962 when he was arrested.'

He had scarcely finished when Yutar, frenzied, was on his feet. 'My Lord! I think that you should warn the accused that what he says from the dock has far less weight than if he submitted himself to cross-examination!'

'I think, Mr Yutar, that counsel for the defence have sufficient expertise to be able to advise their clients without your assistance,' retorted the judge, who generally expressed his irritation with Yutar by calling him 'Mister' instead of 'Doctor'.

'Neither we, nor our clients, are unaware of the provisions of the Criminal Code,' Bram assured the court.

With that, Nelson began: 'My Lord, I am the first accused. I hold a bachelor's degree in arts and practised as an attorney in Johannesburg for a number of years in partnership with Oliver Tambo, a co-conspirator in this case. I am a convicted prisoner...'

He spoke for more than three hours. In the silence of the crowded courtroom, he was watched by the press and VIPs, who faced him from the jury box. His supporters, including his wife and mother, sat behind him, staring at the back of his head, while his lawyers and co-accused sat twisted in our seats.

The judge, Yutar and the entire prosecution team did not look at him once during his address.

Nelson recounted his early life, his political development and his involvement in the ANC. He described the reasoning that led to the formation of MK and the move away from non-violence to controlled violence in the form of sabotage. He articulated his belief in political equality, a belief tantamount to treason for the apartheid state:

> Above all, we want equal political rights, because without them our disabilities will be permanent. I know this sounds revolutionary to the whites in this country, because the majority of voters will be Africans. This makes the white man fear democracy.
>
> But this fear cannot be allowed to stand in the way of the only solution which will guarantee racial harmony and freedom for all. It is not true that the enfranchisement of all will result in racial domination. Political division, based on colour, is entirely artificial and, when it disappears, so will the domination of one colour group by another. The ANC has spent half a century fighting against racialism. When it triumphs it will not change that policy.
>
> This then is what the ANC is fighting. The struggle is a truly national one. It is a struggle of the African people, inspired by their own suffering and their own experience. It is a struggle for the right to live.
>
> During my lifetime I have dedicated myself to this struggle of the African people. I have fought against white domination and I have fought against black domination. I have cherished the ideal of a democratic and free society in which all persons live together in harmony and with equal opportunities. It is an ideal which I hope to live for and to achieve. But, if needs be, it is an ideal for which I am prepared to die.

Nelson sat. His address was followed by a slow moment of deep silence. And then, from the public benches, a sigh, interrupted eventually by sobbing. Justice de Wet turned to Bram and said softly, 'You may call your next witness.'

Brief excerpts of Nelson's statement were published in the newspapers. The *Rand Daily Mail* printed it in full in defiance of the prohibition against quoting restricted persons. For this and other acts of courage, such as exposing the ill-treatment of prisoners, police brutality and abuse of power, Laurence Gandar, the editor, and Benjamin Pogrund, the senior political reporter, would end up paying dearly: they were both later convicted of criminal charges under the Prisons Act and lost their jobs.

The statement became a loved and cherished document, inspiring generations. Often, in future matters, when I asked my clients – young or old – what their defence was to be they would answer proudly: 'The Nelson Mandela Defence'. In recognition of the power of speeches like this, the law would eventually be changed to remove the right of an accused to make a statement from the dock.

Our next witness – the first to give evidence under oath – was Walter Sisulu, led by Bram. Walter was a great man to whom both the accused and the lawyers deferred. He had spent more than thirty years in the ANC and was the best person to testify about its history. Walter lacked formal education – he grew up in a poor district of the Transkei and left school at sixteen to become a cowherd – but he had a brilliant mind. He was a short, pale man – his father, Victor Dickinson, was a white magistrate who had abandoned his two children and their Xhosa mother to move to Johannesburg. Walter would sometimes attend court to watch him preside, but his father never acknowledged him.

Walter proved himself the exceptional witness that we had predicted, giving his calm and careful evidence with great deliberation. He explained to the court that, while he had chosen to testify under oath and to subject his story to cross-examination, he would only answer questions relating to his own beliefs and activities and not those that might lead to the prosecution of others or betray the confidential affairs of the ANC. This position was taken by all the accused.

On the first day of Walter's evidence, Joel interrupted our lunch at the Greek café we frequented to tell us that Walter had been separated from the others. This was an unprecedented move and we were concerned about the effect this would have on our witness. We rushed to consult with our clients. Nelson was not concerned. He had absolute faith in Walter. He reassured us that his friend would handle the situation. He was proved right.

Walter testified about the history of the ANC and its commitment to non-violence before outlining the difficulties inherent in the decision to use controlled violence after the massacre at Sharpeville, the state of emergency and the banning of the ANC. Some of the questions put to Walter by the judge worried us. In response to the assertion by Walter that black people wanted the vote, De Wet asked him: 'Would they really? Is that correct, Mr Sisulu? You think they should have the vote, but how do you know that the ordinary Bantu-about-town wants the vote?'

Yutar had hardly started his cross-examination when Joel whispered in my ear that I had won the bet. In the adjournment, Vernon quoted Damon Runyan: 'Never bet against a Greek.'

Politically naive, Yutar could not confine his questions to the facts of the case he was prosecuting. He was as concerned with establishing the innocence and bona fides of the government as he was of proving the guilt of the accused. He made the strategic error of trying to engage Walter in a political debate. The deputy attorney general and doctor of law, armed with his literary witticisms and often cruel irony, was no match for a man as honourable and politically astute as Walter.

For five days, while isolated in solitary confinement, Walter calmly endured Yutar's attacks on his credibility, integrity and the justness of his beliefs. He appeared to lose his equanimity on only two occasions: the first was when he told Yutar that he wished that 'he could be a black man just for one day so he would be able to understand the plight of his people'. The second was when he asked Yutar how he would feel if 'his teenage son was arrested and held in a police cell'. This was a response to the news that Walter's son Max had been arrested for not having a pass despite being under the prescribed age of sixteen. In his misguided cross-examination, Yutar failed to test key issues arising from the evidence in chief.

Kathy Kathrada testified next, led by Vernon. At thirty-four, he was the youngest of the accused, and his first political home was the Transvaal Indian Congress, an organisation inspired by the teachings of Mahatma Gandhi. The 'Doctors' Pact' between Dr Alfred Xuma of the

ANC and Dr Yusuf Dadoo of the Indian Congress had been agreed before he joined. He was also a member of the SACP. He was not, however, a member of MK and the National High Command. At the time of his arrest he was underground, posing as a ginger-haired and moustached Portuguese businessman going by the name of Mr Pedro Perreira. He was at Liliesleaf to make a tape-recording and improve his disguise.

The state had very little evidence against him. Yutar asked him about a note that Nelson had written in which he said he was met on his return to South Africa by 'K', who had prepared a tasty meal for him at his house and briefed him on the events in the country during his absence.

'Are you sometimes referred to as K?' Yutar asked.

'I am not referred to as K,' Kathy replied. 'I don't know of anybody who refers to me as K.'

'Do you know anybody else who goes under the initial of K?'

'Yes.'

'Who?'

'Mr Khrushchev.'

'So you are trying to be funny at my expense?'

'I wasn't. You asked me if I knew of any Mr K and I told you.'

Kathy's witty replies irritated the judge. Again, Yutar's cross-examination was more political debate than prosecution and he failed to deal with many of the legal issues at stake. He neglected to ask any questions relating to what we considered to be the two critical points necessary to prove Kathy's guilt: Did he attend the meeting to discuss Operation Mayibuye on 11 July 1963? And was the tape-recording that he admitted he had prepared linked to MK? Kathy had acknowledged his membership of the SACP, but this was not a charge in the indictment and we were hopeful for his acquittal.

Raymond Mhlaba was next. He was a widower with three children. A tall, large man, he was quiet, almost stolid, until he found something funny. Then he would let out a great shout of laughter. He was a leading member of the ANC and had been staying at Liliesleaf for a short period before the raid. We were cautiously optimistic that we might be able to secure an acquittal for him.

The key evidence against him was given by a single witness who had taken part in the first operations after the launch of MK and who testified that Raymond was responsible for the coordination of acts of sabotage in Port Elizabeth. Raymond was on an ANC mission out of the country at the time, but would not disclose the details. When Yutar asserted, 'I want to put it to you that you in December 1961 were either in Port Elizabeth or Leipzig', it was clear that the security police knew for a fact that he had been out of the country when the sabotage was committed.

We were more confident of Rusty Bernstein's prospects. There was little evidence against him. He denied that he was on the roof of Liliesleaf on the day the aerials were erected or that he had gone to Durban to set up an MK branch. He had been engaged by Arthur Goldreich to carry out architectural work at the farm, and had arrived shortly before the raid. When Vernon asked for Rusty's acquittal at the end of the case, he said: 'The cross-examination of Bernstein covers a hundred and fifty-three pages of transcript. This is not remarkable in itself. But what is remarkable is that, in that hundred and fifty-three pages, there is not one word of cross-examination as to the facts deposed to by Bernstein.'

Instead, Yutar used his cross-examination of Rusty to impugn Bram before the court. Referring to an article written by Rusty for a magazine called *Fighting Talk*, in which he praised Bram as a white Afrikaner for his commitment to the liberation of all people of South Africa, Yutar asked, 'Who is the secretary general of the Communist Party?' Rusty refused to answer. 'Well, since you are unable to answer that question, perhaps we may conclude that it was the gentleman referred to in the exhibit before you. Will you hand it to the judge?'

Of all our clients, Rusty appeared to have been most affected by his lengthy detention. He was a quiet and articulate man, but he seemed depressed. He had developed a nervous tremor of the hands that persisted long after his detention. The sole witness who incriminated him had also been detained in solitary confinement for an extended period. We wanted to introduce expert medical evidence from two leading psychologists, Dr Danziger and Dr Albino, on the adverse effects of solitary confinement. The judge objected. He did not need a doctor to tell him what weight he should attach to the evidence of a witness. Yutar had obtained a copy of a letter that Rusty had written to his sister describing the use of interrogation to coerce people into making false statements. His plan to use it to expose contradictions in Rusty's evidence backfired when Rusty not only repeated but elaborated on his accusations. He, too, proved an excellent witness.

At fifty-three, Govan Mbeki was the oldest of the accused. He was also the best educated with bachelor's degrees in arts and economics. He had been central to the operations of MK and the National High Command during the relevant period.

We had had more time to prepare him than the earlier witnesses, and I drew up an extensive document from which Bram led him. Yutar had spent much of his cross-examination of Walter trying to downplay the suffering of black people in South Africa. We decided that Govan would give evidence that emphasised how the actions of the ANC were an inevitable response to the brutality and intransigence of an illegitimate regime. His evidence progressed from political oppression to socio-economic conditions, from health to taxation and working conditions. He eloquently elaborated on the evidence of Nelson and Walter, describing how appeals by the African people were met with rejection and scorn by successive prime ministers, who kept their racist policy intact while calling it by different names: segregation, trusteeship, baasskap, apartheid and separate development. In response to a question by Bram as to whether these name changes had heralded any substantial changes, Govan replied: 'No. Apart from that [change of terminology], the leopard has not changed its colours at all. The position was very clearly expressed by the late prime minister, Mr J.G. Strijdom, when he said, "Die wit man moet altyd baas wees."' (The white man must always be the master.)

Yutar, too, appeared unable to change his colours. After announcing, 'I want to remind you that this court is trying issues of sabotage and other offences, it is not a court of enquiry into grievances of the Bantu. So I hope you will forgive me if I don't even attempt to challenge the correctness of some of your complaints', he proceeded to engage in what amounted to a political defence of apartheid with the witness.

Denis Goldberg had an irrepressible sense of humour. He had also tried to escape from detention, but was caught when a prisoner in the cell below him saw him drop past his window. An engineer from Cape Town, Denis was in the lounge of the Rivonia farmhouse waiting for Hazel Goldreich when the police raided. The evidence against him was strong, but his case was slightly different from the others. He claimed that he was in Johannesburg to escape the police harassment he had suffered in Cape Town, prior to leaving the country. He was not a member of the decision-making structures of any of the organisations and was not present at the meeting where Operation Mayibuye was to be discussed. He had, however, admitted in a statement under interrogation that he had visited factories to source components for explosives and other weapons of war. By pure accident, the police had discovered his safe house in Johannesburg after the landlord called them to investigate a broken window, and they had seized a number of incriminating documents. The prosecution alleged that Denis was sourcing material to be used in the imminent guerrilla war, and produced statements by twenty witnesses – factory owners and machinery merchants – who he had approached. He denied that he was amassing material to be used in the imminent guerrilla war. He was, instead, only exploring the possibility of clandestinely manufacturing weapons in the country. His approaches to a number of foundries to enquire about casings and other explosives used in the mining industry were acts of preparation. He was not privy to the conspiracy or any attempt to commit the crimes charged.

Things did not look good for Denis from the moment the judge referred to him as 'Sisulu's clever friend'. The prosecution team reserved their most intense hatred for him, so we were surprised when Yutar delegated the cross-examination of this 'subversive Jew' to his assistant,

A.B. Krogh. Krogh was an experienced prosecutor, but he was not sufficiently fluent in English to successfully pull off his attempt to mimic
Yutar's flamboyant turn of phrase and sharp irony. He conducted an
unremarkable cross-examination.

Andrew Mlangeni and Elias Motsoaledi had continued their membership of the ANC after it had been banned the year before. They were
disciplined members of MK but not the National High Command, and
they admitted recruiting young men for military training outside South
Africa and for other activities of the Johannesburg Regional Command.
The two would inevitably be convicted and so giving evidence under
oath would serve no useful purpose. We agreed that they should both
make short statements from the dock. Both related how they had been
tortured by the security police and affirmed their commitment to the
ANC and to the struggles of their people.

By April 1964, we had led all our evidence. The trial was six months
old. After Nelson's dramatic opening, the remainder of the accused had
given convincing evidence. Inside the country, interest in the trial had
waned, but in the outside world the accused were now famous.

Yutar delivered an offensive and flowery closing address. We were
concerned when his gratuitous insults to the accused met no objection
from the judge. One exchange between them, however, did offer us a
brief moment of hope. When Yutar proclaimed, 'The day of the mass
uprising in connection with the launching of guerrilla warfare was to
have been May 26 1963', the judge immediately interrupted him.

'You do concede that you failed to prove guerrilla warfare was ever
decided upon, don't you?'

'Preparations were being made...' mumbled Yutar, almost inaudibly.

'Yes, I know that. The defence concedes that. What they say is that preparations were made in case one day they found it necessary to resort to
guerrilla warfare, but they say that prior to their arrest they never considered it necessary, and took no decision to engage in guerrilla warfare.
I take it that you have no evidence contradicting that and you accept it?'

'As your Lordship pleases,' replied Yutar in an even quieter voice.

Arthur, the youngest member of the defence team, had already earned himself a reputation as a lawyer's lawyer. He was the first among us to address the court. In a painstaking analysis of the evidence, Arthur demonstrated that of the one hundred and ninety-three acts of sabotage no more than thirteen were proved by proper evidence to have been committed on behalf of the MK National High Command.

Bram argued two main points. First, he urged the court to accept that guerrilla warfare had not been decided upon. Second, that membership of the unlawful ANC did not make one responsible for the acts of MK. The judge stopped him, saying that he accepted both.

Next, Vernon argued for the acquittal of Rusty, Kathy and Raymond. Lastly, Arthur and I argued several other, less important issues in the trial.

Yutar had the right to reply on questions of law only. The judge stopped him when he tried to re-argue the case against Rusty. And stopped him again when he referred to a proclamation promulgated in the course of the trial that equated MK with the ANC. The judge was firm that he would not consider an argument that might allow the defence to re-open the case. Yutar withdrew this argument, submitting that his case was so strong he did not need to rely on any presumption.

Court was adjourned for three weeks for the judge to deliberate. Alan Paton, the writer and leader of the Liberal Party, agreed to give evidence in mitigation. He had wanted to know if the lives of the accused were in danger. When told there was a serious possibility of the death penalty, he had agreed at once.

I met with him at the home of the British consul general, Leslie Minford. As I was leaving, Leslie put his arm around my shoulders and said, 'George, there won't be a death sentence.' I did not ask him how he knew. He had downed several whiskies and I did not feel I could rely on this information enough to report it to our team or our clients. In his biography of Nelson, Anthony Sampson claims that Leslie was thought to have intelligence links and may have had reliable information about the case.

On 11 June 1964, Judge de Wet delivered his judgment:

> I have very good reasons for the conclusions to which I have come. I don't propose to read these reasons. The verdict will be: Nelson Mandela is found guilty on all four counts; Walter Sisulu is found guilty on all four counts; Denis Goldberg is found guilty on all four counts; Govan Mbeki is found guilty on all four counts. Ahmed Kathrada is found guilty on count two and not guilty on counts one, three and four. Lionel Bernstein is found not guilty. He will be discharged. Raymond Mhlaba is found guilty on all four counts; Andrew Mlangeni is found guilty on all four counts; Elias Motsoaledi is found guilty on all four counts. I do not propose to deal with the question of sentence today. My reasons will be made available in a statement. The defence will be given an opportunity to study these reasons and if so required, to address me on the question of sentence. I will deal with the question of sentence tomorrow morning at 10 o'clock.

Bram could not be persuaded to deliver the plea in mitigation and approached Harold Hanson. In the prison consulting room, Nelson was defiant. He spoke for all the convicted men when he said that neither Alan Paton nor Hanson should say anything on their behalf that could be construed as suggesting that the accused regretted what they had done, nor should they make an abject plea for mercy.

If the sentence was the death penalty, the normal procedure would be for the judge to ask if there were any reason why it should not be passed. Nelson said he would be the one to answer. He would tell the court so that their supporters and the world could hear that the liberation movement could not and would not be suppressed by sentencing them to death; their deaths would inspire others to take up the struggle. We pointed out to him that such a defiant approach might be counterproductive. He responded by referring us to his own writing in one of the exhibits: 'There is no easy walk to freedom. We have to pass through the shadow of death again and again before we reach the mountaintops of our desires.'

We discussed whether or not we should immediately give notice of appeal if the death sentence was imposed. Our clients unanimously decided that we should not. It would only have the effect of blunting the process that they expected to commence in the international community against such a sentence.

The following day, amid the solemnity that fills a courtroom when there is the possibility of a death sentence, Alan Paton spoke of the plight of the African people and how their aspirations could only be achieved if they were granted political rights. Asked in court why he had agreed to come and give evidence, he replied:

> Because I was asked to come. But primarily because having been asked, I felt it was my duty to come here – a duty which I am glad to perform because I love my country. And it seems to me, My Lord, with respect, that the exercise of clemency in this case is a thing which is very important for our future.

The judge, irritated by a reference Paton made to the history of the Afrikaner people and their use of violence against the British, interrupted him:

> There were many cases where people resisted and were convicted of high treason and executed. I have in mind the famous gunpowder plot in England. In the light of subsequent history, these people had legitimate grievances. But they are not entitled to break the law by force. And what happens to people like that historically is that they get convicted of high treason and are condemned to death.

This was not a good sign. It seemed to be a warning to expect the death penalty.

Bram whispered that the judge need not have gone back so many centuries and so far away for a precedent. The court had conveniently overlooked the short prison sentence given General Christiaan de Wet in 1915.

I looked across at our clients. They stared ahead, impassive. Nelson took out a piece of paper from his pocket and put on his glasses. He looked at it repeatedly for the rest of the proceedings. When Nelson handed over his file to Joel Joffe at the end of the trial, I saw the notes he had made the previous night. The tremendous stress he was under was evident from the difference in his otherwise legible handwriting. We were never able to decipher the fourth sentence, but before Nelson died, the late Professor Tim Couzens made out the line that appears here (Nelson agreed with this reading). The notes read:

1. Statement from the dock.
2. I meant everything I said.
3. The blood of many patriots in this country has been shed for demanding treatment in conformity with civilised standards.
4. The army is continuing to grow.
4. [sic] If I must die, let me declare for all to know that I will meet my fate like a man.

Yutar's cross-examination of Paton was as scurrilous as the rest of his case. Harold Hanson delivered the final address. Bram had shown him an early draft of Nelson's speech from the dock and Hanson had suggested that, if that was what they were going to say, they would be hanged.

As soon as Hanson finished, the judge signalled the accused to stand:

> The function of this court, as is the function of a court in any other country, is to enforce law and order, and to enforce the laws of the State within which it functions. The crime of which the accused have been convicted, that is the crime of conspiracy, is in essence one of high treason. The State has decided not to charge the crime in this form. Bearing this in mind and giving the matter very serious consideration, I have decided not to impose the supreme penalty which in a case like this would usually be the proper penalty for the crime. But consistent with my duty that is the only leniency I can show. The sentence of all the accused will be one of life imprisonment.

I realised that I had stopped breathing. The men in the dock turned to the public galleries and smiled. Andrew Mlangeni's wife Juni called out, 'How long? How long?'

'Life!' he shouted back.

We had succeeded in our primary objective – our clients would live – but it was a bitter victory. Life imprisonment meant exactly that. I had time for only a faint smile at Nelson before he and his co-accused were led to the cell downstairs. I squeezed Bram's hand in gratitude.

In the gloom of the cell below, Nelson's composure, his calm authority, was not that of a man just sentenced to life imprisonment. He was without regret, anger or bitterness. He thanked us for what we had done. We advised our clients that there were grounds for appealing the sentences of Kathy, Andrew and Elias, but they all refused to appeal. We were interrupted by the prison authorities, who led Nelson and the others away. My appeal to Colonel Aucamp to grant the families a chance to say goodbye was denied despite an earlier assurance that arrangements would be made. The newly convicted prisoners went first to Pretoria Central where they were changed out of their suits and into prison clothes, and went to bed. At about midnight they were taken to a small military base and flown down to Robben Island to serve their life sentences.

Prisoners arriving on Robben Island.

RIGHT: With Isie Maisels (left) and Jonathan Gluckman at the Timol inquest, 1972.

BOTTOM: Nelson with Walter Sisulu on Robben Island.

Chapter 5

⁓

THE ISLAND

'Stay out of trouble and look after my family'

Anyone observing the jaunty squadron as it approached the quayside consulting room where I waited would be forgiven for assuming that the tall man in the centre was in charge. He was certainly setting the brisk pace at which the formation of nine – two in front, two behind and two on either side of him – advanced. It was only on closer inspection that his mid-winter attire of khaki shorts and sandals exposed him as a convicted prisoner under guard.

I had been waiting for some time in the sea-damp wind before I saw the bakkie bringing Nelson approach. It stopped and the squadron formed and came towards me. I stepped off the veranda of the quayside visitors' block and went forward to embrace him. It was a few months after the Rivonia Trial and my first visit since his imprisonment. We hugged. 'How is Zami?' he asked, using his nickname for Winnie. Before I could answer, he pulled back and apologised, saying, 'George, I am sorry. I haven't been here in prison for long, but I seem to have already lost my manners and become a brute. I have not introduced you to my Guard of Honour.' And, with cheerful authority, he introduced each warder to me by rank and name. Surprised into silence, they stepped forward in turn to solemnly shake my hand.

After enquiring after his own family and each of the other lawyers,

Nelson said, 'Unqaphele?' – a Xhosa term for respected persons – and by gesture (lowering his hand to indicate a short person) asked after Bram. Bram and Joel had visited Nelson and our other clients a week after their conviction. On that occasion, when Nelson had asked after Bram's wife, Molly Krige, Bram had wordlessly left the table to compose himself before continuing with the consultation. He had not yet had the equanimity to report that he had attended her funeral the night before: she had died in a freak car accident in the middle of the Free State the day after the Rivonia Trial ended. Bram had been driving and blamed himself. News of her death had since reached the prisoners, and Nelson kept his steady gaze on me, only relaxing when I gave him a thumbs-up.

It was also my first time on the island. The Cape of Storms was well named by the Portuguese explorer Bartolomeu Dias and I was still queasy from the sea crossing from Cape Town. The consulting room where we met was tiny and cheerless, and we sat, cramped and cold, as changing shifts of warders peered in at us through the glass panel at the top of the door.

We assumed that our conversations were bugged and fell back into the unspoken language of our trial preparations. My years of living in a country where I could not speak the language had served me well. I was well practised in the art of communication by means of facial expressions and hand gestures, and our consultations soon had an easy rhythm. Nelson would take my lawyer's pad and write down a name, an event or an organisation. I would respond with a thumbs-up, a nod or, too often, a sad shake of the head.

From the start, Nelson had no interest in talking about himself. His responses to my questions about his health and prison conditions were abrupt. He quickly changed the subject. He had the long-term prisoner's thirst for news of the outside. 'Everything is fine, George, we are all set-tling in well,' he said, waving his hand almost dismissively. I never knew him to complain. 'Tell me, what has been the reaction to our conviction?' I conveyed the massive international outcry and media coverage with a few words and an enthusiastic thumbs-up, drawing a quick and wide smile from Nelson in response.

'Any activity?' I knew he was asking for signs that the liberation movement was still active, and I scribbled down the acts of sabotage for which MK had taken responsibility. 'Have there been any further arrests?' I told him of the fatal bombings at Johannesburg station for which John Harris, a leading member of the African Resistance Movement, was arrested and would be hanged. My report on the detention of members of the MK High Command Reserve, including Wilton Mkwayi, David Kitson, Mac Maharaj, Laloo Chiba and John Matthews, who I would defend before Judge Boshoff in the Little Rivonia Trial, was a blow, reflected immediately by the pause in his questions.

This first consultation determined the rules of engagement for our future meetings over many years. It would change only towards the end of his stay on the island, when the warders would leave us alone and we could talk more freely. If there was ever any input or feedback that I needed from Nelson (even just a broad indication of his attitude), usually for reports to Winnie or the clients that I defended, he would always ask me to wait until after lunch. I knew this meant he wished to consult with Walter Sisulu.

From that first occasion, Nelson and I were separated for lunch. He returned to his cell for mielie-meal porridge, while I was escorted under guard for what would be my first of many liver hamburgers, the signature dish at the warders' canteen. They came with potatoes and pumpkin, which I could never finish, served by 'coloured' common-law prisoners. I ate alone at a table for four in the steely echo of the large canteen.

Our afternoon was more relaxed. I told Nelson that Hilda and Rusty Bernstein had escaped the country to Botswana, and gave my news of Denis Goldberg who, as the sole white prisoner, was kept apart from his comrades in Pretoria Central Prison. We ended the consultation with a discussion of the progress of the newly independent African countries of Zambia, Tanzania and Algeria.

It was clear from that first consultation that Nelson was realistic about what he confronted. Unlike others over the years who sustained themselves with the belief that they would be back home with their families within a few years, he knew that he faced a long imprisonment. The decolonisation process in the rest of Africa encouraged him, but he expected the white regime in South Africa to try to string out their rule for as long as possible. Nevertheless, he was optimistic and did not believe that he would die in prison. Already a master of the art of suppressing his personal feelings, he certainly never expressed despair. Nelson was too imbued with a sense of his responsibility as a leader, and knew that that would have been counterproductive to the people who remained relatively free and needed to continue the struggle.

It was also clear that Nelson was no ordinary prisoner. From that very first visit I was struck by how respectfully yet firmly he insisted that his interactions with his jailers were conducted on a basis that affirmed their common humanity. This was neither expedient nor forced. Nelson's nature, his basic instinct, was to respond to others with generosity. He was a truly decent man. Quite soon after his arrival, many of the warders would be asking him for advice on their marital problems or for his recommendations on what they should study for promotion purposes.

As we said goodbye, Nelson reminded me of my responsibilities to him and the other prisoners. Their families would need support, there would be more arrests and future accused would require legal representation. I needed to be there. 'Stay out of trouble and look after my family,' he instructed. I reassured him that I would.

My return to the mainland was awful. The wind was up and the pitching and rolling of the ferry quickly nauseated me. Determined not to succumb, I faced the stern and concentrated on the horizon, advice given to me as a child on our aborted escape to Crete in 1941. After a while I retreated to the cabin where the tossing boat and the smell of engine oil confirmed this as one of the worst days of my life.

More rock than land, Robben Island lies flat and low in Table Bay, the Atlantic surf colliding endlessly against its cracked contour. Since the time of Autshumato (also known as Harry de Strandloper) in the mid-seventeenth century, the island has confined generations of undesirables in watery exile. Three of the first presidents of democratic South Africa – Nelson, Kgalema Motlanthe and Jacob Zuma – served sentences there.

Prison life was hard, particularly for the first decade. Political prisoners were denied the meagre rights and entitlements afforded convicted murderers. Nelson and the others were required to do heavy manual labour – breaking stones in the startling white of the lime quarry or harvesting seaweed for export to Japan. Nelson washed in cold water and slept on a mat on the floor of his tiny single cell. Stretched out he touched either end. His demand for long trousers was met within months of his arrival, however, when he realised that the authorities had made an exception for him, he returned them and remained in shorts until 1967, when long trousers were issued to everyone.

At first the island delivered the tremendous isolation it promised and there was no news from the world outside. Nelson and his fellow trialists were kept with about thirty political prisoners in B-section, separated from the other inmates by a thirty-foot wall. Nelson was allowed only one letter and one visitor every six months. Both were censored. His first letters to and from Winnie were so blacked out as to be illegible. Visits were observed and, we assumed, recorded. The prison authorities were fickle and punitive in the application of their discretion: visits would be refused without reason, or granted on twenty-four-hour notice. Nelson's predicament was compounded when, a year into his sentence, Winnie was banned for a further period of five years and restricted to Orlando township. Not only did she lose her job as the first black medical social worker in the country (and with it the family's sole source of income), but now also required special permission from the magistrate of Johannesburg to visit Nelson. On one of these visits she was charged and convicted for refusing to identify herself to a policeman she mistook for a reporter. All but four days of her sentence were suspended.

Shortly after my first visit, the head of the prison, Colonel Aucamp, told Nelson that he would never see me again as a lawyer. I would soon be a prisoner in a cell near his. For a while, Aucamp held good to this threat and Winnie's applications to the head of prisons for me to consult on the island were refused or ignored. In addition, the prisoners' letters to me were not posted.

And then, without any explanation, I was again granted permission and my visits resumed. These were lengthy events. The ten-kilometre boat ride across Table Bay took three-quarters of an hour. The ferry left the harbour at seven sharp to collect the children of the prison staff for school and would only return after school hours to drop off the children and return me to the mainland. My time with Nelson was unlimited and I would spend the day with him until the ferry arrived. Then I would join the visitors of other prisoners, who had spent the greater part of their afternoon on the hard benches at the harbour after their short visits, as we filed onto the ferry.

Nelson's first question on my arrival at our consultations was always 'How is Zami?'

For many years, his second, conveyed by hand gesture, was 'How is Shorty?' (our nickname for Bram Fischer). A few months after Nelson's conviction, in September 1964, Bram, together with twelve others, was arrested for belonging to the banned Communist Party. He was released on bail to attend to a trial in London. Soon after his return to South Africa, in defiance of Nelson's advice, he went underground. His lawyer, Harold Hanson, read his note to the court:

> By the time this reaches you I shall be a long way from Johannesburg and shall absent myself from the remainder of the trial. But I shall still be in the country to which I said I would return when I was granted bail. I wish you to inform the court that my absence, though deliberate, is not intended in any way to be disrespectful. Nor is it prompted by any fear of the punishment which might be inflicted on me. Indeed I realise fully that my eventual punishment may be increased by my present conduct [...]
>
> My decision was made only because I believe that it is the duty of every true opponent of this Government to remain in this country and to oppose its monstrous policy of apartheid with every means in his

power. That is what I shall do for as long as I can [...] What is needed is for White South Africans to shake themselves out of their complacency, a complacency intensified by the present economic boom built upon racial discrimination. Unless this whole intolerable system is changed radically and rapidly, disaster must follow. Appalling bloodshed and civil war will become inevitable because, as long as there is oppression of a majority, such oppression will be fought with increasing hatred.

Bram was underground for almost a year before his arrest in November 1965. I represented him in his trial on charges of furthering the aims of the Communist Party and conspiracy to overthrow the government. He was found guilty, sentenced to life imprisonment and sent to Pretoria Central Prison.

Bram was a dear friend to Nelson and me, and we were both hit hard by his conviction and, ten years later, his early death. Nelson would say of him:

> Bram was a courageous man who followed the most difficult course any person could choose to follow. He challenged his own people because he felt that what they were doing was morally wrong. As an Afrikaner whose conscience forced him to reject his own heritage and be ostracised by his own people, he showed a level of courage and sacrifice that was in a class by itself. I fought only against injustice not against my own people.[16]

The most treasured of my many fond memories of Bram is of his kindness to my mother. In 1964 my mother visited South Africa for the first time. By then both of my brothers were living in the country, and Yiannis's impending marriage finally persuaded her to make the trip. My mother always had her own way of doing things and her arrival was brought to my attention only when a Greek-speaking South African Airways official phoned me one morning to ask me to collect her from

Jan Smuts International airport. I rushed to meet her and hugged her as hard and as long as the thirteen-year-old boy who had parted from her some twenty years earlier. She would remain with us for two years, and, although she and my father were not reconciled, it was a very happy time for our family.

One summer Sunday, I invited the Fischers to join us for family lunch, and Bram and Molly arrived with their son Paul. Bram greeted my mother with a warm hug and, while my boys rotated the lamb on the spit, took my mother gently by the arm and led her through the perivoli, the bountiful vegetable patch she had by then planted in the north-western corner of our garden. Assuming that Bram spoke Greek, my mother chatted to him happily all the while, and all the while he smiled, nodded and patted her hand reassuringly. After he left, my mother wanted to know all about that 'good Christian gentleman'.

Once he had checked on Winnie and Bram, Nelson would want news about the rest of the legal team and my own family. And then we would get onto his. Nelson's family matters dominated our consultations. Winnie had a natural talent for finding the reasons required for my visits. The health, education and well-being of Nelson's five children – Thembekile (Madiba), Makgatho and Makaziwe (Maki), from his first marriage to Evelyn; Zenani (Zeni) and Zindziswa (Zindzi), his daughters with Winnie – all required their father's input, counsel and advice. His great regret was the consequences of his political choices for his family. He was too private, too restrained, to talk about the burden of his guilt, but at times it was etched heavy in his silence. Usually, however, he remained sanguine as he interrogated my impressions of his children as they grew up in his absence. Not allowed any photographs for the first six years of his imprisonment, he longed for any news of them.

Nelson's mother died of a heart attack in 1968, a year after her second visit to him. He was refused permission to attend her funeral. When twenty-four-year-old Thembekile was killed in a car accident a year later, Nelson withdrew into silence. Thembekile was a troubled young man, alienated from Nelson since he was ten years old, when he took his mother's side in the divorce. The last time Nelson saw him, he was moved to notice that his son was wearing one of his old shirts, too long at the sleeves. He interpreted this gesture as his son wanting to show his father that he had stepped into his shoes as the man of the house. Thembekile was living in Cape Town at the time of his death, running a shebeen in Retreat. Yet he had never visited his father on the island.

Tragedy hit my family the same year when my father was knocked down in a freak motorcycle accident. His leg was broken in two places so badly that the doctors refused to operate. Instead, they encased it in plaster of Paris in the hope that this would relieve the pain and discharged him. He lived alone in an apartment in Joubert Park. Some days later he fell in the bathroom and was unable to move, perhaps unconscious, when the coffee that he was making on the stove boiled over, extinguished the flame, and he succumbed to the leaking gas.

Nelson's younger son Makgatho visited him quite regularly once he turned sixteen in 1966. Nelson was disappointed when Makgatho left school before matriculating and was anxious for him to continue his studies. Makgatho did not have school Latin, which was then a requirement for law, and Nelson asked me to help.

Arthur's sons were at King David School where there was a gifted Latin teacher, and Arthur and I arranged for her to give Makgatho private lessons. He was not a keen student and rarely kept his appointments. He went on to study law at the University of Zululand and graduated with an LLB. He qualified as an attorney, but never made much of a success in practice.

Prison regulations prevented children between the ages of two and sixteen visiting, so for many years Nelson was unable to see his youngest daughters. They were of particular concern to him, not only because of their vulnerable ages, but also because of the violent police raids on their home and the harassment of their mother to which they were so frequently exposed.

Supporters in the United Kingdom and France offered to pay for Zeni and Zindzi to attend a private school. Winnie selected Waterford, a

United World College institution, in Mbabane, Swaziland. She favoured it for safety reasons and because it was a long way from the disruptions of their home life. Nelson had reservations. Despite the appalling Bantu education curriculum, he was uncomfortable with sending his children to an elitist school out of the country. He canvassed my opinion. The school had an excellent reputation and educated African children from across the continent. Our friend Nadine Gordimer sent her son there and I was confident that it was suitable for the girls. I recommended it. He was eventually persuaded and the girls were sent there for schooling.

At Waterford, Zenani fell in love with Prince Thumbumuzi Dlamini, son of Swazi king Sobhuza II. They wanted to marry immediately after leaving school. As neither of her parents could attend a meeting with the bridegroom, the task of representing the Mandelas was given to me. Winnie guided me through the sort of questions that a senior member of the family should ask a potential husband to determine if he was suitable.

Zeni and Thumbumuzi met me in my office at Innes Chambers in downtown Johannesburg. Thumbumuzi made a good impression on me. He was serious and well educated, with a degree from an American university. Winnie asked me to report back to Nelson and persuade him to give his blessing to the proposed marriage. Nelson interrogated me in careful detail about his potential son-in-law. I tried to answer his probing questions. At some point, slightly exasperated, I said, 'Nelson, you must remember that your daughter is marrying a Swazi prince.' He smiled. 'Tell him he must remember that he is marrying a Xhosa princess.'

The couple had a royal wedding in Mbabane. I was unable to attend. Happily, Winnie was granted permission to go to Swaziland for the full four-day festivities.

The marriage afforded Zenani diplomatic status, a key advantage being that she was allowed to have contact visits with Nelson. When she visited her father the day after her wedding, he was allowed to touch one of his family members for the first time in more than a decade.

Unfortunately, the marriage did not last long, primarily because Thumbumuzi claimed the right to more than one wife. Zenani asked me to sue for divorce in a South African court, as they were living in the country at the time. Thumbumuzi did not accept that a South African court had jurisdiction and opposed the notion that a Swazi prince could be divorced at the insistence of his wife. After a long process, he eventually consented to a divorce.

Nelson really adored Winnie. He was never flamboyant in the expression of his love for her, that was not his style, but it was obvious from the way that he spoke about her. They were happy during their brief, interrupted family life together in the short three years from their wedding in 1958 until he became a fugitive in 1961. After that their time together was confined to clandestine visits in other people's houses. In the chaos that erupted after the life sentences were handed down at the Rivonia Trial, they had not even been able to catch one another's eye before Nelson was led out of court. Winnie said her goodbyes, with their daughters, then five and four, at her side, waving and blowing kisses at the Black Maria as it drove Nelson and the other prisoners away.

At one of the early consultations, not long after his conviction, I arrived on the island to find Nelson grim faced. Once we had settled down, he dispassionately recounted how he had returned to his cell to find that a warder had left a newspaper cutting about a wife who was suing her husband for divorce on the grounds that he was having a love affair with Winnie.

'George, I want you to reassure her that I stand by her,' he said steadily.

I did and went further, appearing on her behalf as an intervening party in the matter. On my next visit, I reported back to Nelson that the magistrate had dismissed the claim. His relief was as immediate as it was plain. 'I do not expect her to lead a monastic life, but I do expect discretion,' he remarked softly, almost whimsically. I chose not to relay this to Winnie. I was under no illusion as to how difficult this concession was or how hurtful the persistent rumours of her lovers were to him.

The authorities soon came to understand that their most effective tool against Nelson was his family. Five years into his imprisonment the campaign of persecution against his then thirty-three-year-old wife began in earnest. Of all his private agonies, his impotence as her protector tormented him the most.

In the early hours of 12 May 1969, Winnie became one of the first victims of Section 6 of the Terrorism Act of 1967, which allowed for indefinite detention and solitary confinement without access to a lawyer. In a nationwide swoop, more than a hundred activists across the country were detained. Zenani and Zindzi, home for the school holidays, watched as their mother disappeared into the midnight darkness in a police car. Winnie would spend the next five months in filthy isolation under the blue glare of a phosphorescent light that was never turned off.

During her detention, Joel Carlson, an attorney and old friend, had made representations to the security police on Winnie's behalf. These had all been ignored. When finally the state was ready to bring Winnie and her co-accused to court, her chief interrogator, Major Swanepoel, not content with the unfair advantage afforded by the panoptic security legislation, devised a plan to subvert the trial. He approached the attorney Mendel Levin and offered to give him access to the accused in exchange for certain promises. Winnie, disorientated and sleep deprived, agreed to appoint him as her lawyer.

Mendel Levin made the fatal mistake of appealing to my friend Professor Gwendolen Carter in the United States for funding for him to brief Vernon Berrangé, Fred Zwarenstein and me as counsel. She contacted me. I already knew Levin by reputation. He had publicly announced his membership of the National Party as proof that it was not anti-Semitic and had avoided a long prison term for fraud by testifying against his co-accused. He was not to be trusted.

I immediately visited Nelson to tell him of my concerns. He was not allowed to communicate with Winnie, so he asked me to approach Joel Carlson and for us both to represent her.

By then, Mendel Levin had secured a brief from all the detainees and advised them to plead guilty in exchange for a lesser sentence. When they arrived at court intending to do just that, Joel was waiting on the steps and they were granted a brief adjournment to consult with him.

After this, Winnie informed the court that her husband on Robben Island had instructed her to withdraw the power of attorney she had given to Levin and to entrust her case to Joel Carlson. All twenty-two accused confirmed Joel's appointment and changed their pleas to not guilty.

Joel brought the indictment to me. The twenty-two defendants, led by three women – Winnie, Joyce Sikhakhane and Rita Ndzanga – were accused of acting to revive the ANC. They were charged with ninety-nine offences under the Suppression of Communism Act and the Unlawful Organisations Act, which prohibited furthering the aims of any banned organisation. The accused faced a jail term of ten years and our preliminary view was that most of them would be convicted. We had three weeks to prepare for trial and my instructions were to consult Nelson. I went to the island.

Nelson was named as a co-conspirator and could be called as a witness. I discussed the indictment and the strategy for the trial with him in the time-consuming way that our monitored consultations required. In line with the legal strategy adopted in political trials since the Defiance Campaign trial, Nelson urged that the accused use the case to put apartheid on trial. The accused should not try to prove their innocence, but rather lead evidence in mitigation of sentence. Of course, he would testify if required.

Nelson had not seen Winnie for almost a year and was concerned about her health. He was reassured when I reported to him on how well she had withstood her five months in detention, but he worried about what imprisonment would mean for her and their daughters.

For all his warmth and spontaneity, all emotion would leave Nelson's face and he would sit dead still, impervious, when discussing a matter of gravity. On this occasion, for all that was at risk, he could not hide his tremendous pride in his wife for her courage and initiative in trying to rekindle the spirit of resistance and set up ANC branches. When he asked me what I thought the outcome would be, I replied, 'Well, we'll try our best to get her off. But I want to tell you that she mirrors your image outside very well.' He beamed with delight, and asked me to convey his love to her and tell her that, at last, he had been allowed to put up a picture of her in his cell.

S v Sikhakhane and 21 others or the Trial of the Twenty-Two, as it was known, started in December 1969 in the Old Synagogue in Pretoria with Judge Bekker, who had acquitted Nelson in the Treason Trial, presiding. Nelson had developed a rapport with him during that trial and spoke of him with respect.

Winnie arrived in court in the black, green and gold of the ANC colours. Never one to listen, she was there to speak. When asked to plead, she told the court, 'I find it difficult to enter any plea because I regard myself as having been found guilty already.' She then added that she and the others, particularly Caleb Mayekiso, who had died during his detention, had already been punished. The judge told her that she was wrong in that assumption and entered a plea of not guilty on her behalf.

Winnie's younger sister, Nonyaniso Madikizela, testified as a state witness. She knew little to assist the state's case, but was threatened with long-term imprisonment if she did not testify. The main reason for her presence in court was not to hear her evidence but to demoralise the trialists and warn them of the power of the state to intimidate and turn families against each other.

Under cross-examination, a number of the witnesses conceded that they had been compelled to sign statements that were untrue. Statements made under duress adversely affect their weight. Many judges of the time would disregard or even disallow evidence of torture or compulsion. Not Judge Bekker. He dismissed the objections of the prosecution to this line of questioning and to their alarm allowed David Soggot to elicit the evidence. Under David's gentle cross-examination, witness after witness testified about how they were tortured – methods that included sleep deprivation, standing for two days and physical assaults – and forced to make false statements. At times, the judge would turn to look at the prosecutor and security police and sadly shake his head.

When Winnie's close friend Shanti Naidoo refused to take the oath, the judge appealed to me, as counsel, for assistance as to what he should do in these circumstances. I told the court of a ruling in the Appellate Division that held it irregular to punish anyone who indicated that they were not prepared to give evidence without giving them the opportunity to consult a legal representative. The judge bristled with anger when the prosecutor confirmed his knowledge of the case. After Shanti consulted a lawyer, she testified as to how she had been interrogated for five days and nights without sleep and had answered questions in a dream-like semi-conscious state. Nonetheless, the judge did not accept her reasons for refusing to testify and sentenced her to two months' imprisonment – a welcome respite from her ongoing detention. In jail she would at least be guaranteed the minimal protections of the penal system.

The court was adjourned until mid-February the following year. Our clients remained in custody for the holiday season and Arthur, David and I visited them regularly.

On the day the trial resumed, the attorney general of the province, Kenneth Donald McIntyre Moodie, arrived at court and put himself on record as the new head of the prosecution team. He then withdrew the charges against the accused. No reasons were given. The judge ruled the accused not guilty and discharged them. Before our clients could move, they were re-detained in terms of the Terrorism Act and led back to the prison cells.

Stunned, I asked Moodie to accompany me to the judges' chambers. I complained that my clients had copies of their confidential statements outlining their defence with them when they were taken away. I wanted to see them. The attorney general submitted that the judge had no power to make such an order. No one had the right to communicate with a detainee. Judge Bekker agreed. The attorney general told us that he would see to it that the statements would not be left with the police but secured elsewhere.

Our attempts to have the documents returned to us and to interdict the police to prevent them from ill-treating our clients failed. Judges Theron and Curlewis saw neither urgency nor legitimate concern about the treatment of the detainees. The accused spent another three months in solitary confinement. We succeeded only in securing their access to proper ablution facilities, and Winnie was able to take her first shower in more than six months.

I would learn only many years later that the Department of Justice and the security police were concerned with the direction that the trial was taking, what with the collapse of the arrangement with Levin and the judge allowing the defence such leeway in exposing torture. When Attorney General Moodie refused the security police's requests for him to intervene, they flew to Cape Town and persuaded the minister of justice to instruct him to do so. It was an order they would come to regret.

Three months after the collapse of the first trial, the accused appeared again, this time on charges of terrorism. With them was a new accused, Benjamin Ramotse. I had represented him on charges of sabotage in the early 1960s. He had subsequently left the country to undergo military training for MK before being abducted in Zimbabwe (then Rhodesia) and detained by the security police. His inclusion as a co-accused indicated to us that the state was going to lead evidence of the activities of MK to prove that the accused were guilty of terrorism. It did not get that far.

I had just received the indictment for the new terrorism charges when Isie Maisels called me into his chambers.

'How similar are the allegations against the original accused in the first and latest indictments?' he wanted to know.

'They are exactly the same in content, but the order of the paragraphs has been reshuffled,' I replied.

Isie showed me a recent United Kingdom judgment in the latest *All England* weekly law reports based on the principle (*autrefois acquit*) that an accused cannot be tried for an offence on substantially the same evidence or facts on which he or she has previously been acquitted. This looked as if it would be available to us as a defence. Joel Carlson briefed Sydney Kentridge, who, after a review of the indictments, jubilantly pronounced our case unanswerable. He paced up and down in his chambers, unable to hide his excitement. I had never seen him so confident, despite knowing that Gerrit Viljoen was to be our judge.

By the time we next appeared in court, two of our clients had been released and we were representing the remaining nineteen. Sydney spent two full court days analysing the fifty-eight-page indictment in meticulous detail and comparing it to the previous indictment. The older one was a mere two pages shorter and the only difference was the allegations against the additional accused, Ramotse.

We had put in a special plea on behalf of Ramotse as he was not properly before the court because the Rhodesian police had kidnapped him and unlawfully handed him over to the South Africans. The court rejected this and found that his trial should proceed.

The others were all acquitted. The accused, having been acquitted and then re-detained in their previous trial, remained in place in dazed bewilderment. In an uncharacteristic display of emotion in court, Sydney exclaimed loudly enough for our clients to hear, 'Let them go! Let them go!' while Joel ushered them out of court and told them to disperse as quickly as possible.

Winnie's acquittal only made the authorities more determined. On her release she immediately applied to visit Nelson but was turned down. A further, even more severe five-year banning order was placed on her. She was under house arrest every night and all weekend and forbidden to receive visitors. She almost immediately fell foul of this and was found guilty and sentenced to six months' imprisonment, suspended for three years, for allowing her sister, brother-in-law and their two children into the house to collect a shopping list for her. On appeal, we indulged in hair-splitting minutiae and semantics: 'receive' was to 'shelter'; a 'visitor' is someone who stays as a 'guest', not a postman or an electricity reader. On the state's version, a security policeman checking on Winnie could be deemed a 'visitor'. The Appeal Court overturned her conviction.

In 1971, I appealed Winnie's conviction for communicating with another banned person, the photographer Peter Magubane, who was found under her bed during a police raid. She was again acquitted. Winnie and I were on a winning streak.

The next year I had just completed the inquest into the death in detention of Ahmed Timol – who was thrown from the tenth floor of police headquarters at John Vorster Square – and the enquiry into how his friend and comrade Salim Essop had ended up comatose in Pretoria hospital, when Jules Browde told me it was time to take a break. 'You may be made of steel, George, but you need a break. Go home to Greece – visit your mother.' I explained to him that I still had neither South African citizenship nor a passport. I had not applied for a Greek one, because I feared that it would jeopardise my status in the country or prompt the minister of justice to strike me from the roll of advocates. Two weeks later the phone rang.

'George, this is Judge Galgut. What the hell is the matter with you?'

'What have I done wrong now, Judge?'

'Jules has spoken to me and I have spoken to the judges. Twenty of the twenty-two at the judges' conference have expressed their opposition to the way that you have been treated. I have called Prime Minister Vorster. He suggested you take out a Greek passport but I refused on your behalf and asked him what he thinks the international legal fraternity would think of the fact that the government has refused for thirty years to grant citizenship to the lawyer who has done some of the most important political work in our country. He says that if you take two photographs to the Department of Home Affairs you can apply for a temporary travel document. Citizenship might take some time. Oh, and George, I told him that he should not expect you to change your ways.'

I still had concerns. The 1967 coup by Greek army colonels had led Melina Mercouri and other Greek exiles to call for tourists to boycott the country. I shared my concerns with Arthur. He had a quick and simple answer. 'Oh George, this is not a tourist holiday. It is a pilgrimage.' Nelson nodded when I relayed this to him. 'Listen to Arthur. He is right.' He smiled.

And so I took the pilgrimage and went home with my family after a thirty-one-year absence. Village life was much unchanged despite the running water, electricity and new primary school. Our days were busy reuniting with relatives and old friends, visiting the family fields and swimming in the gentle waves of the Ionian Sea. In the hot summer evenings we would visit one of the six kafeneia in the village (each with its own television, to the delight of my South African sons who had never encountered one) before falling asleep under the leafy pergola on the veranda of the three-roomed home where my mother now lived.

Our pilgrimage to Arethe's family village of Lia, on the border of Albania, was not as happy. Arethe sobbed as she met her penurious Aunt Anthula in the desolate, near-deserted village, the very place where Nicholas Gage had set his 1983 novel, *Eleni.*

On my return home I was granted South African citizenship and with that the relief of sleeping through the night. Nelson was eager to hear about my trip, in particular my stories of the military dictatorship. He shook his head ruefully as I recounted how my cousin had chastised me for challenging an army captain for jumping the queue at a toilet. My cousin warned me that, if I were a local, I could easily have been arrested on a trumped-up assault charge for putting my hand on the officer's arm to stop him. I had also placed my cousin at risk, as the captain might just as easily have charged him with using his motorcar to transport people other than members of his immediate family.

By then the news flow between Nelson and me was not just one-way. With time, the prisoners on the island had established information and news networks that occasionally surpassed my own, and Nelson would be my source for news from the outside. Oliver Tambo was an honoured guest at Mozambique's independence dinner celebration, although this went unreported in South Africa. On Robben Island, it was common knowledge. Nelson was surprised to hear that I knew nothing about it. He recounted with pride the ANC's diplomatic endeavours. Oliver Tambo and Thabo Mbeki had managed to establish more ANC offices throughout the world than the South African government had embassies or consulates.

There was not much that we were allowed to bring the prisoners and their requests were almost exclusively for writing materials and books. Nelson and certain of the other political prisoners – Walter Sisulu,

Dikgang Moseneke, Neville Alexander and Mac Maharaj – insisted on their right to study under the Prisons Act and registered for correspondence courses. They set an example for the other prisoners, many of whom applied to complete their schooling or study further. The prison authorities resented the additional administration and we were, at times, required to threaten them with court action to allow the students to continue with their ongoing education.

Nelson wanted to speak to the warders in their own language. He learnt Afrikaans and did a two-year correspondence course through Unisa before studying Afrikaans history. He was always clear that his quarrel was not with the Afrikaner people: there were many that he admired.

When Jimmy Kruger, in his capacity as minister of justice, police and prisons, visited Nelson in 1973 and asked him if there was anything he could do, Nelson jokingly replied, 'Well, you can release me.' He then requested the collected works of the Afrikaans poet D.J. Opperman for the prison library. When the publisher supplied the works to the island library, Nelson wrote a letter of thanks. 'Of course for such a wonderful gift, one would not want to thank you in writing. I am sure that I will have an opportunity in the very near future to call on you and thank you personally.' The letter, in Nelson's own handwriting, was published on the front page of *Die Vaderland* newspaper.

When Nelson and his Rivonia co-accused arrived on Robben Island in 1964, most of the political prisoners were senior members of the PAC. Within a couple of years they were joined by hundreds of ANC activists.

Nelson was concerned by the antipathy between the PAC and ANC prisoners on the island, and worked hard to persuade the others that the struggle required the unity of all of the oppressed, particularly those in prison. He wanted all opponents of apartheid to be supported and represented, and had endorsed my earlier efforts to fight the extension of Robert Sobukwe's prison term. He encouraged Arthur and me to defend not only members of the ANC, but also the Black Consciousness Movement and the Unity Movement. His concern was to show those lawyers conducting political trials that all activists needed legal defence.

We were not supposed to discuss politics with the prisoners, but Nelson would listen with great interest to my reports on the trials in which I was involved. He was always concerned about the safety of the people outside and inside the country, yet pleased to hear about those taking the struggle forward, and our discussions about my cases was a way to keep him informed and up to date.

In 1974, my luck with Winnie in her court appearances ran out. She was again charged with communicating with the banned photographer Peter Magubane. He had driven her two daughters to her for lunch and all four were caught sharing a snack in his minibus. This time Winnie and Peter were both sentenced to a year's imprisonment, commuted to six months on appeal. We lost our appeals to the Provincial Division and to the Appellate Division in Bloemfontein. Winnie served most of her six months in Kroonstad Prison. She was released in 1975. Her banning order had expired while she was incarcerated. For the first time in thirteen years she was not restricted and was comparatively free.

At the end of the same year, five leaders of the National Union of South African Students (Nusas) were arrested for calling for the establishment of an egalitarian society, the release of political prisoners and the formation of trade unions by black workers. Glenn Moss, Charles Nupen, Cedric de Beer, Karel Tip and lecturer Eddie Webster were charged with conspiring and committing acts to further the aims and objectives of communism. The state presented a rather contorted argument to justify the charges. The aims of the ANC were illegal because the ANC was illegal. The aims of Nusas were similar to those of the ANC. The pursuit of the aims of Nusas was undertaken to further the aims of the ANC, therefore the Nusas leaders were guilty of furthering the aims of the ANC. We soon realised the significance of the trial. If the state made the charges stick, it would close down what political activity was still permitted. A call for universal franchise or for the release of political prisoners would be unlawful on the basis that the ANC had made a similar call.

The attorney Raymond Tucker briefed Dennis Kuny, Arthur and me to represent the accused. Raymond's articled clerk Geoff Budlender was cited in the indictment. As a student leader at the University of Cape Town, Geoff had participated in the activities of both the local SRC and Nusas, which were under attack. Raymond was concerned that it would not be proper for Geoff to be involved with us professionally on the defence team. Arthur was an expert on difficult legal ethical questions. He had served as a chairman of the Johannesburg Bar Council and as a member of the General Council of the Bar. To our delight he accepted Geoff's assurances that he had done nothing unlawful and sanctioned Geoff's participation in the defence. In Arthur's opinion we should not waive Geoff's right to be presumed innocent. During lighter moments we referred to Geoff as Accused Number 6. When the prosecution team was completed with a comparatively inexperienced prosecutor, Theuns Verschoor, a former student leader who had been prominent in the Afrikaanse Studentebond and president of the SRC, we decided that if anyone raised an objection to Geoff we would simply ask what Verschoor was doing on the other side.

The prosecution team was led by P.B. 'Flip' Jacobs, a relatively unknown prosecutor. When I told my colleagues in the common room that I thought he was competent in housebreaking and cheque-fraud cases, Johann Kriegler said in an imperious tone that he was sick and tired of my cynicism and arrogance, adding, 'I know the prosecutor well and want to assure you all that he can also handle a stock-theft case.'

Key prosecution witness Bartholomew Hlopane spent ten years testifying in one political trial after another, including that of Bram Fischer. Under cross-examination he admitted that he had spent eight months in detention and, while in solitary confinement, had bargained with the security police for his release. This led him to confess to being a member of the ANC and the SACP and to swear that the Freedom Charter was the brainchild of the communists. In the Nusas trial, Hlopane began testifying about the roles played by Nelson, Walter Sisulu and Govan Mbeki before their imprisonment. We asked him to stand down and immediately applied for permission to visit the prisoners on Robben Island. Permission was at first refused, then granted, then, on the eve of our departure, withdrawn, before being granted again in response to the ensuing outcry. Raymond Tucker, Arthur and I flew down to Cape Town.

Nelson, Walter and Govan were delighted to see us and as delighted by the student publications, court evidence and newspaper cuttings relating to the case that we brought with us. It was a rare luxury for them to have access to so much news and we spent a full day together in discussion. We knew from previous trials that Hlopane's evidence was false, so we did not spend much time on it, asking them instead for questions for the cross-examination. Our three clients reminded us that Hlopane was originally one of the accused in the Treason Trial. He knew that Professor Z.K. Matthews had given evidence before three judges of the Supreme Court that the Freedom Charter was his (Matthews') idea. Hlopane would also know that the Supreme Court had found that the Freedom Charter was a document advocating democratic values.

All three prisoners offered to give evidence as witnesses for the defence and to clarify the policy of the ANC. They asked me to thank the young people on trial for risking their freedom to call for the release of political prisoners, and to convey their great admiration for their dedication and courage. In the end we did not call any of them. Govan had been punished with three months in solitary confinement after giving evidence in another trial in the Eastern Cape and we did not want a repeat of this.

A year and a day after the Nusas accused were arrested, all five were acquitted.

On 16 June 1976, a spontaneous student demonstration against a regulation that certain subjects were to be taught in Afrikaans in black schools left at least twenty-three students dead in Soweto. The township and many others in the rest of the country erupted in protest and in some instances violence. Ten days later the death toll would be put at one hundred and seventy-four students, although unofficial figures varied between two hundred and seven hundred deaths. Winnie was again detained under the Terrorism Act and held in solitary confinement at the Johannesburg Fort for more than four months. She was not charged on her release.

A commission of inquiry was established to investigate the causes of the Soweto uprisings. The judge president of the Transvaal Provincial Division, Justice Piet Cillié, chaired the commission. Our old friend Percy Yutar was appointed the evidence leader. He was determined to lay the blame for the uprising on Winnie Mandela.

At the time, I was busy with the trial of students wrongly accused of the tragic death of Dr Melville Edelstein, a white sociologist who had worked in Soweto and who was killed on 16 June. Winnie asked me to see Nelson. I went to the island. He did not even need to ask me whether I would represent her at the commission. Of course I would. I noticed again the immense pride Nelson had for his wife.

Yutar read into the evidence the lengthy affidavits of three young detained activists who alleged that the night before 16 June, Winnie had called for the school uprising at a meeting at her house. Winnie denied the allegations and we protested that the evidence was untested. In response, the judge invited Winnie and her legal representatives to appear before the commission. The witnesses would be recalled and we would be given an opportunity to cross-examine.

When Yutar called the first witness and asked him to confirm that the evidence that he had given before the commission was true, he responded: 'No, Dr Yutar. It was not true and you knew it. We told you so when you consulted with us at John Vorster Square. We told you that the statements had been forced out of us. But you persuaded us to come and allow the statements to be read to the commission for information purposes saying that no one was to be adversely affected by our evidence and more particularly not Mrs Winnie Mandela. But what do we see today – Mrs Mandela sitting there and Mr Bizos in front of her ready to cross-examine us. That is not what we agreed to.'

The other witnesses made similar declarations and we decided that, as there was no case to answer, it was not necessary to call Winnie.

When the commission adjourned, Yutar turned to Winnie and asked, 'Winnie, how is dear Nelson?' Without skipping a beat, she replied firmly, 'We are Mr and Mrs Mandela to you. My husband is well.'

In the course of the commission, Winnie became friends with a young man called Aubrey Mokoena, who would later become a member of the Free Mandela Committee established by Winnie. The campaign would capture the imagination of the world and attract huge international support, but Nelson was never entirely comfortable with the call for his release alone, instead of all political prisoners.

The Soweto uprising saw the prisons filled and the population of Robben Island substantially increased as hundreds of young activists were sent there. In the revived spirit of resistance, the authorities decided that Winnie was too inspirational a presence to remain in Soweto. They had nothing with which to convict her, continued detention would be met with an international outcry, and her banning orders and restrictions had proved ineffective. The state invoked a rare remedy usually reserved to resolve the problem of difficult tribal leaders in the rural areas: banishment.

In the early hours of 16 May 1977, Winnie was taken to the Protea police station and informed that she was being removed from Soweto. She was not told where they were taking her. She and Zindzi watched as the police shoved their belongings into suitcases and boxes before roughly loading them, together with mother and daughter, onto a military lorry. By the time they arrived at their destination, the small town of Brandfort in the Free State, almost every piece of crockery was shattered.

I went to Brandfort to see Winnie as soon as I could. I found her with Zindzi in one half of a tiny shack in the township the locals called Phatakahle ('handle with care'). The family of a security policeman occupied the other half of the flimsy structure and at first the partition dividing the homes did not reach the ceiling. There was no electricity, no running water and no floor. The shack was hardly furnished. The door was too small to allow in most of Winnie's furniture. It was a cold day and Winnie lit a fire in a small coal stove, blowing hard to keep it alight. Smoke billowed into the space designated a kitchen by a flimsy curtain. Our lunch comprised all the food she had in the house: a few eggs, a tin of baked beans and half a loaf of bread.

'How can this be legal?' Winnie asked me angrily. She wanted me to visit Nelson and seek his advice.

It was some time before I was able to see Nelson. By then I could convey the bad news that both Arthur and I did not think there were any legal grounds on which we could challenge the banishment. Nelson asked me to request the local attorney, Piet de Waal, to intervene with the government. De Waal was a loyal Nationalist and a friend of Kobie Coetsee, then a member of parliament for the Free State West constituency. I agreed, but did not think that the intervention would amount to anything. Sadly, I was right. Winnie remained in Brandfort where Piet de Waal and his wife, Adele, became her friends. Adele was once served with a summons for entering a Bantu location without a permit when she dropped Winnie at home one evening. An indignant Piet called Jimmy Kruger to object and the summons was promptly withdrawn.

'They will never succeed in building a wall around her,' Winnie's friend Sally Motlana predicted of her banishment. 'It does not matter where they banish her. This woman is so dynamic she will make the birds sing and the trees rustle wherever she goes.' Sally was right. Winnie stayed in Brandfort until she 'unbanished' herself in 1984, but her influence was undiminished and from the dusty expanse of her remote exile she became an international icon, as recognised and cherished as her husband.

Before the year was out, Stephen Bantu Biko had received a blow to his head of such force that it dislodged his brain inside his skull. He was in detention in the Eastern Cape at the time. The minister of justice's initial account had it that he had died from 'self-imposed starvation'. The party faithful congratulated the minister for being such a good democrat that he had 'allowed Biko the choice of death by hunger strike'. The medical evidence led to a different finding. Biko was, in fact, hit violently over the head, transported more than a thousand kilometres naked in the back of a van, and left to die a miserable and lonely death on a stone floor in a prison cell in Pretoria.

Steve Biko was a great South African. Although more than fifty activists had died in detention before him, it was his death that would finally cause an international outcry and plunge the Nationalist government into crisis. Afrikaner intellectuals, religious leaders, academics and newspaper editors were uneasy about what had happened and voiced their concerns. Sydney Kentridge and I represented the family at the inquest into his death, and I kept Nelson informed of the progress. For decades, the magistrates presiding over inquests had accepted the most implausible of explanations for deaths in detention. These included slipping on soap or lunging out of high windows. Their verdicts were inevitably the same: 'No one to blame.' In his closing argument, Sydney said:

> This inquest has exposed grave irregularity and misconduct in the treatment of a single detainee. It has incidentally revealed the dangers to life and liberty involved in the system of holding detainees incommunicado. A firm and clear verdict may help to prevent further abuse of the system. In the light of further disquieting evidence before this court any verdict which can be seen as an exoneration of the Port Elizabeth security police will unfortunately be interpreted as a licence to abuse helpless people with impunity. This court cannot allow this to happen.

Magistrate Prins did not agree. In a thirty-second verdict he found: 'The available evidence does not prove that the death was brought about by any act or omission involving or amounting to an offence on the part of any person. That completes this inquest.'

Biko and his family were denied justice, but his death had done some damage to the reputation of the regime. It seemed that the authorities wanted to prove that they were not the brutal people that the death of Steve Biko revealed. Conditions for political prisoners began to change – they were allowed to listen to music and play sports. On one visit, Nelson told me that the prisoners were performing *Antigone* and that he had been cast in the role of Creon, the king of Thebes. I was familiar with the play and had participated in it as a member of the chorus of the elders in a production at Wits. We discussed the plot and the fact that the prison authorities must have no idea of the revolutionary nature of this piece of theatre. Creon, we decided, was another Hendrik Verwoerd or John Vorster. In a lengthy speech, Creon lectures his son about the responsibility of a ruler to govern sternly without regard to the views of youth. Famously, his son replies: 'But father, it is not a question of age but what is right and what is wrong.' The chorus ends the play with the words: 'Of the world's virtues reasonableness is above all. And the reasonable man remembers to respect the Gods.'

Nelson would never accept any privileges that were denied to his fellow prisoners. Over time, however, the power of his personality, his insistence on his own and others' dignity, elicited a matching response from the authorities and he was treated with a deference denied his comrades. As his lawyer, the special treatment was extended to me and our consultations were no longer monitored. No more liver burgers either. I was invited to lunch at the officers' club where we dined on seafood cocktail, fresh lobster and chilled white wine, served on starched white linen tablecloths with centre flower arrangements. I would sit among the senior officers and make small talk. I learnt something useful, too. As I was first at the table one lunchtime, I asked my prisoner-waiter what crime he had committed. He shook his head before replying politely, 'You know, sir, it is one thing that we prisoners do not want to discuss. So if you do not mind, I cannot tell you what I am in for and when I expect to be released.'

As a matter of practice, the warders offered tea and sandwiches to the lawyers. In the early years of my visit, I refused the offer because the prisoners with whom I was consulting were not offered anything. Near the end of Nelson's stay on the island, I was asked if I would like some tea.

'You know I do not drink tea alone when I am consulting with someone,' I chided the lieutenant.

The officer appeared genuinely offended when he replied, 'We are really surprised, Mr Bizos, that you would think we would offer you tea and not Mr Mandela.'

'In that case, please,' I answered, and they brought a wonderful tray of sandwiches. I noticed that I had eaten more sandwiches than Nelson and asked him why he was not eating. He replied that he had been beaten at tennis a couple of days earlier and had resolved to become fitter for the rematch.

In Brandfort, or 'Little Siberia' as Winnie called it, she received regular visits from international dignitaries and prominent local supporters. Colonel Johan van der Merwe, the then local head of the security police, contrived to put an end to this state of affairs. He wanted her locked up. Winnie was charged with twelve counts of breaking her banning order and summoned to appear before the Regional Court in Bloemfontein. I was instructed to represent her. Winnie, Zindzi and I booked into the President Hotel. On one occasion, to the undisguised distaste of our fellow white diners in the hotel restaurant, the former president of the ANC, Dr James Moroka, joined us to lend moral support.

The charges Winnie faced were not serious. One related to a visit by her sister and three-year-old niece. Winnie had applied to the magistrate for the required permit for the visit but this had been refused, as had her further appeal to him to allow her family to stay as Zindzi's guests if she undertook not to speak to them. Her sister and niece arrived anyway and, unable to send them out into the veld for the night, she defied the magistrate's ruling and allowed them to stay inside with her. Sergeant Prinsloo, the local policeman charged with monitoring Winnie's every move, was a character straight out of a Tom Sharpe novel. He performed his duties with near psychotic diligence. From his favourite hiding place in the bushes outside her shack, he watched Winnie's sister enter the house and jumped out to arrest her. De Waal was called out and negotiated a settlement in terms of which the sister could overnight in the house if Winnie undertook not to speak a word to her.

Another charge concerned her illegally attending a gathering by asking two postal workers whom she met by chance in the street to buy her a chicken from a local farmer. Yet a further one concerned a visit by Priscilla Jana, a close friend but also an attorney awaiting admission.

I was confident of a favourable result. The day before the trial I approached the senior prosecutor and disclosed my defence to him. He told me that he would withdraw the charges against my client in open court the following day. Winnie and I were delighted. The next morning, however, there was no sign of the prosecutor in court. He eventually arrived at 11.30 a.m. and, embarrassed and apologetic, explained that Colonel van der Merwe had insisted that the trial proceed.

The state's star witness, Sergeant Prinsloo, performed poorly in court. Winnie, by now something of a trial veteran, was accomplished. She testified that as Priscilla Jana had visited her in the Johannesburg Fort, she assumed that she could do the same in Brandfort. After all, surely her rights could not be less than those of a convicted prisoner? 'Actually,' she added, 'it seems that I enjoyed more rights in prison than I do in Brandfort.'

Winnie testified that she had told the magistrate that she was not there to defy his authority, but that the circumstances had given her no choice, as she could not send her sister and her niece out into the night. The prosecutor challenged her on this point.

'If you do not want to be defiant, why do you come to court dressed in the colours of the ANC every day?'

'Sir, I have few freedoms, but of the very limited rights available to me, the choice of wardrobe is still mine,' she replied.

The magistrate convicted Winnie on two counts: no matter how trivial and spontaneous the conversation about the chicken, it still constituted an unlawful gathering that she was forbidden to attend. And a child could not receive a visitor as the head of a household. On appeal, the Provincial Division of the Orange Free State Supreme Court set aside the convictions.

Pressure from the white residents of Brandfort for Winnie to be relocated increased over the years. They complained that she had made their servants uppity and difficult – they wanted higher wages and to form trade unions. General Johann Coetzee, then commissioner of police, visited Winnie on his way to the opening of parliament in Cape Town. He offered her a position as a social worker in Welkom. She refused. 'My home is in Soweto. You brought me to Brandfort against my will. I will only leave it to go home to Soweto,' she explained firmly.

In 1981, more than sixty young men and women of all races were detained under the Terrorism Act. The Rabie Commission of Inquiry into Security Legislation was appointed to investigate the conditions under which detainees were held. Two days after the report was released proclaiming their conditions most favourable, the doctor and trade unionist Neil Hudson Aggett was found hanging from the bars of the steel grille in his cell in John Vorster Square police station. I represented his family at the inquest. Once again, the inquest magistrate found that there was no one to blame.

Around this time, the authorities realised that they could no longer afford these inquests into deaths in detention. While the judgments might be in their favour, they were neither legitimate nor credible, not even to many of their own supporters. The state formed covert police hit squads and resorted to killing their opponents, some of the details of which would only be revealed more than a decade later at the Truth and Reconciliation Commission (TRC).

It was not only detention without trial that was no longer working that well for the authorities. Jailing convicted activists together was also not having the desired effect. The authorities had apparently overlooked the tremendous influence that Nelson and his colleagues would have on the newly convicted youths flooding the prisons. Robben Island became a de facto university as the younger activists joined their leaders. In the main, whatever ideological tendency the new prisoners may have favoured when they arrived, the vast majority soon came under the influence of Nelson, Walter Sisulu, Govan Mbeki, Ahmed Kathrada and others. Most emerged staunch supporters of the ANC, and on their release played an important role in the formation of the United Democratic Front (UDF) and its affiliated organisations.

The Department of Prisons resolved to end Nelson's influence. On 31 March 1982, Nelson, Walter Sisulu, Raymond Mhlaba and Andrew Mlangeni were, without warning, explanation or opportunity to say goodbye, told to pack their things. They were leaving the island.

TOP: Winnie Mandela in Brandfort.

BOTTOM LEFT: A poster on the death of Ahmed Timol.

BOTTOM RIGHT: At Steve Biko's funeral.

Zindzi Mandela, wearing a yellow UDF T-shirt, delivering the
'My Father Says' speech that inspired a nation on 10 February 1985.

Chapter 6

~

PRISONER 46664

'My father says'

Nelson, Walter, Raymond and Andrew were transferred to Pollsmoor Maximum Security Prison in Cape Town. After a few months, on 21 October, Kathy joined them. In the beginning they were kept together on the top floor. Their quarters were more spacious than their cells on Robben Island, and for the first time in eighteen years they were given beds. To Nelson's delight, a terrace allowed him to continue the gardening hobby that he had cultivated on the island. Half a dozen half-drums were supplied and were soon producing peppers, onions, spinach and beans.

Winnie sent Zindzi from Brandfort with instructions for me to bring an urgent application for Nelson to return to the island. Mother and daughter, together with millions of others, feared that the move from Robben Island was aimed at isolating Nelson, breaking him down to induce him to agree to proposals detrimental to the struggle for freedom. I told her that I did not want to rely on second-hand reports, and so Ismail Ayob and I went to get instructions from Nelson.

Flanked by the eastern slopes of the Constantiaberg and the edges of Tokai forest, the drab three storeys of Pollsmoor Prison stood discordant among the poplars and pines. It was autumn when I first consulted Nelson there and the tarred prison grounds were dappled in a kaleidoscope of fallen leaves.

My visits to Robben Island were always unknown to the other prisoners who could not see or be seen by visitors other than their own. At Pollsmoor, we arrived to a few prisoners milling around the foyer. They had heard who I was and who I wanted to see and their joy was so obvious as to cause the chief warder to hurry me out of sight and into the offices of the commanding officer.

I was taken up the steps to the third floor where I waited in a small, sparsely furnished room until Nelson was brought in and we were alone. He was relaxed and cheerful and as anxious as ever to hear my news.

'How are Winnie and the rest of the family? How are Arethe and your sons Kimon, Damon and Alexi?'

After I explained the purpose of the visit, Nelson told me that they had not been given any reasons for their transfer, although he believed it was an attempt to weaken both the influence of the ANC among prisoners on the island and the symbolic power of the island in the imagination of the world. Nelson was not unhappy with the move. Their treatment at Pollsmoor was, in many respects, better than on the island. Brigadier Munro, the Pollsmoor commanding officer, arranged visits more frequently and with less fuss than his counterparts on the island.

Nelson did not want any steps to be taken to change the situation. 'I am fine here, George. Tell Winnie and the others that we are all fine. They do not need to worry. I can handle any proposals from the regime. I will not, under any circumstances, agree to being released before the others.'

I reported back to Winnie and Nelson stayed at Pollsmoor.

The president of the ANC, Oliver Tambo, declared 1983 the 'Year of United Action'. The incarcerated ANC leadership endorsed the call. In January of that year, the charismatic president of the World Alliance of Reformed Churches, Reverend Allan Boesak, called for the formation of a united front to organise joint opposition to proposed constitutional reforms for the establishment of a tricameral parliament with two additional houses of parliament for coloured and Indian South Africans. Albertina Sisulu, Walter's wife, whose banning order had recently expired, accepted a leading role in the organisation.

Nelson was encouraged by the formation of the United Democratic Front, a coalition of over six hundred anti-apartheid organisations, and urged Arthur and me to make ourselves available for the advice and defence of its members. Winnie, however, was not favourably disposed towards the UDF. She resented the organisation, more particularly her exclusion from the leadership while Albertina was patron, and refused to become an ordinary member. I did not discuss it with her, but Nelson confided in me that he was disappointed that Winnie would not come to terms with Albertina's seniority.

Locally and internationally the call for the release of all political prisoners grew louder. On Nelson's sixtieth birthday, thousands of letters from well-wishers across the world had arrived on Robben Island. He was given only the six that came from members of his family. Ten years later, in 1988, the Nelson Mandela 70th Birthday Tribute concert at Wembley Stadium in London would be broadcast to an audience of six hundred million people in sixty-seven countries. As each year went by, the outcry intensified. I recalled the words of Captain van Wyk (who had arrested most of the accused at Liliesleaf) shortly after the Rivonia Trial sentences. 'Here we are Mr Bizos, we arrest these people, we convict them and the world is not against them. The world is against us. What are we doing?' he had said with some resignation. Time had only served to emphasise his point.

African leaders of the Bantustan homelands called for the release of all political prisoners, and even the Afrikaner Broederbond recommended to President Botha that he find a way of releasing Mandela. International opposition to apartheid intensified with louder calls for boycotts and economic sanctions from the United States, the United Kingdom, Europe and the newly independent African states. Oliver Tambo played a key role as the leader of the ANC in exile. On a visit to the United States, he was told that the student daughter of a multi-billionaire banker was leading the anti-apartheid campaign at her university. Oliver asked to see her. Within days of meeting her, her father's bank announced that it would not extend the repayment period of a large loan to South Africa. Other banks followed suit. The rand lost more than half its value against foreign currencies.

In January 1985, P.W. Botha offered to release Nelson to the Transkei and all other political prisoners on condition that he 'unconditionally rejected violence as a political instrument'. In parliament, Botha announced that, 'It is no longer the South African government which now stands in the way of Mr Mandela's freedom. It is he, himself.'

Nelson dictated his response to Botha's proposal to Winnie during a visit and instructed her to consult Arthur and me as to the form and manner in which his statement should be released. When Winnie flew back to Johannesburg, she, together with Zindzi and Ismail Ayob, met us in my office at Innes Chambers on Pritchard Street.

Winnie wanted to deliver Nelson's statement herself at a UDF rally the following weekend in Soweto's Jabulani Stadium. The event was to cele-brate and honour Nobel laureate Archbishop Desmond Tutu on his return from the prize-giving ceremony in Oslo. Arthur and I advised her against this. By then she was back in Soweto, having unilaterally 'un-banished' herself from Brandfort. However, there was still uncertainty about the status of her banning order. She would place herself at great risk by speaking at a public rally. Winnie had an answer: her daughter Zindzi, then sixteen, would speak. Arthur and I agreed. We thought that it was unlikely that the authorities would punish Nelson's teenage daughter. We spent the afternoon in chambers working on the notes that Winnie had brought. Arthur added the statement: 'Only free men can negotiate. Prisoners do not enter into contracts.'

When Arthur also suggested the addition of the final statement, 'I will return', I asked him if he knew who else in history had made the same promise to his people. Arthur did not. 'Christ,' I informed my Jewish friend mischievously.

Winnie's suggestion was inspired. On 10 February 1985, speaking with the bold confidence she inherited from both of her parents, Zindzi, wearing a yellow UDF T-shirt, delivered the speech that inspired a nation. 'My father says,' she began:

I am a member of the African National Congress. I have always been a member of the African National Congress and I will remain a member of the African National Congress until the day I die. Oliver Tambo is much more than a brother to me. He is my greatest friend and comrade for nearly fifty years. If there is any one among you who cherishes my freedom, Oliver Tambo cherishes it more, and I know that he would give his life to see me free. There is no difference between his views and mine.

I am surprised at the conditions that the government wants to impose on me. I am not a violent man. My colleagues and I wrote in 1952 to Malan asking for a round table conference to find a solution to the problems of our country, but that was ignored. When Strijdom was in power, we made the same offer. Again it was ignored. When Verwoerd was in power we asked for a national convention for all the people in South Africa to decide on their future. This, too, was in vain.

It was only then, when all other forms of resistance were no longer open to us, that we turned to armed struggle. Let Botha show that he is different to Malan, Strijdom and Verwoerd. Let him renounce violence. Let him say that he will dismantle apartheid. Let him unban the people's organisation, the African National Congress. Let him free all who have been imprisoned, banished or exiled for their opposition to apartheid. Let him guarantee free political activity so that people may decide who will govern them.

I cherish my own freedom dearly, but I care even more for your freedom. Too many have died since I went to prison. Too many have suffered for the love of freedom. I owe it to their widows, to their orphans, to their mothers and to their fathers who have grieved and wept for them. Not only I have suffered during these long, lonely, wasted years. I am no less life loving than you are. But I cannot sell my birthright, nor am I prepared to sell the birthright of the people to be free. I am in prison as the representative of the people and of your organisation, the African National Congress, which was banned.

What freedom am I being offered while the organisation of the people remains banned? What freedom am I being offered when I may be arrested on a pass offence? What freedom am I being offered to live my life as a family with my dear wife who remains in banishment in Brandfort? What freedom am I being offered when I must ask for permission to live in an urban area? What freedom am I being offered when I need a stamp in my pass to seek work? What freedom am I being offered when my very South African citizenship is not respected?

Only free men can negotiate. Prisoners cannot enter into contracts. Herman Toivo ya Toivo, when freed, never gave any undertaking, nor was he called upon to do so.

I cannot and will not give any undertaking at a time when I and you, the people, are not free.

Your freedom and mine cannot be separated. I will return.

After twenty-two years of silence, Nelson had spoken to his country. If ever there was doubt before, there was certainly no doubt now about whom the majority in the country considered their leader.

The same year, Nelson became ill. He had a serious prostate problem requiring surgical intervention and the prison authorities appointed Dr Willem Laubscher to perform the operation. Winnie again approached me to make an urgent application to stop the procedure. She did not want an Afrikaner surgeon working for the authorities to operate on her husband. She wanted top physicians to be consulted. I understood her anxiety but suggested that we first ascertain Nelson's opinion.

I went to see Nelson who reassured me that he considered Dr Laubscher both a competent surgeon and a man of honour. He also believed that the times demanded trust and he did not want to appear suspicious of the good faith of either the doctor or of Afrikaners in general. Winnie's concern was assuaged when Nelson's own doctor recommended that a leading urologist assist in the operation. The operation was a success and for the lengthy period of recuperation Nelson was accommodated in a private nursing home in Cape Town.

He had not been in hospital long when I was summoned to see him. I found him sitting in an easy chair in pale pyjamas and a dressing gown. He was in good spirits and pleased to be having unrestricted visits from Winnie. He praised Dr Laubscher and the nursing staff, and thanked Brigadier Munro, sitting opposite him, for facilitating the visits. He asked the brigadier to remain in the room while we discussed certain important matters.

Nelson told me that the minister of justice, Kobie Coetsee, had visited him in hospital. The minister claimed that he was approaching him without the knowledge or consent of the president to discuss both his conditional release and the possibility of a settlement of the conflict between the liberation movement and the government. Nelson had told the minister that he wanted to be the last prisoner released and that he could not negotiate with him without first consulting with Oliver Tambo. He had told him that he wanted to send me to Lusaka to speak to Oliver on his behalf. He asked me if I would be prepared to leave as soon as possible. Of course I agreed to go.

Nelson interrupted our meeting at noon. He told me that there was to be a change in the nurses' shift and he did not want to delay those who needed to attend to him before they left. At this, two noticeably pretty, young nurses came into the room. From their coy smiles, it was clear that Nelson had charmed them. He asked me to take an early lunch and return a bit later. I did as he asked and we continued our discussion once the new shift had arrived.

Nelson was steadfast from the first. The choice of his own freedom over that of his country's was unthinkable. He was not seduced by the small tastes of freedom that he was allowed after the island nor tempted by the offers of release. He was not corruptible and understood that his continued incarceration posed a difficulty to the government that would strengthen his hand in the challenging negotiations process that lay ahead. He wanted me to reassure Oliver.

When I left the hospital that afternoon, I found Winnie, Zindzi and Ismail Ayob outside surrounded by television cameras and journalists.

'What is wrong with Mandela?'

'Can you confirm that you are here to arrange the release of Nelson directly from the hospital bed?'

'Is it true that he has agreed to go into exile?'

'Where are you going after Cape Town? Do you intend to travel beyond the borders to talk to the ANC and make the necessary arrangements?'

My replies were curt. 'What was said between Nelson Mandela and me is both privileged and confidential. I am going home.' I was evasive about what I would do after that.

First, I had to meet the minister of justice. H.W. van der Merwe, a Quaker professor at the University of Cape Town, served as the go-between. He telephoned the minister's secretary from my hotel room and discovered that, quite by chance, Minister Coetsee and I were travelling on the same flight to Johannesburg that very afternoon. The minister would be up front in a first-class seat. He would see to it that the seat next to him was empty and I was instructed to walk up to greet him as a fellow lawyer. He would then invite me to sit down next to him and we would talk.

I did as told, and the minister and I spent the longer-than-expected flight together. Weather diverted our flight to Durban and back to Johannesburg again, and we were on the plane for some five hours. It was just as well. We had a lot to talk about and used the extra time to our advantage. Minister Coetsee insisted that he was acting without the knowledge of the president and requested that our discussions be kept confidential. He displayed the same exquisite Afrikaner manners that I had come to know through my friendship with Bram Fischer, and our mutual wariness dissipated quickly. We were soon engaged in a frank and earnest conversation.

First, the minister wanted to talk about Nelson. It was apparent from his many questions that his understanding was not limited to intelligence reports compiled by the security police, but was influenced by the more sympathetic and nuanced reports from the Department of Prisons, more particularly Brigadier Munro. He did not need to tell me that Nelson had impressed him. This was clear.

'How far is Nelson prepared to go?' he wanted to know.

'How far is the apartheid government prepared to go?' I asked in return.

'Could Nelson be persuaded to accept release before the other political prisoners?'

'No.' I was emphatic. That was easy. I reminded the minister of Nelson's recent statement read by Zindzi. They could perhaps consider releasing Govan Mbeki first. He had served more than twenty years and the practice of releasing prisoners after fourteen years was well established. Besides, there was Mbeki's age to bear in mind. (Not long after this, Mbeki became the first of the Rivonia trialists to be released.)

The consequences of Nelson's release concerned him. 'Would Mandela, Sisulu and Mbeki accept conditional release to the Transkei?'

'No.' Just as emphatic, just as easy.

'Would those in exile accept a fourth chamber to represent blacks as a first step towards a settlement of the conflict and the end of sanctions and the sports boycott?'

Again, a clear emphatic 'No'. I reminded Coetsee that the majority of coloured and Indian people had rejected the 1983 constitution. They would settle for nothing less than meaningful participation in the affairs of the country, universal suffrage, free and fair elections, and a democratic constitution. The minister was affronted by this comment and told me not to preach to him.

Coetsee wanted an assessment of Oliver Tambo. Like his government, he was concerned that Oliver was not strong enough to withstand the communist influence of Joe Slovo and the others.

As the plane neared Johannesburg for the second and final time, the conversation took on a lighter note. We talked about legal practice, colleagues known to both of us and some recently appointed judges. We parted on good terms.

On my drive home through the midnight streets of Johannesburg, uneasiness settled on me. If the minister was really acting without the knowledge or authority of the president, then the security police and their agents in Lusaka would be unaware of the purpose of my visit. Would they be waiting for me when I returned? I was concerned that I would be detained and interrogated on the reasons for my visit and the content of my discussions with Oliver Tambo.

Johann Kriegler, then a judge of the provincial High Court, was a close friend. When he was appointed as a judge, I had moved into his chambers and he had given me most of my office furniture. He had intervened on my behalf on at least two previous occasions, once when the police sought to ban me from seeing my clients in prison and again when they subpoenaed me to give evidence against Barbara Hogan, a client charged with treason. I trusted him implicitly. Now, once more, I turned to him for advice. He recommended that I take an attorney with me as a defence against a potential charge of conspiracy. I could argue that I was performing a professional legal duty rather than a political function. On a subsequent visit to Nelson, we agreed that I should ask Ismail Ayob to accompany me.

A meeting was arranged for February 1986 and Ismail and I flew to Lusaka. We were welcomed at the airport by ANC representatives who were indistinguishable from any other highly placed diplomats abroad receiving important guests from their country. They cleared our entry into Zambia, and at the hotel produced a letter on an ANC letterhead stating that we were their guests and agreeing to settle the account. I was no stranger to these letters – they had been used as evidence against many a client in the past and I could not help fearing that I might see this particular letter again if things went wrong. Ismail left to attend to other business with one of the Zambian attorneys while I waited in my hotel room.

At 10 p.m., Oliver arrived. It was a delightful reunion for us both. We had not seen, spoken or written to one another in the twenty-six years since his hurried departure from the country in 1960. We were silent as we embraced, fighting back tears of joy and regret.

After we had asked after each other's families, Oliver wanted to know about Nelson, who had by then been discharged from hospital and was back at Pollsmoor Prison. He was anxious to know about the state of his health and the conditions under which he was being held. He asked what was behind the rumours of his possible release and whether his illness and isolation could lead to an embarrassing arrangement.

I reassured him that the conditions of Nelson's incarceration had improved. He was not isolated, but very much in touch with political developments in the country. He had access to the Rivonia trialists, as well as the leaders of the UDF. He now had contact visits with Winnie, a radio and television, and, of course, was enjoying his rooftop garden.

I outlined Nelson's attitude as he had instructed me. There would be no early release. He stood by the speech Zindzi had read out in Soweto. At this, Oliver smiled. He knew the speech well and said that it had dispelled any concerns he might have had. The ANC in exile was also pleased by what Nelson had said and welcomed the support that the speech had garnered for the liberation movement out of the country.

I told Oliver that Walter and most of the other prisoners, with the exception of Govan Mbeki and Harry Gwala, agreed with Nelson's approach. At the time I was busy with the Delmas Treason Trial of twenty-two UDF members, including three of the top leaders, and was also able to report to Oliver what I knew of their attitude.

Oliver asked if I really believed that the minister was acting without the knowledge of the president. No, I did not. Neither did he. The improbability of the minister endangering his own political career by keeping secret from the president discussions to which so many other people were privy strengthened our belief that talks about talks might be in the offing.

Oliver confirmed that he did not regard Nelson's intentions a departure from the policy of the ANC since the 1950s to bring the government to the negotiating table. He understood that any exploratory talks needed to remain secret to avoid their floundering in public debate at that early stage. I was to assure Nelson that the ANC in exile had full confidence in him and that he had Oliver's full support. The national executive would support specific proposals when they were put on the table. He also urged me to ensure that Coetsee and his government did not suffer under any delusions that the struggle would stop just because there was the possibility of talks.

Once we had finished with the meat of the meeting, we talked as old friends. Oliver was well informed and pleased with the political situation in the country and the positive popular response to the UDF. Internal ungovernability, coupled with an intensification of the economic and sporting boycotts, was having an impact.

With some awe, he remarked on what an international icon Nelson had become despite his lengthy incarceration, confiding softly, 'I sometimes ask myself if it might not have been better if Nelson had gone into exile instead of me.' I reassured him that he was undervaluing his contribution. I knew of no liberation movement that was as united as the ANC had become under his leadership.

Oliver and I talked for over five hours until past three the next morning, when his security officials, who had been standing sentry outside the door, interrupted the meeting from concern that it was becoming a security risk.

I visited Oliver the next morning at his home in the guest cottage in the lush grounds of the presidential residence. President Kenneth Kaunda was there and Oliver introduced me as a friend and lawyer. I told the president that I brought him greetings from Nelson. He was moved and, wiping tears from his eyes with his customary white handkerchief, he said, 'Tell my friend Nelson that none of us in Africa feel free while he is in jail. We will do whatever we possibly can to gain his freedom.'

As we sat down to lunch, the grandfather clock in the dining room struck one and an aide brought a small transistor radio tuned to the BBC news for Oliver. He waved him away. The aide returned a few minutes later and whispered in Oliver's ear. Oliver burst into sudden tears and told us that Olof Palme, the prime minister of Sweden, had been killed. He asked his secretary to book him a flight for the funeral and stopped eating. Our conversation came to an end and our questions were left unanswered. Had a South African agent done it? Where was the ANC to find such a good friend again?

Later, as he bade us farewell in the airport lounge, Oliver asked us not to divulge where he was living. South Africa's hit squads had assassinated ANC leaders in the neighbouring states of Swaziland, Lesotho, Botswana, Mozambique and Zimbabwe. Unsuccessful attempts had also been made in Zambia. Oliver Tambo was the number one target on every hit list and we recognised that every precaution had to be taken.

I returned to South Africa and to a visit from Winnie. Since his discharge from hospital, Nelson was being kept separate from his comrades. 'What are you going to do about it?' she asked me.

'I am going to visit him,' I replied, without adding that the primary reason was to report back to him on my trip to Zambia.

Nelson had been moved again. He was now imprisoned on his own in a ground-floor section of Pollsmoor, with three rooms and a toilet for his exclusive use. He did not want to agitate to rejoin the others. He missed them, as well as the rooftop garden and fresh air, but he had been assured that the four would be brought together whenever he requested it.

He was pleased to hear of Oliver's confidence and endorsement. He was also delighted with the message from KK, as he called the Zambian president. He instructed me to report back to the minister of justice.

Once again, I sought Johann Kriegler's advice and this time he agreed to accompany me to the meeting with the minister. Should we be recognised, it would not be considered unusual for a judge to meet with the minister of justice. The minister's home was at Bryntirion, a ministerial suburb in Pretoria. As we drove up to the barbed wire, security boom and policemen guarding the property, I remarked to Johann, 'The ministers live in similar conditions to the ANC leadership in exile.' 'Yes,' he agreed, 'they both live in military camps.'

Kobie Coetsee was alone. He opened a bottle of fine KWV wine and served us himself, his patrician manners delaying the asking of any questions until we had emptied the first glass. His response to my report was clearly aimed at establishing whether Tambo spoke on behalf of everyone associated with the ANC in exile. The South African establishment believed that the communists dominated the ANC and the minister wanted to know if the SACP were in agreement. I reassured him that Tambo was highly respected by the national executive committee and its structures, and that, from what I knew of the ANC, it operated by consensus.

The minister's sanction of my visit to the president of the ANC in exile emboldened me. After that, I served as a messenger and courier for Nelson. On his behalf, I travelled to London and Athens to see Oliver, Chris Hani, Albie Sachs and other members of the ANC national executive, as well as various international leaders.

Conservative British prime minister Margaret Thatcher had her reservations about the ANC and about Nelson. These were not shared by her ambassador, Sir Robin Renwick, or the undersecretary for Africa, Lynda Chalker. On Nelson's instructions I visited Chalker to thank her for her efforts in persuading her prime minister to put pressure on the apartheid government for the release of political prisoners. As I entered her office, she embraced me and asked warmly, 'George, how is dear Nelson?'

When the Eminent Persons Group – led by Nigerian president Olusegun Obasanjo – visited the country, they met with Nelson in Pollsmoor Prison. However, any hopes of a meaningful outcome from their visit were sabotaged by a series of deadly raids ordered by the minister of defence, Magnus Malan, into refugee camps in Zambia, Botswana and Zimbabwe.

In November 1987, the process of freeing prisoners began with the release of Govan Mbeki. He immediately took up a public leadership role on behalf of the still-banned ANC in flagrant disregard of its unlawful status. Many in the security establishment were angered by his behaviour and the fact that they could not censor him, ban him or confine him under house arrest in Port Elizabeth. It is arguable that his busy political agenda delayed the release of the rest of the Rivonia trialists and other political prisoners by a few years. If so, they never complained about his conduct but appreciated that he did what was expected of an ANC leader.

In December 1988, after more than six years at Pollsmoor Prison, Nelson was transferred to Victor Verster Prison in Paarl. Here, he stayed at the end of a meadow in the relatively isolated splendour of the house of a senior prison officer. His new home was fully furnished in the style of an early Holiday Inn and had its own swimming pool. Nelson had a key to the front door, a telephone and a television, and, to his utter astonishment, a microwave oven. On Walter's first visit to the house, Nelson immediately rushed him to the kitchen to marvel with him at a cup of cold water emerging boiled after half a minute.

His time here was such that when he built his home in Qunu after his release it was designed on the same floor plan.

Nelson welcomed his many guests wearing suits and ties, his collared shirts perfectly starched. He would take his daily constitutional along the garden paths and sometimes I would join him for the more confidential of our conversations. We learnt only later that the flowers were bugged.

Nelson was now assigned a personal cook. Warrant Officer Jack Swart and warder James Gregory and his son attended to him. They were really more butlers than jailers. As we sat down for lunch one day, Nelson called Gregory junior to bring the wine to the table so that I could select one. I indicated my preference, a bottle of dry white. Nelson thanked the young man for having tipped him off that I would not drink the semi-sweet wines that he and most of his other guests preferred. He chuckled as he warned me to be careful. 'The authorities know a lot more about you than you might suspect, George,' he teased.

On 18 July 1989, Nelson celebrated his seventy-first birthday surrounded by his entire family.

By the time he moved to Victor Verster, Nelson's relationship with Winnie was not a happy one. She visited him frequently but refused to spend the night with him, although this was permitted. From around the time of the 'My Father Says' speech, Winnie's lack of judgement had progressively diminished her stature and sullied her reputation. For Nelson, the movement and the nation it was a serious embarrassment. For Winnie, it was nothing less than a tragedy.

Winnie distanced herself from the rest of the democratic movement and became a law unto herself. Her speeches were angry and provocative, often in defiance of Nelson and contrary to the policies of the liberation movement. She undermined her husband's negotiations for a peaceful settlement with the government and made inflammatory calls for 'neck-lacing' in the townships. Nelson established the Committee of Three, comprising Archbishop Desmond Tutu, Dr Nthato Motlana and Dr Beyers Naudé, to advise her. She rejected their counsel. When her conflict with Nelson started, she cut contact with me and refused to take my calls.

Informants and rumours were powerful weapons in the dark and suspicious atmosphere of the 1980s. Winnie surrounded herself with a number of people, not all of whom were either trustworthy or honourable. Nelson was particularly troubled by reports of the activities of the Mandela United Football Club. He suspected Jerry Richardson, the coach and head of Winnie's security, of being a police plant and of inciting the young, supposed football players to commit crimes against people in Soweto. The UDF accused the football club of the abduction in December 1988 of five young men from the home of a Methodist minister, Paul Verryn. The youths were subsequently kept in an outhouse at the back of Winnie's Soweto home and assaulted. One of the five, the fourteen-year-old Stompie Seipei, was later found murdered. Winnie tried to justify the abduction by claiming that she had believed the reports of Verryn's housekeeper, Xoliswa Falati (herself a suspected informer), that the minister had sexually molested the youths.

When the UDF issued a statement that no democratic lawyer should represent Winnie against the allegations of abduction and assault, I felt compelled to contact her. I knew that the UDF statement was intended mainly for me, but I was not affected – I was accustomed to criticism – and I considered myself honour bound to defy it. I thought it wrong for some of my friends and colleagues to declare that anyone was not worthy of being defended by a lawyer of their choosing. I also believed it my duty to remain true to my undertaking to Nelson to look after his family.

I invited Winnie for a consultation. She chose the middle of the afternoon and arrived overdressed, accompanied by a number of guards. Winnie denied that she was present during the assaults. No charges were brought against her at that stage, and Richardson was charged with and convicted of the murder.

For Nelson, Victor Verster had become not so much a jail as an office from which the leader of the ANC conducted his business. Here, he took charge and proved himself an accomplished negotiator. The government seemed to have mistaken Nelson's gentle, reasonable manner with weakness and had not recognised how tough, or how stubborn, he was. They started their engagement with him on the assumption that he was corruptible, that they could strike a bargain, but in their arrogance and misjudgement of him they soon lost control of the direction of the negotiations.

From March 1989, Nelson started meeting in prison with a committee of four representatives from government: justice minister Kobie Coetsee, head of the National Intelligence Service Dr Niel Barnard, director general of Justice Fanie van der Merwe and commissioner of prisons General Willemse. They would meet forty-seven times before Nelson's release in February 1990, and Nelson would be required more than once to make it clear that 'the majority need the minority. We do not want to drive you into the sea.'[17]

Nelson met with President P.W. Botha only once, in July 1989. The meeting was cordial but short and lasted less than half an hour. In August, President Botha had a stroke and resigned. President F.W. de Klerk replaced him.

In October, I was invited to speak in the UN plenary hall at a special meeting of the anti-apartheid committee attended by ninety ambassadors and other dignitaries. Before the session began, I was told by a group of excited South African exiles that the Pretoria government had just announced the release of Walter Sisulu and other Rivonia trialists, but that nothing had been said about Nelson. I told them of his determination not to accept his own release before the other political prisoners were free.

As I was led through the august assembly, I decided to abandon my speech and talk off the cuff. I praised the work of the United Nations, recounting the morning that Bram had arrived with the front page of the *Rand Daily Mail* reporting that the UN had called for the release of the Rivonia trialists and of his certainty that they would not be hanged. When I then announced the news that I had just heard, the auditorium broke into joyful applause.

Still, I was not prepared for President de Klerk's announcement at the opening of parliament on 2 February 1990 that he would lift the ban on the ANC, PAC and SACP, place a moratorium on the death penalty, lift the state of emergency restrictions, and limit detention periods to six months. I was as taken aback by his declaration that:

> The agenda is open [...] Among other things, those aims include a new, democratic constitution, universal franchise, no domination, equality before an independent judiciary, the protection of minorities as well as of individual rights [...] I wish to put it plainly that the government has taken a firm decision to release Mr Mandela unconditionally.

I did no work for the rest of the day, which was spent in speculative conversations with my colleagues about the motives, and consequences, of this move.

Nelson was released in the early afternoon of Sunday 11 February 1990. The sixty kilometres from the gates of Victor Verster Prison on the outskirts of Paarl to the Grand Parade in the centre of Cape Town were lined with thousands of supporters. Sadly, I had a trial the next day so could not fly down to Cape Town to welcome him. Instead, I joined thousands of others across the world and watched Nelson walk out of prison from home on the state-controlled television.

Arthur Chaskalson and I at the Soweto rally
to welcome Nelson home.

Chapter 7

~

FREE NELSON MANDELA

'Take your guns, knives and your pangas and throw them into the sea'

'Today, my return to Soweto fills my heart with joy. At the same time I also return with a deep sense of sadness...'

'Welcome home, our leader, welcome home!'

Eighty thousand people cried as one at an exuberant rally in Soweto, two days after Nelson's release. Arthur and I arrived at Soccer City football stadium together and were ushered through to the VIP section just in time to watch Nelson's helicopter land on the playing field. From the podium, Nelson instructed the master of ceremonies, Cyril Ramaphosa, to announce over the public address system that George Bizos and Arthur Chaskalson should come forward. It took a good twenty minutes for us to make our way under marshal escort through the crowd and up to the stage to join the seated dignitaries. When we finally got there, a free Nelson Mandela flung his arms around me in a tight embrace.

The next day I called his home in Soweto. Winnie answered the telephone. Complaining that the house was no longer hers, she told me that she was determined to have a family lunch on Sunday but that I should come over in the morning. I arrived to long queues of supporters and media lining Vilakazi Street. Thirty years her junior, Winnie's young lover Dali Mpofu was standing sentry at the gate. He waved me in past a number of UDF office bearers who had been denied entry and were waiting

TOP: Arthur and I mounting the podium with Cyril Ramaphosa.

BOTTOM: Arthur and Nelson.

outside. Mirella Kalostipi of ERT, the Greek national broadcaster, was with me. I had told her that there was no possibility of her meeting Nelson, but she had asked to accompany me and film me arriving at the house.

Winnie welcomed me warmly and took me to a bench under the tree that dominated the small garden. There in the shade sat Nelson, the Sunday newspapers spread out before him. Wearing one of the colourful tunic shirts with which his sartorial style would become synonymous after his release, he looked as casual, as at ease, as any other suburban grandfather relaxing into a familiar weekend routine. We talked as old friends do, sharing news of our families and friends, reminiscing about Bram. Nelson asked me whether Arthur and I would be prepared to assist him and the ANC with the drafting of the new democratic constitution. I confirmed that I would, and would approach Arthur, confident that he would too.

When I stood up to leave, Nelson asked me what my hurry was. I explained that I had a Greek journalist and cameraman waiting in the car. Nelson was indignant. 'George, how could you leave them waiting outside? They must believe that I have no manners. Bring them in and let me meet them!' he chided. And so, in one of Nelson's first exclusive interviews, a delighted Mirella asked him how he was going to spend his first Sunday at home after twenty-seven years. The fifteen-minute interview was broadcast across the world.

A few days later, Cyril Ramaphosa called me to tell me that the national executive committee of the ANC had appointed Arthur and me as members of the legal and constitutional committee. I asked Cyril whether that meant that we had to get ANC membership cards.

'No, that is not necessary, George. We do not need your twelve rand,' he answered cheerfully.

'But what are we to do as members of the constitutional committee?'

'Everything,' he replied, adding, 'I will try and get you an exemption from toyi-toying.'

The ANC did not yet have an office. The newly established constitutional committee met in a small boardroom at the Holiday Inn in downtown

Johannesburg. Our group comprised lawyers, legal academics and legal activists, and included Albie Sachs, Zola Skweyiya and Dullah Omar. Our first task was to draft a constitution and a bill of rights consistent with the Freedom Charter and universally accepted social democratic principles. We all supported the establishment of a Constitutional Court to enforce the constitution and guarantee the fundamental rights of every individual even, if necessary, against a majority of the voters and members of parliament. Nelson arrived at the first session to thank us for participating.

'We in the ANC do not want a charter that favours any particular group of people in the country,' he instructed. 'The constitution must incorporate those universally accepted principles that will ensure the democratic ideals of all South Africans. Make it fair. This is for everyone.'

Nelson had wanted to be the last political prisoner in the country. He was distressed that he was not and that political prosecutions and detentions without trial continued after his release. I received a call one morning from the office of the commissioner of prisons to inform me that my applications to see prisoners in Johannesburg and Pretoria had been granted. I was taken aback. I had not made any applications. Nevertheless, I thanked him. As I put the phone down, it rang again. It was Nelson calling from Zimbabwe. Political prisoners had embarked on a hunger strike for their release. He wanted me to meet with them to tell them that negotiations over their release were advanced but at a delicate stage, and that threats of a strike could derail them. He dispatched me to Johannesburg and Pretoria prisons and Arthur to Robben Island.

My reception by the fifty or so young prisoners at 'Sun City' – the ironic nickname for the new Johannesburg prison – was reserved. They did not know me and clearly did not trust me. Fortunately, Patrick Maqubela, slightly older than the rest, was among them. He had been a candidate attorney for Griffiths and Victoria Mxenge and sentenced to five years' imprisonment for refusing to testify against his colleagues. Our mutual delight at seeing each other after so many years relieved the tension. The group decided to stop their strike and asked me to convey their good wishes to Mr Mandela. The outcome on Robben Island was the same.

No agreement was reached on political prisoners and they remained imprisoned. President de Klerk used his presidential prerogative to release a few high-profile struggle leaders as well as a few right-wingers convicted of racist murders. For the rest, a committee of three retired judges ruled slowly on applications for indemnity. In the end it took mass action and sustained international pressure to secure the release of most of them.

Once the ANC established offices at Shell House on Plein Street, Johannesburg, I would visit Nelson regularly. Although I was well known, the climate was such that my car was routinely searched and the undercarriage examined for explosives. In his office adjacent to Walter's on one of the upper floors, he would consult me on legal and constitutional issues or we would share a meal, usually both. As I perused press statements and drafts of speeches, we would chat.

Nelson wanted to know how to handle a mixed cabinet in a unity government. 'How many heads of government have handled such cabinets in the past and how did they do it?' he wondered. 'Do you think everything will have to be put to the vote?'

I recounted how the French leader, Georges Clémenceau, had handled his. 'He used to canvass opinion and then announce his decision as a cabinet resolution, simultaneously asking if there were any resignations.' Nelson looked dubious.

Next he rejected the apartheid practice of judicial appointments by the executive and wanted suggestions for an alternative. Arthur proposed the establishment of an independent body for judicial promotions and appointments on which political parties and the legal profession were represented. His suggestion would be accepted and evolve into the Judicial Service Commission. As president, Nelson would later be entitled to appoint four of the twenty members and would nominate me as one.

My participation on the ANC constitutional committee was followed by my appointment, in December 1991 , as advisor to the ANC negotiators, seconding Zola Skweyiya, at the World Trade Centre in Kempton Park. I would spend much of the next three years attending lively meetings debating the terms of the interim constitution – a negotiated transitional constitution that would provide for an elected constitutional assembly to vote in a new government and draw up a permanent constitution for the country.

Around the same time, a rich man briefed me to represent him in his divorce. He had left his wife of many years for his beautiful young secretary. On the date the matter was to be heard, the wife did not appear at court and a divorce was granted in her absence. She applied for a *rescission* of the judgment and I was briefed to oppose it. The wife explained to the judge that she had not been at court because her hairdresser had misinformed her that if she did not appear the divorce could not be granted. At the end of the first day, the judge called counsel into his chambers. 'Your client was prepared to be generous before his wife's stupidity left her with nothing,' he said to me. 'He is wealthy. He is also estranged from his two daughters because of the way he has treated their mother. Why don't you advise him to settle? He does not need to give her everything he originally intended, but he should give her something.' I reported this to my client and told him that I agreed with the judge.

'But you told me that I have an iron-clad case!' he barked rudely. 'Have you changed your mind?'

'No, I haven't, but this is what the judge suggests and I happen to agree with him.'

'No! I do not want to hear another word from you. Now get back into the court and do your job and win my case!' he ordered.

I did as instructed.

By the time I got home that evening I had made up my mind. I telephoned Arthur. 'I have decided to come and work with you. Write a letter of appointment for me for the Legal Resources Centre – I will do seven months at the centre and five months private work every year. But Arthur, I won't do any administration or fundraising.' I had done some work for the non-profit public-interest legal firm that Arthur had started in 1979. Now we formalised the arrangement.

Shortly after his release, Nelson confided in me that his relationship with Winnie was strained. She refused to share his bed. They spent little private time together and most evenings she would leave the house without telling him where she was going. She drank heavily. He cast no judgement and placed no blame, but in a voice flat with regret said simply, 'We cannot seem to agree. Things are not good, George.' Within a few months, he had moved into a suite at the Saxon Hotel in Sandton. Not long after that he bought a house on 12th Avenue in Houghton.

The tension between them sometimes went public. Winnie countered Nelson's calls for national reconciliation with calls to arms. When Nelson took her on a European tour, she contradicted him on a public platform in Germany. Asked about the prospects of a peaceful settlement, Nelson replied, 'We will find one another, there will be no civil war and peace will reign.' Winnie did not agree. 'The struggle will continue. The government only understands violence.'

On their return to South Africa, I reminded Winnie of her claim to her German biographer that she would listen only to Nelson and George Bizos. 'Follow the example of Prince Philip and not Evita,' I told her. 'The Duke of Edinburgh always walks at least one step behind the queen [of the United Kingdom].'

'I am no Prince Philip,' she said, laughing me off.

Winnie would also have nothing to do with those who criticised her. At Nelson's request, she headed the ANC's social welfare desk, yet she refused to acknowledge certain of the ANC leadership. Nelson, ever a loyal and disciplined member of the ANC, continued to work closely with her foes. She considered this a betrayal: he should make her enemies his. The conflict was untenable.

A year after Nelson's release, Winnie was charged with the abduction and assault of Stompie Seipei and four others. Nelson and Winnie were hardly on speaking terms by then, but he called me and told me that his daughters had reported that she wanted me to represent her but was too proud to ask. He wanted me involved to strengthen the public perception that she had his support despite their estrangement and asked me to defend her.

I took on the case at once. Advocates Pius Langa and Dikgang Moseneke, who would later become chief justice and deputy chief justice respectively, were briefed with me. The matter was heard in the Johannesburg Supreme Court on Pritchard Street. Nelson did not want to create the impression that he had abandoned her. Every day he walked from the ANC headquarters at Shell House to attend the trial, often accompanied by leading members of the ANC. He would emerge with Winnie at lunchtime, return to follow the proceedings and leave with her in the afternoon, all before the hundreds of enthusiastic supporters and television cameras waiting outside. He would not, however, attend our consultations in my office at Innes Chambers across the road from the court. Dali Mpofu, the young lawyer with whom she openly continued her love affair, was a member of her defence team and he was always present.

The defence had irrefutable evidence to prove that Winnie was in Brandfort at the time that Stompie and the other youths were abducted in Soweto.

At the murder trial of Jerry Richardson, the Mandela United Football Club coach, three of the abducted youths had given evidence alleging that they were assaulted in Winnie's presence. My colleagues carefully went through the record of the youths' evidence and prepared notes for me to use in cross-examination to establish the improbability of their allegations. The trial judge could not reject Winnie's alibi for the poor testimony of the prosecution witnesses. He ruled that Winnie was not present at the time of the assaults, but that she was aware that the youths were being held in her Soweto house. He found her guilty of kidnapping and as an accessory after the fact to the assault.

The Supreme Court of Appeal set aside Winnie's conviction as an accessory after the fact to assault, but let the conviction for kidnapping stand, although it qualified its findings in Winnie's favour. Although the court found that there was no evidence to support her claims about Verryn, it disagreed with the trial judge that there was no evidence to support her claim that she had believed the allegations of her co-accused, Xoliswa Falati. The six-year jail term was set aside and replaced with a fine and a suspended sentence.

In 1992, between Winnie's conviction and her appeal, Nelson handed me a three-page letter. It had been sent to Nelson by the *Sunday Times* newspaper for comment and confirmation that it was written by Winnie to Dali Mpofu. Nelson asked me to take the letter to Winnie and find out if she had written it. I met Winnie at Zindzi's Bezuidenhout Valley home one Sunday morning. We sat together at the kitchen table and I wordlessly passed her the note. Winnie glanced at it, burst into tears and said that she had been betrayed. It was not necessary for her to say anything more. Nelson showed no emotion, least of all surprise, when I reported back to him. He called the editor to confirm that the letter was indeed from Winnie to Dali.

The *Sunday Times* published the letter as front-page headline news. In it Winnie warned her lover: 'Before I am through with you, you are going to learn a bit of honesty and sincerity and know what betrayals of one's love means to a woman. Remember always how much you have hurt and humiliated me [...] I keep telling you the situation is deteriorating at home, you are not bothered because you are satisfying yourself every night with a woman. I won't be your bloody fool, Dali.' The newspaper report included details of cheques made out to Dali from the ANC's Department of Welfare, which Winnie headed.

Several months earlier, on 13 April 1992, a sombre Nelson, flanked by his old friends Walter Sisulu and Oliver Tambo, announced his separation from his wife. I had only ever seen him wear so grave an expression once before: twenty-eight years earlier as he waited to hear if he and his comrades had been condemned to death. Now, as then, he fumbled with the notes in his hand. On this occasion, he was required to read them.

During the two decades I spent on Robben Island she was an indispensable pillar of support and comfort to myself personally [...] She endured the persecutions heaped upon her by the government with exemplary fortitude and never wavered from her commitment to the struggle for freedom. Her tenacity reinforced my personal respect, love and growing affection. It also attracted the admiration of the world at large. My love for her remains undiminished [...] I part from my wife with no recriminations. I embrace her with all the love and affection I have nursed for her inside and outside prison from the moment I first met her.

He stood. 'Ladies and gentlemen, I hope you'll appreciate the pain I have gone through.' I had witnessed Nelson sit out a twenty-seven-year prison sentence, but this was as close to despair as I had seen him.

In the early days of his separation, Nelson would occasionally join our extended family Sunday lunches on our sunny stoep at home, usually accompanied by a grandson and sometimes his secretary, Barbara Masekela. He was particularly fond of lamb on the spit, which he would eat with a small glass of the sweet white wine he preferred. After our meal, he and I would visit the vegetable garden and discuss the state of the spinach or share ideas for managing hail damage.

I was also a fairly regular visitor at his home, dropping in on my way home from work in the evenings. On one occasion, I popped in on a Sunday afternoon to deliver a speech I had drafted for him. I left my mother-in-law, who I was taking home after lunch, waiting in my car. It took a bit longer than expected for Nelson to read the draft and comment on it. When he saw me out to the car, he was astounded to see her there. I introduced her to him. 'What kind of mother are you that you allowed your daughter to marry such a rude man who leaves you outside in the car while he comes in to visit me?' he teased. He never lost his dry sense of humour, but over this period he was rarely his usual exuberant self.

For some time after they separated, Winnie could still cut him to the quick. He could not disguise his anguish as he told me about how he had phoned Winnie during an official visit by her to the United States and Dali had answered the phone of her hotel bedroom. A broken undertaking made the betrayal all the worse. 'Before she left I had made it clear that she was not to take him with her and she had agreed. I believed that she would respect her word,' he said tersely, before descending into a stony silence.

The next year, Nelson suffered another terrible loss. I was in the village in Greece on the Easter weekend of 1993 when the café owner told me that my brother had phoned from South Africa to say that one of the ANC leaders had been killed. I thought it was Nelson. I immediately contacted my son Damon, who told me that Chris Hani had been shot outside his house in Dawn Park, Boksburg.

Chris Hani was a popular leader of the ANC. He and Nelson had a natural affinity and Chris became like a son to him. His assassination by the Polish immigrant Janusz Waluś and right-winger Clive Derby-Lewis brought South Africa to the brink of civil war. On the night of Hani's killing, Nelson took to television to appeal to his country:

> Today, an unforgivable crime has been committed. The calculated, cold-blooded murder of Chris Hani is not just a crime against a dearly beloved son of our soil. It is a crime against all the people of our country [...] We are a nation in mourning. Our pain and anger is real. Yet we must not permit ourselves to be provoked by those who seek to deny us the very freedom Chris Hani gave his life for. Let us respond with dignity and in a disciplined fashion.

Three days later, in another televised address, Nelson told the nation:

> Tonight I am reaching out to every single South African, black and white, from the very depths of my being. A white man, full of prejudice and hate, came to our country and committed a deed so foul that our whole nation now teeters on the brink of disaster. A white woman, of Afrikaner origin, risked her life so that we may know and bring to justice this assassin.

211

I had never seen Nelson so alarmed. His public appeal to his supporters not to be provoked into committing acts of revenge was successful and Hani's death proved to be a turning point for the negotiations process. De Klerk realised that he could not control the country without the help of Nelson and the ANC. Nor could he put off the timetable for the adoption of the interim constitution and the elections. Dates were finally agreed: December 1993 and April 1994 respectively.

In his speech after his release on 11 February 1989, Nelson had told the world that President F.W. de Klerk was 'a man of integrity'. Not long afterwards, he confided in me that he was mistaken. Nelson never really liked De Klerk and there was no personal warmth between them. Their relationship was fraught from the time of their first meeting in Cape Town when De Klerk told Nelson that the government would not negotiate with Joe Slovo or any other known communist. Nelson was quick to explain to him that the choice of who represented the ANC was not De Klerk's.

The relationship deteriorated over time, causing Nelson to remark publicly of De Klerk: 'He has sometimes very little idea of what democracy means' and 'Even the head of an illegitimate discredited minority regime as his has certain moral standards to uphold'. Never one to speak with different tongues to different people, Nelson's public ambivalence was unusual. He was walking a tightrope. He knew that De Klerk was needed to see the negotiations process through, but he did not trust him. At the same time, Nelson faced criticism from his own side for not doing enough to pressurise him.

When Nelson was awarded the Nobel Peace Prize jointly with De Klerk in 1993, he was not sure whether he should accept it. He felt that the Nobel Prize should have been awarded to him and the ANC alone, and that he should not have to share it with a man who had spent most of his political life upholding apartheid. His hesitation was compounded by his personal difficulty with De Klerk's lack of humility or self-reflection and apparent failure to recognise the plunder of the spirit that was the essence of apartheid.

At the time, Nelson also believed that, not only was De Klerk not doing enough to stop the violence that raged across the country, but also that he was allowing the 'third force' – members of the security forces who were involved in organised killings of activists and innocent civilians – to continue with its activities. He accused De Klerk of allowing the slaughter of innocent people because they were black.

In the end, despite his concerns, Nelson decided to accept the award. He invited me to attend the prize-giving ceremony in Oslo as part of a group of family and friends that included his daughter Zenani, Nadine Gordimer and then ANC publicity secretary Carl Niehaus. We were booked into the Grand Hotel on Karl Johans gate, Oslo's central plaza, together with De Klerk's delegation.

The potential for reconciliation between the two parties that the occasion presented was not fulfilled and the event served to further sour relations.

The difficulties started almost immediately. De Klerk's wife, Marike, cancelled a joint shopping spree organised by our host after Zenani implied to a journalist that her father alone, and not De Klerk, deserved the award.

Nelson expected De Klerk to acknowledge the immorality of apartheid and the suffering it had caused the majority of South Africans in his acceptance speech at the awards ceremony. Instead, De Klerk said only that 'both sides had made mistakes', causing Nelson to shake his head grimly.

The two recipients of the prize, together with three members each from their entourages, were invited to a private audience with the king of Norway. De Klerk introduced Pik Botha to the king as 'the longest-serving foreign minister of all democratic countries'. Nelson, as was his wont, introduced me as 'the lawyer responsible for his twenty-seven-year imprisonment'.

'Perhaps Mr de Klerk was more directly responsible,' I remarked as I bowed to the king.

'No. I was in nursery school at the time,' De Klerk lied to his majesty.

213

From the balcony of the Grand Hotel where the playwright Ibsen famously addressed the crowds, the prize-winners stood to acknowledge the cheers of the symbolic torchbearers and those members of the public gathered on the snowy streets below. The placards, freedom songs and shouts of praise left no doubt as to whom the people were there to see. The evening torch procession from the palace to the cathedral ended with the singing of what would soon become the South African national anthem – 'Nkosi Sikelel' iAfrika' – enthusiastically sung by the Norwegian crowd. In stark contrast, De Klerk and Marike talked to each other throughout the singing. Their chitter did not escape Nelson's attention.

We were all tired on the day of the prize-giving ceremony. Carl Niehaus and I asked Nelson's secretary if he was available for a short discussion on what was to be said at the dinner that evening. 'Come in,' she said. 'But don't make it a long one, because it's going to be a private dinner. The press won't be there.' When Nelson heard that, he said, 'Ah, if that's going to be the case, don't write a speech. I'll take it in my stride.' We were happy to do that, and rested for the afternoon instead.

At the private dinner hosted by the Norwegian prime minister to honour the two laureates, Nelson's patience finally snapped. Before the one hundred and fifty invited guests, he spoke off the cuff. In horrible detail he described the treatment of political prisoners on Robben Island, recounting an incident in which prison warders buried a man in the sand up to his head and urinated on him. He attacked the apartheid regime for the oppression of black people and for the murders committed by its hit squads. 'What mistakes did we make when you were brutalising us and locking us up and banning us and not allowing us to vote?' he asked angrily of De Klerk. This was the one and only occasion that I would ever see Nelson lose control and allow his personal feelings to spill out in public. After he had finished, a furious Pik Botha approached me and said that in future he would make sure that his president spoke last. 'If there is any such a performance by Mandela again, President de Klerk will give it back in kind,' he warned.

The next morning the breakfast seating arrangements at the hotel had been changed and the two South African delegations sat separately to eat. Minister Botha publicly accused the ANC of hijacking the awards ceremony by putting up posters in the hall where the event was to take place. He claimed that the Nobel Prize committee had been forced to intervene and remove them. This in turn led to denials by the Norwegian organising committee that there were ever any posters or that they were asked to intervene. The domestic media pointed out that in Norway, at least, the citizens were free to show their support for whomever they wished. The De Klerk delegation left the country early without saying goodbye to us.

Back home, the violence continued. In Natal, the Inkatha Freedom Party (IFP), armed and assisted by elements in the security forces, was at war with the UDF. Two weeks after his release, Nelson had called for peace at a rally in Durban.

> My message to those of you involved in this battle of brother against brother is this: Take your guns, knives and your pangas and throw them into the sea. Although there are fundamental differences between us, we commend Inkatha for their demand over the years for the unbanning and release of political prisoners as well as their stand for refusing to participate in a negotiated settlement without the creation of the necessary climate. If we do not halt this conflict, we will be in grave danger of corrupting the proud legacy of our struggle. We endanger the peace process in the whole of the country. We recognise that in order to bring the war to an end, the two sides must talk.

We knew that the violence was fuelled by government-assisted hit squads, but did not have sufficient legal evidence to take the matter up in court. At around ten one night, Nelson called me at home and asked me to fetch him and accompany him to the ANC offices. A young man had arrived at Shell House with a story of being abducted and forced to become a hit-squad member. He wanted to show the ANC where the hit squads were based. He told the ANC officials that he feared for his life and wanted an assurance from Nelson Mandela himself that he would be protected. We arrived to find Advocate Paul Pretorius already there, preparing the application for a court order based on the statement.

I asked whether there was any reliable information about the man. We needed to verify his story before he met with Nelson. He needed to give us full details of who he was. Where did he come from? What school did he go to? How had he ended up at Shell House?

The young man claimed that he came from a small township outside Kroonstad in the Northern Free State. He gave the name of a school and a street address. We called someone from the ANC office in Kroonstad who confirmed that there was such a street, but that the house number was too high, there were not that many houses on the street. And there was definitely no school by that name in Kroonstad. In addition, the story of how he had arrived at Shell House was suspicious. He claimed that he had run away from the farm where he was being held in the Eastern Transvaal, caught a train to Johannesburg and been directed by a passer-by to the ANC.

The security police had pulled this kind of trick on me before. I was convinced that the young man was a police plant sent to the ANC to trick them into embarking on a flawed court application that would discredit Nelson and the ANC, together with the claims about the existence of a third force. Neither Nelson nor I met the young man. I advised the ANC to send him away and have nothing further to do with him. I drove Nelson back home.

In March 1994, the ANC intelligence department reported to Nelson that it had received information that the organisers of an Inkatha march planned to attack Shell House. Nelson telephoned De Klerk the night before to warn him of the intended attack and to request that the police take steps to prevent it. Despite this, only two junior policemen were present when two large groups of Inkatha supporters armed with traditional weapons deviated from the march route and converged on the ANC headquarters from different directions. ANC security guards armed with AK-47s opened fire and nine marchers were killed and many others injured. Inkatha leaders declared it an unprovoked massacre reminiscent of Sharpeville.

The minister of justice established a judicial inquiry, headed by Judge Robert Nugent. Nelson was angered by the police's failure to heed his warning and upset by false propaganda alleging that he had instructed the guards to shoot. He asked me to represent the ANC and the guards, and I led a legal team comprising the attorney Caroline Nicholls and advocates Karel Tip, Kgomotso Moroka and Daniel Berger. Nelson wanted to testify, but we persuaded him to file an affidavit instead. In a careful ruling leaving no room for either side to claim a political victory, the judge and his assessor found the ANC guards not culpable for the deaths of the nine marchers.

Still, the violence continued. Nelson blamed the president for his failure to intervene more effectively. A few months before the 1994 elections, incensed by television footage of armed Zulus rampaging through the main streets of Durban, he demanded a meeting with De Klerk. Why wasn't he exercising his powers as president to put an end to this violence? Somewhat to Nelson's bemusement, De Klerk replied, 'Mr Mandela, when you join my government after the election, you will see how little power a president has.' While the remark did little to end the violence, it was a useful indication of De Klerk's thinking: he assumed that Mandela would still be his junior partner after the election.

Nelson enjoyed a better relationship with General Constand Viljoen. Viljoen, the former commander of the South African Defence Force, was the scapegoat of the South African government when the media exposed its continued support of the Mozambican National Resistance (Renamo) in breach of the Nkomati Accord. He was forced to resign and became a bitter opponent of De Klerk's Nationalist government. In May 1993, he had emerged as the leader of the Afrikaner Volksfront, a coalition of a number of unambiguously named extreme groupings, including the Afrikaner Weerstandsbeweging, the Boer Resistance Movement, the Boer Republican Army, Resistance Against Communism, the Foundation for Survival and Freedom, the White Wolves, White Security and the

South African branch of the Klu Klux Klan. In the small army town of Potchefstroom, at a meeting of about fifteen thousand heavily armed white men, Viljoen declared himself ready and willing to die in defence of the fatherland.

He told his assembled people:[18]

> You must pray for forgiveness for your sins and you must defend yourselves, for no one else will. Every Afrikaner must be ready. Every farm, every school is a target. If they attack our churches, nowhere is safe. If we are stripped of our defensive capacity, we will be destroyed. A bloody conflict which will require sacrifices is inevitable, but we will gladly sacrifice because our cause is just.

Nelson's intelligence sources reported to him that the Volksfront could call up an army of one hundred thousand men. He had a number of options as to how to respond to the threat posed by Viljoen and his supporters and chose the distinctly Mandela one. Working through Viljoen's twin brother, Abraham, he invited him to his home in Houghton for talks.

John Carlin recounts Viljoen's description of his meeting with Nelson in his book *Knowing Mandela*. A smiling Nelson welcomed Viljoen and three of his retired generals at the front door, and suggested that they talk privately before their delegations met. After pouring a cup of tea for the general,[19] Nelson, in fluent Afrikaans, told his guest how, despite the great harm that Afrikaners had done to him and his people, he retained a great respect for them as a people. He then went on to warn Viljoen of the dangers of a civil war. It would be a war that no one would win. The numbers of the ANC would match the military capacity of the right wing, and the outcome would be only the peace of graveyards.[20]

Nelson counselled him not to sabotage the reconciliation process but to rather contest the elections. 'Everyone says they are speaking for the Afrikaners, but why don't you form a party for Afrikaners?'

Eventually Viljoen would call off the armed action, the plans for which were already well advanced, and stand for election on behalf of his newly formed parliamentary party, the Vryheidsfront (Freedom Front). Not all his people obeyed his call or followed him into the general election, and far-right bomb attacks disrupted the weeks leading up to the 1994 elections. Nelson had, however, averted a well-organised armed insurrection that would surely have ended in a bloody civil war.

Nelson often asked me to attend election meetings that he addressed, particularly if the audiences were predominantly white. A number of ANC branches nominated me for parliament and I was asked if my name could be put forward for the ANC election list. I was honoured, but declined. Nelson asked me instead to join the government with him or seek a judicial appointment to the bench. I declined again. I wanted to retain my independence and continue my human rights work at the Legal Resources Centre. I would be more than happy to serve on the Judicial Service Commission if appointed; in the meantime, I would remain available as counsel to Nelson and the ANC.

I did not sleep the night before the elections on 27 April 1994. Nelson cast his vote outside Durban near the grave of John Dube, one of the founders of the ANC. He chose this polling station in honour of all those who had died for this day. I joined the ten-deep queue at the local primary school.

Nelson was concerned to secure the support of the judiciary for the new order and was worried by the threats of a small number of judges that they would not serve under the new dispensation. He was concerned that the judiciary should remain as intact as possible and asked me to ascertain whether Chief Justice Michael Corbett would be prepared to remain on as chief justice after the elections. On the morning of the inauguration, Judge Richard Goldstone, who sat with him on the Court of Appeal, happened to be waiting for the visitors' bus up to the Union Buildings when I arrived with Arethe. I asked his wife if I could sit next to him and sounded him out on his view as to whether he thought that the chief justice would accept the extension of his tenure. After the ceremony, at which the chief justice took the oath from Nelson, Richard reported to me that he had discussed the matter with Michael, who had confirmed that he would remain.

I think it was only at the inauguration that I realised how remarkable were Nelson's achievements. After twenty-seven years in prison and just four years of freedom, there sat President Mandela, the first black president of South Africa, next to the then head of the police, General van der Merwe (the very policeman who had so persecuted Winnie in Brandfort), with the head of the South African Defence Force in full uniform nearby. The crowd applauded as a number of helicopters trailing the bold new flag emerged from above the Voortrekker Monument on the western side of the Union Buildings. When several air-force jets appeared and screeched past them, the massed thousands below, mostly black South Africans, cried out loud enough to drown their noise, 'Viva the South African Air Force! Viva!' Now, I thought, we've arrived!

We breakfasted in Nelson's new home, the presidential residence in Pretoria. He told me that he found it far less comfortable than the home he had left behind in Johannesburg. 'Still, I will only have to endure it for four years,' he added. He was always clear that he would not serve as president for more than one term to set an example for South Africa's future politicians.

Winnie was not invited to sit next to Nelson when he was sworn in as president; his daughter Zeni was at his side. At first Winnie was in the same section of the audience as me, but then someone ushered her onto the stage where she took a seat behind and at some distance from Nelson.

For many years, Nelson blamed himself for the breakdown of the marriage. He believed that he was responsible for Winnie's excesses, that he had driven her to them by failing her as a husband and as a father to their children. Over time, his feelings for her calcified into a bitter hardness and Winnie became the blind spot on his great generosity of spirit. It is perhaps ironic that the great love of his life became the one person who Nelson could never forgive.

In 1996, Nelson sued for divorce in the Rand Supreme Court in Johannesburg. He asked me to represent him, but I thought it inappropriate. I told him that I would not go to court as his counsel but as his friend. I attended court with him every day and sat by his side to support him. Nelson appointed Advocate Wim Trengove as his counsel instead. Advocate Ishmael Semenya represented Winnie. Winnie opposed the divorce, claiming that there were only minor differences between her and Nelson. On her behalf, her counsel filed a counterclaim for maintenance of R107 000 per month and other relief if a divorce was granted. Postponement for mediation by the Thembu chief, Kaiser Matanzima, was also requested.

Nelson gave evidence to oppose Winnie's application for an adjournment. Under cross-examination by Semenya, he conceded that Winnie had endured much, but said that this was not uncommon. 'There were many women in this country who suffered far more than she did,' he testified.

He described himself as the 'loneliest man' during the period he stayed with Winnie after his release, adding, 'Can I put it simply, My Lord? If the entire universe tried to persuade me to reconcile with the defendant, I would not [...] I am determined to get rid of this marriage.'

The court granted the divorce the following day. Winnie did not appear in court and no reasons were given for her absence. I was no longer Uncle George to her and we lost contact. When Mrs Madikizela-Mandela, as she was later known, appeared before the Truth and Reconciliation Commission, there was some speculation that I had refused to represent her. The truth is that I was not asked.

The new democratic order and the shift from parliamentary to constitutional sovereignty brought with it two significant changes in the administration of law in the country: the constitution, the supreme law in terms of which all other law is to be consistent; and the Constitutional Court, a court of final instance over all matters related to the interpretation, protection and enforcement of the constitution.

The Constitutional Court consisted of a president and ten judges. Nelson, after consultation with the chief justice and his cabinet, appointed Arthur Chaskalson as the president. At the inauguration of the court,

Nelson spoke. After remarking that the last time he had appeared in court was to hear whether or not he was going to be sentenced to death, he said:

> Judge Arthur Chaskalson and other members of the Constitutional Court, let me say the following: Yours is the most noble task that could fall to any legal person. In the last resort, the guarantee of fundamental rights and freedoms for which we have fought so hard, lies in your hands. We look to you to honour the constitution and the people it represents. We expect from you, no, demand of you, the greatest use of your wisdom, honesty and good sense – no shortcuts, no easy solutions. Your work is not only lofty, it is also lonely. In the end you have only the constitution and your conscience on which you can rely. We look up to you to serve both without fear or favour.

The next day the court would begin work on what I consider the most legally significant case on which I have ever worked: *S v Makwanyane and Another*, the case to determine the constitutionality of the death penalty. Few issues are as controversial in South Africa and the mixed cabinet of the Government of National Unity was as divided on capital punishment as the country. The ANC wanted it abolished; the National Party wanted it retained. Cabinet decided to resolve the issue in court, allowing the government to brief counsel to argue for its abolition and the attorneys general to exercise their independence – they argued that it was a valid punishment.

The matter was not just academic. Themba Makwanyane and Mavusa Mchunu were two convicted criminals who had been sentenced to death and their appeals had been dismissed. They had not yet been executed because of the moratorium on the death penalty, but if the court ruled that capital punishment was compatible with the constitution, they would be hanged. Wim Trengove, briefed by Geoff Budlender and Thandi Orleyn of the Legal Resources Centre, represented the appellants. Ten prosecutors from the different provinces led by the deputy attorney general of the Witwatersrand Local Division, Klaus von Lieres und Wilkau SC, represented the prosecution. The prosecution was supported by Johannesburg advocate Emmanuel Zar SC representing a member of the public, Ian Glauber, with strong views on the matter. Advocates F.E. Davis and G.M. Makhanya appeared for the Black Advocates Forum and argued for the deferment of the decision to allow for further investigation and research into the provisions of customary law. Dennis Davis and Danny Berger appeared as *amici curiae* (friends of the court) on behalf of Lawyers for Human Rights, the Centre for Applied Legal Studies and the Society for the Abolition of the Death Penalty. In the first government brief of my career, I represented the cabinet of the government of South Africa.

We were all a bit awkward when the registrar called counsel into the chambers of the president of the court. Smiling nervously, Arthur told us that the members of the court did not want us to address them as Milord or Milady, but rather as Justice.

Those of us opposed to the death penalty argued that it violated a number of the fundamental rights contained in the interim constitution (the rights to life and dignity), and the prohibitions on physical, mental or emotional torture and cruel, inhuman and degrading treatment. Furthermore, these violations were not permitted by the limitations clause in the bill of rights because they negated the essential content of the rights to life and dignity, and were not necessary or reasonable and justifiable in an open and democratic society based on freedom and equality. Wim quoted the Canadian judge John Sopinka:

> At the very heart of this appeal is a conflict between two concepts. On one side is the concept of human dignity and the belief that this concept is of paramount importance in a democratic society. On the other side is the concept of retributive justice and the belief that capital punishment is necessary to deter murderers. A historical review reveals an increasing tendency to resolve this tension in favour of human dignity.

Arguing that South African public opinion was in favour of retaining capital punishment, Von Lieres cited the British judge Lord Denning.

> Punishment is the way in which a society expresses the denunciation of wrongdoing: and in order to maintain respect for law it is essential that the punishment inflicted for grave crimes should adequately reflect the revulsion felt by the great majority of citizens. It is a mistake to consider the objects of punishments as being deterrents or reformative or preventive or nothing else [...] The truth is that some crimes are so outrageous that society insists on adequate punishment because the wrongdoer deserves it, irrespective of whether it is a deterrent or not.

It was clear that our new justices had studied and mastered the voluminous court papers. They proved themselves a participatory and engaged audience. Each of the eleven justices delivered a separate ruling and unanimously declared the death penalty unconstitutional.

In his ruling, delivered on 6 June 1995, Judge President Chaskalson wrote:

> Most accused facing a possible death sentence are unable to afford legal assistance, and are defended under the *pro deo* system. The defending counsel is more often than not young and inexperienced, frequently of a different race to his or her client, and if this is the case, usually has to consult through an interpreter. *Pro deo* counsel are paid only a nominal fee for the defence, and generally lack the financial resources and the infrastructural support to undertake the necessary investigations and research, to employ expert witnesses to give advice, including advice on matters relevant to sentence, to assemble witnesses, to bargain with the prosecution, and generally to conduct an effective defence. Accused persons who have the money to do so, are able to retain experienced attorneys and counsel, who are paid to undertake the necessary investigations and research, and as a result they are less likely to be sentenced to death than persons similarly placed who are unable to pay for such services [...]
>
> The Attorney General argued that what is cruel, inhuman or degrading depends to a large extent upon contemporary attitudes within society, and that South African society does not regard the death sentence for

224

extreme cases of murder as a cruel, inhuman or degrading form of punishment…The question before us, however, is not what the majority of South Africans believe a proper sentence for murder should be. It is whether the Constitution allows the sentence [...]

Those who are entitled to claim this protection include the social outcasts and marginalised people of our society. It is only if there is a willingness to protect the worst and the weakest amongst us, that all of us can be secure that our own rights will be protected [...]

We would be deluding ourselves if we were to believe that the execution of the few persons sentenced to death during this period, and of a comparatively few other people each year from now onwards will provide the solution to the unacceptably high rate of crime. There will always be unstable, desperate, and pathological people for whom the risk of arrest and imprisonment provides no deterrent, but there is nothing to show that a decision to carry out the death sentence would have any impact on the behaviour of such people, or that there will be more of them if imprisonment is the only sanction. No information was placed before us by the Attorney General in regard to the rising crime rate other than the bare statistics, and they alone prove nothing, other than that we are living in a violent society in which most crime goes unpunished – something that we all know.

The greatest deterrent to crime is the likelihood that offenders will be apprehended, convicted and punished. It is that which is presently lacking in our criminal justice system; and it is at this level and through addressing the causes of crime that the State must seek to combat lawlessness.

In the debate as to the deterrent effect of the death sentence, the issue is sometimes dealt with as if the choice to be made is between the death sentence and the murder going unpunished. That is of course not so. The choice to be made is between putting the criminal to death and subjecting the criminal to the severe punishment of a long term of imprisonment which, in an appropriate case, could be a sentence of life imprisonment. Both are deterrents, and the question is whether the possibility of being sentenced to death, rather than being sentenced to life imprisonment, has a marginally greater deterrent effect, and whether the Constitution sanctions the limitation of rights affected thereby.

In the course of his argument the Attorney General contended that if sentences imposed by the Courts on convicted criminals are too lenient, the law will be brought into disrepute, and members of society will then take the law into their own hands. Law is brought into disrepute if the justice system is ineffective and criminals are not punished. But if the justice system is effective and criminals are apprehended, brought to trial and in serious cases subjected to severe sentences, the law will not fall into disrepute. We have made the commitment to 'a future founded on the recognition of human rights, democracy and peaceful co-existence...for all South Africans'. Respect for life and dignity lies at the heart of that commitment. One of the reasons for the prohibition of capital punishment is 'that allowing the State to kill will cheapen the value of human life and thus [through not doing so] the State will serve in a sense as a role model for individuals in society'. Our country needs such role models [...]

[The Attorney General] contended that it is common sense that the most feared penalty will provide the greatest deterrent, but accepted that there is no proof that the death sentence is in fact a greater deterrent than life imprisonment for a long period [...] 'A punishment as extreme and as irrevocable as death cannot be predicated upon speculation as to what the deterrent effect might be' [...]

Retribution is one of the objects of punishment, but it carries less weight than deterrence. The righteous anger of family and friends of the murder victim, reinforced by the public abhorrence of vile crimes, is easily translated into a call for vengeance. But capital punishment is not the only way that society has of expressing its moral outrage at the crime that has been committed. We have long outgrown the literal application of the biblical injunction of 'an eye for an eye, and a tooth for a tooth' [...]

In the balancing process, deterrence, prevention and retribution must be weighed against the alternative punishments available to the State, and the factors which taken together make capital punishment cruel, inhuman and degrading: the destruction of life, the annihilation of dignity, the elements of arbitrariness, inequality and the possibility of error in the enforcement of the penalty [...]

The rights to life and dignity are the most important of all human rights, and the source of all other personal rights in Chapter Three [of the Constitution]. By committing ourselves to a society founded on the recognition of human rights we are required to value these two rights above all others. And this must be demonstrated by the State in everything that it does, including the way it punishes criminals. This is not achieved by objectifying murderers and putting them to death to serve as an example to others in the expectation that they might possibly be deterred thereby.

I welcomed the decision. I have represented too many good men facing the death penalty to consider it anything short of abhorrent. As an office bearer of Don't Touch Cain (an Italian-based non-governmental organisation campaigning for abolition of the death penalty), I have long associated myself with the hope that the international campaign will one day succeed. Many of my fellow citizens have opposing views and still today there are calls for a referendum on the issue. I am sure most of them have not read the judgment rejecting their arguments, and suspect, sadly, that many of those among them would not be persuaded by the judges' reasoning even if they did.

In September 1995, on the eve of the first democratic local elections, the Constitutional Court ruled that a part of the Local Government Transition Act was unconstitutional, together with two presidential proclamations issued in terms of it. Nelson went on national television to apologise and announce to the nation that, although he was unhappy with the result, he accepted the decision of the court without qualification. He said parliament would be recalled and that the constitutional defects in the legislation and proclamations would be rectified.

On 8 May 1996, four hundred and twenty-one members of the constitutional assembly voted on the Constitution of the Republic of South Africa Bill. Two of those present opposed it and twelve abstained. The approval by such a large parliamentary majority was not enough, however. An internationally unique politico-legal stipulation, aimed at reassuring South Africa's minorities, required the Constitutional Court to certify that the new constitution complied with thirty-four constitutional principles agreed to at the Convention for a Democratic South Africa (Codesa) and annexed to the interim constitution. If it did not, it would be referred back to the assembly for revision until it did.

I headed a large team of counsel – Wim Trengove, Marumo Moerane SC, Nono Goso and Kgomotso Moroka – in the application for certification on behalf of the constitutional assembly. Cyril Ramaphosa and Fink Haysom sat behind us. In the event that the court refused certification, they needed to understand the reasons and take them back to the assembly.

Five political parties that had participated in the assembly opposed the certification, mainly because their views were not incorporated into the final text and they wanted to re-open the debates that had already occurred. F.W. de Klerk's National Party and Mangosuthu Buthelezi's IFP contended that the draft did not comply with the principles requiring meaningful provincial powers. Many other special interest groups, representing a broad cross-section of society that had not been part of the constitutional assembly (the South African Police, traditional leaders, and campaigners for the death penalty and the prohibition of abortion), applied to court for their objections to be heard. Small Afrikaner groupings produced maps with their arguments for their right to an independent homeland. The Congress of South African Trade Unions, represented by Martin Brassey, argued that management's right to 'lock-out' should be scrapped. Business South Africa claimed a constitutional protection equal to that of their employees so that they could counter aggressive behaviour by workers. I found myself in a protracted and slightly uncomfortable debate with certain of the justices defending a position that was, against my instincts, in favour of the extensive emergency provisions relating to the declaration of a state of emergency.

There was an inherent difficulty in the notion of an unelected court being required to certify a draft constitution that was the will of the democratically elected representatives of the majority of the people. There were also others: a constitutional principle could be interpreted or complied with in more than one way. Surely the court should respect the constitutional assembly's interpretation? The court was anxious to hear argument on when it was entitled to substitute its opinion for that of the will of parliament. It could not afford to be accused of having elevated itself into a 'dikastocracy' – a rule by judges. The court wanted as far as possible to resolve the difficult jurisprudential issues that it predicted future courts would face.

In the end, we lost. The court delivered a lengthy single decision ruling that nine clauses of the new constitution did not satisfy the constitutional principles and were of sufficient importance for the text to be sent back to the constitutional assembly. These included the powers and functions of the provinces; the majority provisions for the amendment of certain sections of the bill of rights; the appointment and removal of the public protector, the auditor general and the Public Service Commission; and the emergency provisions for which I had argued.

The constitutional assembly produced a new draft and we applied again to the Constitutional Court for certification. This time it was an easier and quicker process. Despite the objections of the Democratic Party and the IFP, the new constitution was certified.

Of it, Nelson would say:

> The Constitution of South Africa speaks of both the past and the future [...] The Constitution commits us to build a nation based on the democratic values of human dignity, equality and freedom, through constitutionalism and the rule of law. It describes the mechanisms and institutions which we have created to ensure that we achieve this. There are no short cuts on the road to freedom. The Constitution describes the

path which we must and shall follow. A Constitution is a living document. Our understanding of its requirements will and must adapt over time. But the fundamental principles are and must be unchanging. A full understanding of how and why those principles were adopted will help us to ensure that we remain true to the solemn undertakings which we have made to each other and to those who will follow us.[21]

The Promotion of National Unity and Reconciliation Act 34 of 1995 established a Truth and Reconciliation Commission to investigate gross human rights violations perpetrated under apartheid. The Azanian People's Organisation, Mrs Biko, Mr Mxenge and Mr Ribeiro challenged the constitutionality of the provisions that allowed the amnesty committee of the TRC to grant amnesty from both civil and criminal liability to perpetrators who could show that their crimes were committed in 'furtherance of a political objective' and that they had 'given full disclosure'.

The Constitutional Court dismissed the application and found that 'amnesty was a crucial component of the negotiated settlement itself, without which the interim constitution would not have come into being [...] If the court kept alive the prospect of continuous retaliation and revenge, the agreement of those threatened by its implementation would never have been forthcoming.' In a unanimous judgment delivered by the deputy president of the court, Justice Mahomed, the relevant sections of the Act were upheld.

Much of what transpired in this shameful period is shrouded in secrecy and not easily capable of objective demonstration and proof. Loved ones have disappeared, sometimes mysteriously, and most of them no longer survive to tell their tales [...] Secrecy and authoritarianism have concealed the truth in little crevices of obscurity in our history. Records are not easily accessible, witnesses are often unknown, dead, unavailable or unwilling. All that often effectively remains is the truth of wounded memories of loved ones sharing instinctive suspicions, deep and traumatising to the survivors but otherwise incapable of translating themselves into objective and corroborative evidence which could survive the rigours of the law. The Act seeks to address this massive problem by encouraging these survivors and the dependants of the tortured and the wounded, the maimed and the dead to unburden their grief publicly, to receive the collective recognition of a new nation that they were wronged, and, crucially, to help them to discover what did in truth happen to their loved ones, where and under what circumstances it did happen, and who was responsible.

I would spend several years representing old clients and the families of friends before the amnesty committee. The security police, whose lies and cover-ups at the inquests of Steve Biko and the Cradock Four – Matthew Goniwe, Fort Calata, Sparrow Mkonto and Sicelo Mhlauli – had contributed to findings by the magistrates of 'no one to blame', now came forward to confess to their murders. An apparent combination of shame and arrogance prevented them from telling the full truth of what they had done, and their amnesty applications were refused. So, too, Janusz Waluś and Clive Derby-Lewis, whose applications from prison for amnesty for the murder of Chris Hani were denied.

I was disappointed when the TRC granted amnesty to Craig Williamson for the murders by letter bomb of Ruth First, Jeanette Schoon and her daughter Katryn. I opposed his applications on behalf of Ruth's three daughters – Shawn, Gillian and Robyn – and Marius Schoon, the husband of Jeanette and father of Katryn. I still regret that we did not pursue an application for review.

No-one applied for amnesty for the death of Ahmed Timol, yet his family never accepted that he committed suicide. Thanks to their persistence, forty-six years later, the inquest into his death was re-opened before Judge Billy Mothle in the Gauteng Division of the High Court in Pretoria in 2017. Advocate Howard Varney, assisted by Advocate Musatondwa Musandiwa appeared for the family, instructed by the law firm Webber Wentzel and the LRC. Respected private investigator, Frank Dutton, investigated the case on behalf of the family. His investigations were supported by the Foundation of Human Rights (FHR). I became a witness and gave similar fact evidence about torture and deaths in detention, which the judge accepted. As I write, the court has not yet delivered its verdict, but I am confident that we will succeed.

The TRC report was released in 1998. The government accepted its findings. Deputy President Thabo Mbeki, then president of the ANC, like De Klerk before him, wanted to interdict its publication. He approached me to bring an application on behalf of the ANC. I consulted with Nelson before refusing to take the brief. The court dismissed the application and the final report was published.

Nelson and I still met up regularly during his presidency. He said publicly that Thabo Mbeki was 'the real ruler of South Africa, the de facto ruler', but my impression was that Nelson was more engaged in the nitty-gritty business of governing than he admitted.

The relationship between Nelson and Thabo Mbeki had soured by the time Nelson stood down as president. I attended the ANC conference in Durban at which Mbeki was elected as the leader of the party to succeed Nelson. The chairman welcomed Mbeki to the position and remarked that he would now have to step into Nelson's shoes. Mbeki retorted that he was not going to do that as 'Madiba wears ugly shoes'. It was a poor attempt at a joke and Nelson was not pleased. I do not remember anyone laughing.

With Nelson and Winnie at the Stompie Seipei Trial.
On the right is Dikgang Moseneke.

TOP: Greek composer Mikis Theodorakis greets Nelson at the signing of the call for Universal Peace in preparation for the 2004 Athens Olympics.

MIDDLE: In Greece, with Arethe and Graça Machel.

BOTTOM: Nelson and I with Ngoako Ramathlodi, and Cosmas and Penny Cavaleros.

Chapter 8

~

AT LAST

'Greece is the mother of democracy
and South Africa, its youngest daughter'

The four years after his release were the loneliest of Nelson's life. More than ten thousand people were killed in political violence. Estranged from his wife, Nelson's relationship with his children was strained. He lived with his secretary, Barbara Masekela, and four grandsons from his son Makgatho in his large home in Houghton. I would visit him often and we would eat together at the waxed dining-room table in the silent house. It was sometimes painful to witness the solitude of this warm and generous family man. He was always courteous and engaged, yet in repose his face could look stony, even hard, and his unspoken sorrow immense.

Nelson shared his bed with his grandson Mbuso, who was only eight when Nelson was released. When a high-profile American visitor came to the country, I was asked to arrange a meeting with Nelson. I organised a dinner attended by about fifteen people at the Three Ships Restaurant at the Carlton Hotel. Nelson arrived first, just before 7 p.m., with Mbuso. He explained that, while he was dressing, the boy had asked him if he was going out again, and started crying. To pacify him, Nelson had brought him along. We arranged a special chair at the table with a couple of cushions on it and Mbuso ordered sausages and chips. He was unimpressed with the elegance of the service when his meal arrived, asking only, 'But where is the tomato sauce?'

Nelson was coy at first about his relationship with Graça Machel, the widow of President Samora Machel of Mozambique. They had met in 1992. He was reluctant to make a public announcement about their intentions, although he did disclose in a television interview that 'I am in love with a remarkable lady'. There was a certain period when it was not generally known that she had moved in with him. Archbishop Desmond Tutu, as a close friend, tried in private to persuade Nelson to marry her, but when he declined, Tutu said publicly that it was unbecoming of the president of the country not to marry the person with whom he was living.

I knew that a marriage was imminent in 1998 when Nelson mentioned to me, as though in passing, that Graça's relatives were arriving the following weekend. Respectful of his desire for privacy, I refrained from further questions. The next weekend, on his eightieth birthday, they married in a private ceremony on the lawn of his home.

I met Graça at the Houghton house. She has never accepted that the death of her first husband was an accident and I was impressed by her determination to prove that the South African military was responsible. Samora Machel had died in a plane crash on the border between his country and South Africa. The Mozambicans claimed that the South African military had put up false beacons to confuse the pilot, who descended thinking that he was soon to land. Instead he was approaching a mountain. The South African government alleged that the Russian pilot was drunk. There was a strong denial from the Russian ministry of foreign affairs and a call for evidence of the allegation of drunkenness. Foreign minister Pik Botha would later acknowledge that he was 'misinformed'.

Nelson accepted and understood why Graça wanted to retain the Machel name. He was an admirer of Machel, who had gained freedom from the Portuguese colonial occupation in Mozambique while Nelson was in prison. He had made his country available to South Africans in exile. Nelson also knew the reasons that had led Machel to sign the Nkomati Accord and to agree to stop helping exiles in exchange for the South Africans ceasing to support Remamo (an undertaking that the South African government would break).

My wedding gift to Nelson and Graça has an interesting provenance. Well-known artist Cyril Coetzee, a lecturer at Wits, had signed a contract with a local gallery for the distribution of his work. But the gallery failed to promote his pictures and left them in a storeroom. On top of this, he was obliged to pay one-third of anything he earned – mainly from portraits of academic heads and others – even though he was not getting commissions through the gallery. His father-in-law was a close friend and asked for my help. I negotiated the termination of the contract on Cyril's behalf. In return, he painted a portrait of me in my senior-counsel robes and refused payment as he felt it was the least he could do after I had liberated him from the contract. He would, however, allow me to pay, at a highly reduced rate, for a life-size portrait of Nelson and Graça. The portrait was hung on the wall of the staircase leading to the bedrooms at the house in Houghton.

Nelson's marriage to Graça was a very happy one. They were caring and compatible companions. If asked to do anything, he would happily reply that he would have to get permission from his wife first. Graça paid special attention to Nelson's friends, and we were always warmly welcomed into their home.

She did all she could to promote the unity of the extended family. After the divorce, Nelson and Winnie were not on speaking terms and she was not included in family gatherings or celebrations. When Graça arranged a party to celebrate the graduation of one of Nelson's grandchildren from initiation school, she insisted that Winnie be invited. 'How would the young man feel if his grandmother is excluded?' she asked. 'This is a great day for the boy who is becoming a man and he is entitled to be proud before both his grandmother and his grandfather.' Nelson reluctantly agreed.

After this Graça insisted on inviting Winnie to every family occasion, often giving her pride of place in the seating arrangements, including at the wedding of Nelson's eldest grandson, Mandla Mandela. Winnie would often attend, although Nelson would not receive her with any enthusiasm.

237

TOP: Cyril Coetzee's portrait of me in my senior-counsel robes.

BOTTOM: The life-size portrait of Nelson and Graça by Cyril Coetzee I gave to them as a wedding gift.

Internationally, Nelson was a hero, and no more so than in Greece, where he was regarded not only as a world statesman, but also as a friend. On Sharpeville day in 1983, the ancient Greek city of Olympia (the birthplace of the Olympic Games in the valley of Ilias in the Peloponnese) had conferred honorary citizenship on him. The prison authorities had withheld the official letter notifying him and he was oblivious to the recognition. I discovered the award quite by chance when the Association of European Parliamentarians with Africa invited me to a conference in Athens. Our delegation visited Ancient Olympia and I was asked to translate the mayor's speech from Greek into English. After I had finished, he asked me where I was from that I could speak such good Greek. I told him that I was born in Greece, but lived in South Africa. 'Your Nelson Mandela is an honorary citizen of Ancient Olympia,' he told me, before adding that Nelson had never acknowledged it. I told him that I was Nelson's lawyer and friend, and assured him that Nelson would have responded if he had known. The mayor then took me by the arm and led me into his office to show me the large portrait of Nelson that took pride of place behind his desk. On my return, I informed Nelson. He would later tell me that he considered it one of the most important awards conferred on him.

It is fitting that the first and only holiday that Nelson and I ever took together was in Greece. In 2002, he and Graça were invited to Athens as guests of the minister of foreign affairs, George Papandreou. Arethe and I accompanied them and the four of us planned to holiday together after the official business of the trip was concluded. Our itinerary included a yacht trip to certain of the Aegean and Ionian islands, and a stop in the Venetian-built harbour of Koroni, the port town near my family village of Vasilitsi.

Arethe and I arrived a few days before Nelson and his party. Our room was on the floor above his in a luxury hotel on Constitution Square in Athens. After Nelson had settled in from the airport, he rang me and asked me to come down. I found him in the semi-darkness of the draped lounge of the presidential suite and I drew back the heavy curtains to allow

239

in the white heat of noon. Before us the panorama across Constitution Square stretched from parliament to the Parthenon.

'George, are you sure that I have not been here before?' Nelson said in a voice barely above a whisper. He was staring as if dazed at the Acropolis. After a long silence, he confessed that he had now forgotten what he had wanted to discuss.

'Greece is the mother of democracy and South Africa, its youngest daughter,' Nelson proclaimed to the large audience at the first event to welcome him to Greece and to honour his support for the Olympic Truce campaign, as well as for his contribution to the advancement of universal peace.

George Papandreou had campaigned to restore the spirit of the ancient Olympic Games by calling on the nations of the world to adopt what was in antiquity known as Ekeheiria – 'the Olympic truce'. The terms of this truce required all hostilities to cease for seven days before and after the games to allow the athletes, officials and spectators to travel to Olympia, participate in the games, and return home in safety. Papandreou hoped that the initiative would demonstrate the positive contribution that sport could make to global peace. In 2001 he had asked me to approach Nelson to be a sponsor of the initiative together with other international dignitaries, including Kofi Annan, then secretary general of the UN, and Jacques Rogge, then president of the International Olympic Committee. Nelson had agreed. The initiative received enthusiastic high-level support and was officially announced during the flame-lighting ceremony for the Olympic Winter Games in Olympia in November 2001. In December of the same year, all one hundred and seventy members of the UN general assembly passed a resolution in its favour.

The opening function for Nelson's visit took place at the Megaro Mousikis, the largest concert hall in Greece. Ambassador Stavros Lambrinidis, the director of the International Olympic Truce Centre, asked us to stand as George Papandreou and Nelson Mandela appeared on stage. Nelson was already seated between Lambrinidis and Papandreou when he asked audibly, 'Where is George? Let him come here.' I was sitting with the rest of his party in the area reserved for diplomats, but was called up to join him. Slightly embarrassed, I whispered short summaries of the speeches delivered in Greek into Nelson's ear in the hope that my sudden elevation would not offend those who preferred strict adherence to protocol.

Ambassador Lambrinidis read out the final paragraph of the truce:

> Humanity's quest is for a world free of hatred, terrorism and war, where ideals of peace, goodwill and mutual respect form the basis of relations among people and countries. The goal may still remain elusive, but if the Olympic Truce can help us bring about even a brief respite from conflict and strife it will send a powerful message of hope to the international community [...] we pledge to support and disseminate, individually and collectively, the symbolic call for the Olympic Truce throughout all future Olympic Games and beyond, and to exercise our best efforts within our communities, countries and relevant international organisations to achieve its recognition and observance.

As Nelson took his pen from his inside jacket pocket to sign the declaration, already endorsed by presidents, prime ministers, members of parliament and religious leaders from across the world, he received a standing ovation. The world-renowned composer Mikis Theodorakis, who had survived the German occupation, civil war, detention without trial, torture and exile, came forward. He stretched out his hand to Nelson, who grasped it firmly to enthusiastic applause. 'Your example shows us that everything is possible, even world peace,' Mikis told Nelson.

After George Papandreou had signed he invited me to do the same, followed by a number of intellectuals, academics and artists. The few among them who made speeches addressed themselves to Nelson, describing him as a hero, icon, world leader, peacemaker, reconciler and (could there be higher praise from such an audience?) 'a committed philhellene'.

The next day, Prime Minister Costas Simitis gave a lunch in Nelson's honour. Nelson, members of the cabinet and the head of the 2004 Olympic organising committee, Gianna Angelopolous-Daskalaki, were soon engaged in intense conversation about ancient Greece, the four-hundred-year occupation by the Ottoman Empire, Greece's fight against fascism, the suffering of its people during the occupation, and the civil war. Nelson questioned the assembled dignitaries about the country's electoral system and the role played by opposition parties to the left and right of the socialist government.

President Konstantinos Stephanopoulos also hosted a function for Nelson. He expressed his regret that Nelson had not managed to visit Greece while he was president of South Africa despite the efforts of both ministers of foreign affairs and the ambassadors of the two countries, but assured Nelson that in the eyes of the Greeks, if not the whole world, he was still President Mandela.

Our party visited the Parthenon and the Temple of Poseidon on the cliffside of Cape Sounion, from which, legend has it, King Aegeas threw himself to his death in the mistaken belief that his son had been killed by the Minotaur of Crete. It is a popular tourist attraction and on a Sunday afternoon there are thousands of visitors. Officials kept the crowds at some distance from where we were enjoying lunch, but Nelson insisted that the cordon be removed so that he could meet the children, who queued up and greeted him one by one.

There was one more official engagement planned for the following day with the trustees of the Alexander S. Onassis Foundation, before we were to board the yacht. Ambassador Economides and his wife Athena, Nelson's personal assistant Zelda la Grange, my sister Vaso, and my son Kimon were to join the party.

As I readied myself for the Onassis Foundation meeting, the phone in my hotel room rang. It was Zelda. She asked me to come down as Nelson was not well with a stomach ailment. The military doctor who travelled with Nelson consulted Kimon, who was a fellow of the Royal College of Surgeons, and they recommended that the appointment with the foundation be postponed and the yacht trip cancelled. An unknown source alerted the media and it was reported that Nelson had been admitted to the Onassis Cardiac Surgery Centre in a critical condition. We assured the ambassador that the information was false and a press conference was hastily convened in the foyer of the hotel to set the record straight.

We changed our holiday plans and booked into a quiet seaside resort on the east coast outside Athens instead. The well-wooded hotel gardens sprawled onto a secluded beach and Nelson was able to relax and recuperate. Within two days, his stomach had cleared up and he was in good spirits.

Each morning he and Graça would breakfast in their suite, but we would lunch and dine together, usually in the cool breeze of the open-air restaurant on the edge of a cliff overlooking the sea. Nelson was fond of quoting the advice of an eastern philosopher that you should have a hearty breakfast, share your lunch with a friend and make a present of your dinner to your enemy. Nevertheless, he would join us after sunset as the bright August moon rose over the horizon and invariably have something to eat.

We spent our days at the shaded garden tables edging the powdery sea sand of the Aegean. Graça, Zelda and I would swim while Arethe sketched and Nelson read. Nelson was frequently interrupted, but responded with his customary grace to the solicitations of the hotel staff: the chef wanting to know what was his favourite dish, the general manager recounting the names of the many royal figures and heads of state who had occupied the suite made available to him. The number of kings and queens Nelson met who deferred to his actually rather humble royal connection and requested that he call them by their first names rather than Your Majesty or Royal Highness bemused Nelson. I teased him about this, reminding him of how he had referred to his warders on Robben Island as his guard of honour. 'And, Nelson, didn't you also instruct me to remind the Swazis that they were getting a Thembu princess when you gave permission for your daughter to marry a Swazi prince?'

We had already been at Vouliagmeni a few days when I noticed that the South African flag was not up at the hotel. I reported this to Ambassador Economides who immediately set off to have it rectified. A couple of hours later, I looked up to see the blue, white and orange of the old South African flag waving next to the blue and white of the Greek one. Anxious to avoid a minor diplomatic incident, the unflappable Ambassador Economides rushed to secure its removal and replacement with the proper one.

Unfortunately the Aegean cruise was not the only event that had to be cancelled. The honorary citizen of Ancient Olympia was unable to pay it a visit and see his portrait in the council chamber as we had planned. Nelson and I agreed that we would return together to Athens for the Olympic Games.

As it turned out, both Cape Town and Athens wanted to host the 2004 Olympic Games. When Cape Town was eliminated, Nelson canvassed members of the International Olympic Committee, particularly the Africans, to use their votes in favour of Athens. His efforts to secure the games for Greece won him even greater admiration there and ultimately helped bring the Olympics home. It was anticipated that he would be a guest of honour in Athens in 2004.

I was honoured to be invited to be part of the delegation to the games in Athens. Nelson and Graça were invited as expected and I looked forward to being with them, but things did not work out as I had hoped. At a late stage, their trip was cancelled when Nelson's doctor cautioned against the heat and the strain of a visit.

Nelson's philhellenism extended to the Greek community in the country. He attended a number of functions at the South African Hellenic Educational and Technical Institute (Saheti) school with me and was impressed with the non-racism and curriculum. He was pleased when the daughters of Chris and Limpho Hani became pupils at the school. I recently saw Limpho at a school function. Her grandchild is now a pupil. I went up to greet her and welcome her back to Saheti as a grandmother. She shook her head. "No, I am not a granny," she chided me, "I am a yiayia" (granny in Greek).

In December 2004, Nelson's son Makgatho was hospitalised. I visited him at the Linksfield Clinic Hospital on the eastern side of Johannesburg. Makgatho and Nelson were estranged, but I arrived to find Nelson in the ward with Graça. Nelson, utterly silent and inscrutable, stared into the middle distance over the bed of his then comatose son. None of us spoke.

Makgatho would die as a result of HIV complications in January 2005. To the anger of some of the members of the family, Nelson made his cause of death public. It was in the middle of Thabo Mbeki's denialism and Nelson's decision was an effort to destigmatise the disease. 'The health of the nation is more important than our personal feelings,' he said. 'We must admit it and we must fight it with provision for prevention and treatment.'

When anyone asked Nelson for his opinion during Mbeki's presidency he was quick to answer, 'Go and ask the president.' The ANC remained his church and he would not comment publicly, although in our private conversations he expressed his concerns about the divisions in the ranks of the ANC. HIV/AIDS was the only exception to his decision to stay out of politics when he retired. The problem was too big to ignore and he found fault with Mbeki for not doing enough to deal with it. He could not in good conscience remain silent.

Nelson never lost his dry self-deprecation, even in relation to his own presidential achievements. I remember telling him about how *Time* magazine had given Thabo Mbeki a glowing reference after a visit to the United States.

'You know, Thabo has made a very, very good impression,' I said. 'They had some words of praise for you as well, but also a criticism.'

Nelson frowned. 'What was that?'

'They said you know nothing about economics.'

Nelson looked at me, then looked away. After a pause he met my eye. 'George,' he said, 'why do you say that as if you do not believe it?'

Nelson did not want money for himself, but welcomed financial assistance for the benefit of disadvantaged people. Whenever anyone asked

245

if Nelson would accept a donation, I told them that the best way to please Nelson Mandela was to build a school or a clinic. Nelson would sometimes ask me to get involved in discussions with benefactors. In 2000, he and I took a helicopter with Cosmas and Penny Cavaleros to attend the opening of a school in Limpopo that they had funded. Nelson told the delighted pupils of Naletsana School in Warmbaths that the youth were a national asset and the future. On another occasion, I liaised on his behalf with a German international firm that built and supplied the medical equipment for a clinic in the Transkei.

Nelson would never commercialise his name. He was offered millions for its use in the promotion of products, including liquor and tobacco. He would not hesitate to refuse. He would also decline offers by members of high society to make paid guest appearances at their functions. He would, however, meet with international celebrities – film stars, rock stars and artists – and clearly enjoyed the accompanying glamour. Graça would insist that these events take place at the Nelson Mandela Foundation and not at their home.

There was one instance where Nelson's name was used in the promotion of a product. Ismail Ayob had been an articled clerk in the firm Patel Cachalia Loonat. They were Nelson's attorneys while he was in prison on Robben Island and Ayob was sent to the island from time to time to visit their client. After Ayob was admitted as an attorney, he continued to visit Nelson without disclosing to him that he was no longer associated with the firm of attorneys to which he had been articled. When Nelson eventually found out, he was somewhat taken aback, but he accepted the situation and retained Ayob to manage his financial affairs. I would work with Ayob – he arranged my transport to Cape Town from time to time and would accompany me to Robben Island, Pollsmoor and Victor Verster prisons. Over the years, he was also my instructing attorney in a number of cases involving Winnie.

The three of us enjoyed a warm relationship. Nelson relied on Ayob as an attorney and a friend, and we both enjoyed the samosas his wife made. After Nelson's release, Ayob was responsible for the management of practically all of Nelson's personal affairs, including the trusts he had registered in his name and in the names of family members.

At Ayob's suggestion, Nelson agreed to collaborate with an artist to produce limited-edition paintings that he would sign. The venture was essentially aimed at raising funds for charities bearing his name and espousing various causes, including fighting AIDS, bringing up orphans and advancing rural education. Ayob registered two companies and a trust to manufacture and trade in the artworks. He and his marketing agent, Ross Calder, were the directors of the two companies, while two of Nelson's daughters – Maki and Zeni – were appointed as co-directors of the trust.

Nelson was horrified when it emerged that Calder and Ayob had photo-graphically reproduced innumerable copies, stamped with a mechanical signature, that were then sold at exorbitant prices across the world. He told me that the books did not add up, he had not been given a proper accounting. He needed me to find out from Ayob and Calder what had been sold and at what price. He invited me to his home early one Sunday afternoon before a scheduled signing ceremony of the works that was to be filmed by the media. We met with Ayob and Calder in the lounge with its large picture window overlooking the lawn. But that quiet subur-ban garden belied the tension inside the house.

Nelson wanted Ayob to cease fabricating and trading in the so-called artworks. I did not want to be seen as the one responsible for Ayob's termination and asked Nelson to consult with Dikgang Moseneke, then head of the Nelson Mandela Children's Fund. Dikgang recommended that Nelson appoint Bally Chuene as his attorney and we asked Advocate Wim Trengove to write a letter to Ayob terminating his mandate. In short, Ayob would have to hand over everything that he had in his pos-session relating to Nelson's affairs. Ayob refused and Nelson had to resort to court to obtain an interim order to prevent him from trading in the artworks and abusing his name for commercial purposes.

In 2007, we reached a settlement in terms of which Ayob agreed to pay part of the money he was alleged to have disbursed, and Nelson appointed me, Tokyo Sexwale and Bally Chuene to replace Ayob in the companies.

I would still see Nelson two or three times a month, often for lunch at his home in Houghton. The menu rarely changed: oxtail or chicken accompanied by a glass of white wine, semi-sweet for Nelson, dry for me. Afterwards we would sit in the afternoon garden at the shaded south-eastern side of his house. He would drink tea, while I preferred a coffee. Near the end, Nelson's memory failed him. On my arrival for a visit he would soon ask me whether I had seen Walter recently. I would reply no, and explain that Walter had passed away. Nelson would contemplate this in grave silence for a while. Once we had resumed our conversation, it would not be long before he would enquire again, 'Any news of Walter, George?'

Sometimes our conversations would turn to death and what the mutual friends we had discovered at the Little Swallow had to say on the subject. In Plato's *Apology*, Socrates spoke of why we should not fear death:

> [...] there is great reason to hope that death is a good; for one of two things – either death is a state of nothingness and utter unconsciousness, or as men say, there is a change and migration of the soul from this world to another. Now if you suppose that there is no consciousness, but a sleep like the sleep of him who is undisturbed even by the sight of dreams, death will be an unspeakable gain. For if a person were to select the night in which his sleep was undisturbed even by dreams, and were to compare with this the other days and nights of his life, and then were to tell us how many days and nights he had passed in the course of his life better and more pleasantly than this one, I think that any man, I will not say a private man, but even the great king, will not find many such days or nights, when compared with the others [...] But if death is the journey to another place, and there, as men say, all the dead abide, what good, O my friends and judges, can be greater than

this? If indeed when the pilgrim arrives in the world below, he is deliv-ered from the professors of justice in this world, and finds the true judges who are said to give their judgment there, Minos and Rhada-manthus and Aeacus and Triptolemus, and other sons of God who are righteous in their own life, that pilgrimage will be worth making. What would not a man give if he might converse with Orpheus and Musaeus and Hesiod and Homer? Nay, if this be true, let me die again and again [...] What infinite delight would there be in conversing with them and asking them questions! In another world they do not put a man to death for asking questions; assuredly not. For besides being happier than we are, they will be immortal, if what is said is true...no evil can happen to a good man either in life or after death.

Nelson told me that when he died he would join the nearest branch of the ANC in heaven. In particular, he looked forward to meeting up with his old friend Walter.

On one of my visits to him, he called to the staff as I entered: 'Get me my boots.'

'What do you want your boots for, Tata?' one asked.

'George is here. He will take me to Qunu,' he answered. It was clear that he wanted to go home.

Our last meeting was at his home in Houghton. Nelson no longer fin-ished his sentences and our conversations were not about politics, but confined to news of our families and friends. Nelson and Graça were having a late lunch. Nelson sat at the head of the table, while Graça, on his left, gently helped him eat. It was a warm winter's day and I had left my jacket in the car.

At the end of the meal, I embraced both of them as I said goodbye. Suddenly Nelson said, 'George, don't leave your jacket behind!'

Those words touched me. He was being thoughtful and wanted me to protect myself from the winter chill that would set in as the afternoon lengthened. They were the last words that I heard him utter.

Graça telephoned me a couple of days later. She said that Nelson had been taken to a Pretoria hospital. The doctors described his condition as 'serious but stable'.

I asked her if I should visit him. She told me that the doctors recommended only brief visits by members of the immediate family. In any event, his condition was deteriorating, he would not recognise me and he was incapable of meaningful conversation. I took Graça's advice and did not try to see him.

When Nelson came back home after the doctors had given up on him, I again decided not to see him. I was still moved by his last words of concern that I was shielded from the cold.

When Nelson died, I could not bring myself to join the long lines of people viewing his body on exhibit in the garden of the presidential offices at the Union Buildings. I waited to go to the place where he would be buried.

The drive from Mthatha airport to Qunu is about an hour. My son Alexi joined me and we spent the night in a hotel in town. The next morning at the house in Qunu I was with Zelda la Grange, Nelson's long-time personal assistant, when, to my surprise, Nelson's daughter Maki stopped her at the door and told her that she was not allowed in as she was not a member of the family. Zelda broke into tears and left.

After the service, I shunned the motorcars on offer and, in the Greek tradition, followed Nelson's cortège on foot up the gravel road to the hill where he would be buried.

I am still Nelson's lawyer and he has kept me busy since his death.

I was appointed the executor of his estate, together with former deputy chief justice Dikgang Moseneke and Judge President Sangoni of the Eastern Cape High Court. I am also a trustee of the NRM Family Trust, which oversees Nelson's estate and image rights.

Although Nelson provided in his will for relatives and various institutions, Winnie was not mentioned. She instructed her attorney to write a letter in which he said that his client was not challenging the validity of the will, but contended that the house in Qunu was hers as the second wife in terms of the provisions of customary law. She brought an application to court, which I, together with the other executors, opposed. The claim was dismissed. Graça has refused to be drawn into the dispute.

I saw Graça recently. She asked how I was feeling. I said that I was concerned because I had lost four close friends over the last three years: Nelson Mandela, Arthur Chaskalson, Nadine Gordimer and Jules Browde. Each one of them had played an important part in my life. Frequently I wondered how long I would outlive them.

'I dream that the bell may soon toll for me,' I told her.

'Stop thinking about the bell tolling for you and think what your dear friends would want you to continue doing. And stop crying,' she added, referring to the tendency of my eyes to tear up involuntarily.

I am trying.

With Arthur and Nelson at the Fort on Constitution
Hill, the site of the Constitutional Court.

EPILOGUE

There is a small group of ill-informed South Africans who accuse Nelson Mandela of having 'sold out' the rights of black people in the country because he was 'trounced' by the De Klerk government during the Codesa negotiations.

They are obviously ignorant of our history and Nelson Mandela's attitude to all our people, which is clearly stated in the Freedom Charter's opening words:

> We, the People of South Africa, declare for all our country and the world to know:
>
> that South Africa belongs to all who live in it, black and white, and that no government can justly claim authority unless it is based on the will of all the people;
>
> that our people have been robbed of their birthright to land, liberty and peace by a form of government founded on injustice and inequality;
>
> that our country will never be prosperous or free until all our people live in brotherhood, enjoying equal rights and opportunities;
>
> that only a democratic state, based on the will of all the people, can secure to all their birthright without distinction of colour, race, sex or belief;

And therefore we, the People of South Africa, black and white to-gether – equals, countrymen and brothers – adopt this Freedom Charter. And we pledge ourselves to strive together sparing neither strength nor courage, until the democratic changes here set out have been won.

Nelson Mandela was a prominent leader of the ANC and made a sub-stantial contribution to the adoption of the Freedom Charter. He was banned when it was adopted by six thousand people at Kliptown, but watched the proceedings at a distance in disguise.

As an accused on a charge of treason in the late 1950s, Nelson, led by Sydney Kentridge, gave evidence in support of the adoption of the Freedom Charter, which was alleged by the state to be a communist-inspired document. Judge Tos Bekker asked him while he was in the wit-ness box whether he was aware that his organisation's slogan of 'one man, one vote' was frightening to the majority of white people in the country. Would Nelson and the ANC settle for something less?

Nelson would answer the question most cogently in his statement from the dock at the Rivonia Trial.

Above all, we want equal political rights, because without them our disabilities will be permanent. I know this sounds revolutionary to the whites in this country, because the majority of voters will be Africans. This makes the white man fear democracy.

But this fear cannot be allowed to stand in the way of the only solution which will guarantee racial harmony and freedom for all. It is not true that the enfranchisement of all will result in racial domination. Political division, based on colour, is entirely artificial and, when it disappears, so will the domination of one colour group by another. The ANC has spent half a century fighting against racialism. When it triumphs it will not change that policy.

This then is what the ANC is fighting. Their struggle is truly a national one. It is a struggle of the African people, inspired by their own suffering and their own experience. It is a struggle for the right to live.

From its inception, the ANC made it clear that it did not regard whites as its enemy. It knocked on the doors of successive white governments for generations without receiving any response and was prepared to negotiate decades before the white government agreed to do so.

It would do Nelson's critics well to consider the preamble of our constitution [emphasis my own]:

> We, the people of South Africa,
> Recognise the injustices of our past;
> Honour those who suffered for justice and freedom in our land;
> Respect those who have worked to build and develop our country; and
> **Believe that South Africa belongs to all who live in it, united in our diversity.**
>
> We therefore, through our freely elected representatives, adopt this Constitution as the supreme law of the Republic so as to
> - **Heal the divisions of the past** and establish a society based on democratic values, social justice and fundamental human rights;
> - Lay the foundations for a democratic and open society in which government is based on the will of the people and every citizen is equally protected by law;
> - **Improve the quality of life of all citizens** and free the potential of each person; and
> - Build a united and democratic South Africa able to take its rightful place as a sovereign state in the family of nations.
>
> May God protect our people.
> Nkosi Sikelel' iAfrika. Morena boloka setjhaba sa heso.
> God seën Suid-Afrika. God bless South Africa.
> Mudzimu fhatutshedza Afurika. Hosi katekisa Afrika.

And, just as importantly, Chapter 1 of the founding provisions of our constitution:

1. Republic of South Africa

The Republic of South Africa is one, sovereign, democratic state founded on the following values:

(a) Human dignity, the achievement of equality and the advancement of human rights and freedoms.

(b) Non-racialism and non-sexism.

(c) Supremacy of the constitution and the rule of law.

(d) Universal adult suffrage, a national common voters roll, regular elections and a multi-party system of democratic government, to ensure accountability, responsiveness and openness.

Have those who criticised Nelson Mandela read the constitution?

Do they recognise that certain portions of the constitution, including the sections set out above, are probably non-amendable and other portions require either a seventy-five per cent or two-thirds majority from the democratically elected parliament?

I am sure that I am not alone in believing that most South Africans do not share the views of those who are critical of the constitution. It was, after all, adopted by a parliament elected by a vast majority. Only two people in that parliament voted against it, while twelve abstained.

Much of the current criticism of the constitution arises in relation to four issues: the death sentence, the punishment of criminals, the land question and tribal law.

Perhaps these critics need to be reminded that our court has considered these issues in some detail.

Our Constitutional Court has ruled that capital punishment offends the rights to dignity and not to be subjected to cruel, inhuman and degrading punishment. There is no evidence that the death penalty is a greater deterrent to offenders than life imprisonment – indeed, the evidence is clear that it is the likelihood of conviction, rather than fear of the sentence, that serves as the deterrent to crime. I hope that most South Africans would reject debasing our society by condoning the taking of another's life under the guise of moral righteousness or retribution.

The Constitutional Court has also circumscribed the use of deadly force. Sadly, that did not prevent the death of thirty-four and the injury of more than seventy-nine striking miners at Marikana. On 16 August 2012, eight hundred police fired over five hundred rounds of live ammunition into a largely unarmed crowd. It is disappointing that, in this context, there are still calls for the police and property owners to be unrestrained in their response to threats from criminals. This call to sanction the firing of a firearm by a policeman or individual amounts to a return of the death penalty, and one that is imposed in a split second by the person firing the gun. Likewise, those critics of the rights to due process for those accused or convicted of crimes need to be reminded that the constitutional safeguards apply to all – including those wrongly accused of offences that they did not commit. Rights are not up for barter. Affording rights to one person does not take away the rights of others. And the protection that the constitution affords 'the worst and the weakest among us' is testament to its character.

The call for the amendment of the property clause, Section 25 of the constitution, is perhaps the most popular. I do not believe that an amendment to this clause will solve the difficulties we face, because our transformative agenda has fallen short and because the wealth disparity in the country is alarming. Our constitution might prohibit the arbitrary deprivation of property, but the section does contemplate the expropriation of land for a public purpose or in the public interest, including the nation's commitment to land reform and to reforms to bring about equitable access to all South Africa's natural resources. Our Constitutional Court has ruled that this provision must be interpreted with 'due regard to the gross inequality in relation to wealth and land distribution in this country' and that the obligation imposed by this section is not to over-emphasise private property rights at the expense of the state's social responsibilities. We do not want to make the same mistake as Zimbabwe: the expropriation of productive land without any compensation is not a sensible solution either. Section 25 is a careful attempt to balance complex and competing interests. I would urge us to tread this difficult path gently.

Lastly, I believe that the establishment of a fourth arm of government comprising traditional leadership structures together with the executive, legislative and judiciary is untenable. Of course, I believe that traditional leadership is a well-respected institution that has a role to play. This, however, cannot be in the guise of a separate body distinct from the framework of the constitution which declares that 'the Republic of South Africa is one, sovereign democratic state'. Affording executive powers to traditional leaders would lead to a lack of certainty and accountability, and appointments to positions of power outside the democratic electoral process. It would erode the founding values of the indivisibility of South Africa if certain parts of the country were subject to a different executive leadership than the rest. Traditional leadership as it presents itself today is, in part, a product of our colonial past and plagued with issues of patronage and lack of gender representation.

Where does the power of the constitution lie? As a question of fact, it is merely a document containing words on paper. As a question of law, we know it to be supreme, but supremacy is an intangible concept. For me, it is a question of values. Our constitution entrenches the deepest values that we share as a people. It is our common ground, our shared history and our optimism for the future. A constitution does not depend on the text alone, but on turning that text into a reality for us all to enjoy.

Nelson enjoined those of us on the ANC constitutional committee to draft a constitution for 'South Africa as a whole, not just the ANC'.

I believe that this is what we did. Our constitution is good for our country and all its people. It is not an obstacle to transformation or reform. It does not stifle wealth creation and prosperity. It is the product of a collective effort, negotiated for the benefit of all, founded in the common values of those who fought so hard to see it realised.

The principles upheld in the constitution are only the first step in a long and arduous journey to put into practice the ideals that these principles embody. There is no doubt that this is in no small part the role of government, but there is also a role for civil society to see the realisation of these rights. We have failed a large number of our people who still live in poverty and are unable to vindicate the basic rights that they are promised. But the constitution is a framework; it is for us to give it life and meaning.

I would urge that we all respect the provisions of the constitution adopted by millions of our citizens.

~

ACKNOWLEDGEMENTS

I want to thank those who have helped me write this book, in particular Miriam Wheeldon. I met Miriam in 1997 when she joined the Constitutional Litigation Unit of the Legal Resources Centre as an attorney. We worked on the Cradock Four and Biko amnesty cases before the Truth and Reconciliation Commission to which she applied herself with great commitment and energy. I recall one night being too tired to continue working and calling it a day at about 11 p.m. The next morning, in the same clothes from the day before, Miriam presented me fully prepared cross-examination notes. When I was briefed to appear on behalf of the Legal Resources Centre before the Marikana Commission of Inquiry, I asked her to work with me on the case for what I thought would be three months. It turned into more than two years. When I decided to write this book, she remained at the Legal Resources Centre in part to assist me.

My gratitude to publisher Fourie Botha, editors Mike Nicol and Bronwen Maynier, and proofreader Rhonda Crouse. Gratitude is also due to Sahm Venter of the Nelson Mandela Foundation, who so fastidiously fact-checked my manuscript.

My memory is not what it used to be. I have already written two books, one an autobiography, on which I have relied in telling this story. The many interviews that I have given over the years have also been a useful aide memoir and I have drawn from these. I thank the many journalists, students, and researchers, too many to name, who have so diligently recorded my words and recollections over the years.

I also wish to thank the Legal Resources Centre, in particular the national director Janet Love, and the colleagues with whom I work, for their support, assistance and encouragement to finish this book.

Lastly, but by no means last, my thanks and love to my late wife Arethe, my sons Kimon, Damon and Alexi, and my six grandchildren.

With the team at the Legal Resources Centre.

With my wife and sons Damon, Kimon and Alexi
at Kimon's wedding in 1994.

With Janet Love.

GEORGE BIZOS
IN CONVERSATION

Janet Love (JL):[22] George, it is wonderful that you are publishing this book in the same year that you celebrate your ninetieth birthday, although perhaps you could explain why it is only nine years since we celebrated your eightieth?

George Bizos (GB): Yes, well, my date of birth was a subject of some confusion for many years and it is still not reflected correctly on my South African identity documents. All of the village records, including those of my parents' marriage and my birth, were burnt during the war. When my father and I arrived in Egypt, my father declared my year of birth as 1928, not 1927, to the officials issuing my refugee permit. I am still not sure if this was an innocent mistake or an attempt by him to make me a year younger to protect me from conscription into the army.

And then my father and my mother had a dispute about the actual date of my birthday – he recorded the date as 28 December, but my mother was insistent that I was born on Saint Philip's feast day, which was 14 November. When finally we retrieved the records much later, it seems that I was actually born on 15 November 1927. And so this is the birthday we will celebrate this year.

JL: I thought that we should start this interview at the beginning – when we first met, George. I am not sure if you remember that that was in 1975 during the Nusas Five Trial. I was a friend of Cedric de Beer.

GB: Ah yes.

JL: So I thought that we could begin there, as it is a good example of the interconnectedness of the network of people who weave their way through your story. The Nusas Trial took place against the backdrop of the revival of the independent trade-union movement, and two of the accused, Glenn Moss and Eddie Webster, were both involved in the Industrial Aid Society (IAS) of the Nusas Wages Commission. Felicia [Kentridge] was also involved with the IAS, as she was one of the people who first arranged for lawyers to assist the trade-union advice offices and enabled them to function as law clinics.

GB: Yes, well, I seem to remember that when Felicia was lecturing at Wits University she became involved with the student law clinics – I think she might have started the one at Wits. And then she worked with the university clinical services and the IAS, before going on to establish the Legal Resources Centre with Arthur [Chaskalson] and Geoff [Budlender].

JL: Yes. Both Arthur and Geoff were also involved in the Nusas Trial. Geoff was also in Nusas, but was not on trial himself; he was the articled clerk for the defence attorney, Raymond Tucker. I remember the cross-examination of Bruno by you and Arthur. As I recall, Arthur started the cross-examination. You were not around at the time but some of us went to lunch. I think Geoff was there. But there was a discussion as to whether Arthur had finished with Bruno. And I remember so vividly that Arthur got an unmistakeable twinkle in his eye when he said, 'I have, but George must have his turn.' And he smiled in a way that made it clear that he felt that your time for dealing with this man had come.

GB: Well, Arthur and I were very different kinds of lawyers. We worked well as a team, but our approaches differed. At the Nusas Trial, there was a Hungarian doctor, Doctor Recsey, who came to give evidence about how he had fled Hungary when it became a communist country, and how he was very concerned that what happened in Hungary would happen here and that the communists were going to take over. Arthur was my senior, and a careful cross-examiner, and he said, 'We will ask him to stand down.' I said, 'No, I want to take him on.' Our discussion prompted the presiding officer to ask: 'Would you two gentlemen like to take an adjournment to resolve your differences?' Arthur said no, and told me to go ahead. So I asked Dr Recsey whether he had taken any steps to oppose tyranny in his country, when he was a student in the 1930s, when there was a dictatorship. And when he said no, he hadn't, I asked him whether he had ever thought that his failure to oppose tyranny, the attitude to authority shown by him and other students, might be responsible for the poor democratic record of his own country. He had no answer to that.

JL: And two of the accused from the Nusas Trial, Karel Tip and Charles Nupen, would also both go on to work for the LRC. In fact, I think that it was his experience in that trial that may have led to Karel's decision to study law.

GB: Yes, that is right.

JL: You write about how the trial was important because if the state had secured convictions, a legal precedent would have been set that would have criminalised anybody making any of the same political demands as the ANC on the basis that this was furthering the aims of a banned organisation. But it was also an important trial for you on a more personal level, because it gave you and Madiba a pretext to confer. It must have been your only chance while he was on the island to examine media reports, student publications and other documents together?

GB. Yes, it was. Arthur, Raymond Tucker and I went to the island to consult and we met with Nelson, Walter [Sisulu] and Govan [Mbeki]. We spent the whole day together. They were thrilled to see all of the material. Arthur explained to them how Nusas stood accused of furthering the aims of the ANC, and we considered whether we might call one of them to say what we said at the Rivonia Trial to challenge the evidence of Hlopane and to oppose the charge that the ANC was intent on the violent overthrow of the government. But Govan warned us to be careful because of what had happened to him – he had volunteered to give evidence in a trial in the Eastern Cape and they punished him for it by putting him in a small cell for three months before he was sent back to the island. So we decided not to call them.

JL: It must also have encouraged them to see what this group of white students were up to.

GB: Yes, Nelson was delighted. And he asked me to thank them all for their efforts, for the calls that they had made for the release of political prisoners in general and of him in particular, for the risks that they were taking on their behalf.

JL: The list of cases that you took on while Madiba was imprisoned is impressive – beginning soon after his imprisonment with the treason and sabotage trials of the 1960s, including Little Rivonia and the trial of Bram Fischer, the 1970s inquests into the deaths in detention of Ahmed Timol, Steve Biko and Neil Aggett, and then into the 1980s, the Delmas Trial.

GB: I discussed all of these cases with Nelson. He was always hungry for news from the outside and I would report to him on the trials that I was involved in. Once we had finished dealing with his family matters, we would spend a large part of our consultations discussing my political cases, which was one way for him to get a sense of political developments in the country. Of course, he had other sources as well.

JL: He must have been encouraged to hear about the people you represented, for example, Ahmed Timol, who, as a young Indian teacher, had joined Umkhonto we Sizwe.

GB: Yes, although Nelson was always concerned about the safety of people, he was buoyed by those who were taking his legacy forward. I would report to Nelson on all of these trials, and sometimes I would come with a query about political strategy, sometimes an issue that one of my clients had raised, and Nelson would say, 'Let me consider this and I will tell you after lunch', and I would know that he wanted to discuss the matter with Walter. We had to be careful – our consultations were monitored. I did not jeopardise my position by taking risks. Our discussions were measured; there was always a certain restraint.

JL: I realise that this was necessary during the trial and Madiba's subsequent imprisonment, but when I read the book I was struck by how phlegmatic your friendship was from the very start. I got a sense of an almost tacit stoicism to your relationship, which was perhaps a consequence not only of the circumstances and the times, but also because you were both private men.

GB: Well, I suppose, there was never much opportunity for the normal pastimes. When we first met and were getting to know each other, the intrusions of apartheid denied us many of the simple pleasures of friendship – we could not watch sport or go to the bioscope together; I could not even visit Nelson at his home in Soweto without a permit. And when I met Nelson he was already rising fast in the ranks of the ANC, so there were security reasons why it was better for me not to know too much about what he was up to. One didn't ask unnecessary questions.

JL: But it also seemed to have been compounded by your discreet personalities and the fact that you were men of your generation, born between two world wars.

GB: Yes, I think neither of us was ever keen on small talk. There was too much else going on around us that interested us. Of course, we were always concerned to know about the well-being of each other's families. After Nelson's imprisonment, I was in regular contact with Winnie and defended her in her many trials, so I knew about what was happening with his family. And Nelson always asked after Arethe and my sons. In 1980, I recall his interest when I recounted to him how my sons Damon and Alexi had been arrested with a group of other Wits students for protesting in favour of his release. But neither of us liked to discuss our personal lives much.

JL: And yet, there seems to be much in your personal lives that you had in common – your country childhoods, your separation from your mothers at an early age, your stubborn fathers. You both arrived in Johannesburg in the same year and were pretty much left to your own devices, and then you found yourselves at Wits University,

269

studying law, which was a career choice that both your own father and Madiba's guardian opposed.

GB: Yes, there were some experiences that we had in common, but there were important differences. I suffered discrimination because I was a refugee, I was marginalised, I was poor, but I was still white and because of that I was privileged. But there was a strong sense of solidarity that developed between us early on.

JL: It is clear that you also laughed together. You were both a bit self-deprecating.

GB: Yes, we shared the same dry sense of humour. We would sometimes tease each other. Of course, things changed over time and so did our relationship. Once Nelson was released, we could talk freely about everything; and then at the end, when his memory was failing, we only really talked of family and our mutual friends.

JL: That is another thing that is striking about your book. The sixty-five years of friendship refers of course to the friendship between you and Madiba, yet there are so many other consequential and abiding friendships that you shared and that thread themselves through the years. I am struck by the quality and endurance of many of them. It is impossible to discuss them all, but let's start with the others from Wits.

GB: Well, there was Arthur [Chaskalson], Bram [Fischer], Duma [Nokwe]…I became an advocate in 1954, Arthur in 1955 and then Duma in 1956.

JL: Can you tell us a bit about Duma?

GB: Duma was a good friend to both Nelson and me. He also had a very good sense of humour. In fact, it was through our mutual friendship with Duma that Nelson and I really got to know each other so well. He had been a mathematics teacher before he studied law, and when he was admitted to the Bar, he and I shared chambers. I was fortunate to join the Maisels group – there were twenty-two advocates who applied, but I was chosen – I don't know why…perhaps the fact that I was a refugee.

Duma was a very clever advocate. Much to the surprise of the Afrikaner magistrates and judges, he was also fluent in Afrikaans. His mother was from the Free State. Nelson and Duma were in the ANC together – Duma became the acting secretary general of the ANC when Walter [Sisulu] was banned, and he was also involved in the Defiance Campaign. And then when they were both accused in the Treason Trial, they, together with Oliver [Tambo], Walter and others, would meet in our chambers to discuss the trial and other ANC business. I would be there when they arrived in the afternoon or early evenings, and then leave them there for their meetings. At that time, we were sure that our offices were not bugged – although they were later. It was Duma who approached me about Nelson's problem with the Kempton Park magistrate and asked me to help.

JL: Duma went into exile in 1963.

GB: Yes. One morning he left our office at about ten o'clock saying that he would return in an hour, but he was back ten minutes later. The security police had been waiting for him at the gate to His Majesty's Building, and when they searched him they found a document on him saying that the 'Time has come for V to be met with V'. They took the document, but the policeman was not of a rank to arrest him so they left him. When he left the country, he left his family behind and told me to try to do something for them, which we did, until they joined him. And Duma became Oliver's secretary. I had no contact with him after he left the country. It was too dangerous to make contact with him when he was in exile. I heard news of him from time to time.

JL: And then when he died in Lusaka in 1978, did you tell Madiba?

GB: He knew. I went to the island every two or three months, but Nelson had other people who visited him and told him what had happened; or they didn't tell him but they told another prisoner who told him, so he was well informed.

271

JL: Another person who threads in and out of your story is Bram Fischer.

GB: Yes, he was also a good friend to us both. And he was a hero to Nelson. He was one of the people who persuaded Nelson of the commitment of some whites to the struggle against apartheid. He was also one of the lawyers that inspired Nelson's belief in the legal profession and the potential of the courts. Bram was the chairman of the Bar Council and a brilliant, highly respected lawyer – one of the great lawyers this country has produced. He was Afrikaner royalty, yet he risked it all, and lost it, for his political beliefs. Nelson admired him for that, for the courage and sacrifice of standing up for what was just even against his own people. That was something that Nelson was not required to do, and he admired Bram immensely for that.

JL: They were both your friends who were sentenced to life imprisonment and I seem to remember something about their having both turned to you for guidance on their respective daughters' choice of husband.

GB: Yes, well I recount how Nelson asked me to represent the family and meet her suitor when Zeni wanted to marry. And then, after Bram's daughter Ilse got married, Bram asked me my impressions of her new husband – the prison visit had been so short that he had not had the chance to get a real impression. He wanted to know if he was worthy of his daughter. I said to him, 'Bram, he managed to persuade your daughter to walk down the aisle of a church.' He shed tears and said, 'That is a good judgement.'

JL: Bram was disbarred for his political beliefs...

GB: Yes, he was. For conduct 'unbefitting a member of the Bar and the Society' for absconding while on bail during the course of his trial when he was facing charges of contravening the Suppression of Communism Act. He was very, very hurt by that. And then, in 2003, a full bench of the Johannesburg High Court reinstated him. But there were only four advocates from the Johannesburg Bar who flew down to Bloemfontein for his funeral: Maisels, Lewis Dison, Arthur and I. Nobody from Bloemfontein came. Arthur delivered the funeral oration – André Brink was supposed to deliver it, but on the day of the funeral his father said to him that he needed to go to the doctor. And when André asked if his brother could not take him instead, his father said to him that he would not go to the doctor unless André took him. 'You would rather go to the funeral of *that traitor* than take your own father to the doctor.' As we were going up the steps of the airport, Arthur, Maisels and I, we saw Judge Rumpff. And Isie [Maisels] went to talk to him. He asked Isie: 'What are you guys doing in my city? Court is not in session.' And when Isie told him that we were there to bury Bram, Rumpff, the arch Afrikaner, said: 'He will be remembered long after all of us have died.' Which was something that Arthur and I took to heart.

JL: How did you get to know Bram?

GB: Before the Rivonia Trial, I became friendly with him. I called on him in his chambers and he was interested in my refugee status and my story. I think my sharing chambers with Duma Nokwe had an effect on Bram; he was impressed with my volunteering. Bram had impeccable manners; he was unflinchingly polite. My mother referred to him as that 'Good Christian gentleman' after he took her by the arm and walked with her through the garden of our Parktown North home, nodding as she spoke to him in fluent Greek, when of course he could not understand a word.

JL: There is another charming story about your mother and your friend Advocate Jules Browde.

GB: Yes, Jules was another good friend to Nelson and I. We became friends at university. He was about eight years older than me, and had been in the army, so he had qualified by the time I graduated. He obtained the temporary permit for the firm Mandela and Tambo to retain its offices in Chancellor House and then tried to obtain ministerial permission for them to remain, which he did not succeed at doing, but somehow he managed to persuade the authorities not to kick the firm out and they did not charge them for being in unlawful occupation, so they managed to stay on. And he was responsible for the fact that I was finally granted South African citizenship in 1972 and returned to Greece for the first time after thirty-one years.

JL: But before that, he visited your mother in Greece?

GB: Yes. Selma and Jules visited Greece and they went to see my mother and they thought that I had warned her that they were coming, but I hadn't. Nonetheless, when they knocked on her door, she welcomed them in with great enthusiasm and sat them down at the table and offered them refreshments. It was only after they were fed, and they handed her the letter that I had given them for her, that she realised they were friends of mine from South Africa. Although she did not know that they were South African and she could not speak English, or they Greek, she was simply extending her usual generosity and hospitality to two foreigners who had appeared on her doorstep.

Then they arranged for someone to interpret for them and they asked my mother when last I had visited the village. They were shocked to hear that I had not been back since I left in 1941 and had only seen her once when she visited us in South Africa in 1964. And so, on his return, Jules asked about this and I told him how I had applied for a South African passport, which had been refused. As a refugee I was stateless. Although I could have applied for a Greek passport, I feared that this would jeopardise my residency status in the country. I would be given a one-way exit visa, and prompt the minister of justice to strike me from the role of advocates. And so Jules spoke to Judge Galgut, who spoke to Prime Minister Vorster, and I was eventually granted citizenship.

JL: Nadine Gordimer was another Wits student...

GB: Yes. I met Nadine at the university; she was also a member of the 'left'. She was at least a year ahead of me in her BA, but she did not finish her degree.

JL: She also assisted your efforts in both the Rivonia and Delmas trials?

GB: Yes. She did the biographies at Rivonia – each accused wrote a biography and I handed the batch to Nadine, who edited them and we gave them to the media. She was a close friend of Anthony Sampson and he was staying with her when I gave him the draft of Nelson's speech from the dock, which he edited.

She gave evidence in mitigation at the Delmas Trial and testified that she supported the ANC, which gave her husband a terrible fright. He was in the audience in court and he was so afraid that the security police would come and arrest her that he tried to arrange for her to sleep somewhere else. She would not have it. 'If they come they can come!' she said. I was also a close friend of her husband – he was a refugee from Nazi Germany and his family were dealers of French art from the late-nineteenth and twentieth centuries.

JL: And then there is the story of how Nadine facilitated a cameo based on you in court for the movie *A Dry White Season...*

GB: Yes, Nadine invited me to meet a filmmaker from the United States who was doing a film of the book by André Brink. Marlon Brando was to play the role of the lawyer. I spent a couple of hours with the filmmaker and Nadine. And then, when I went on sabbatical to Columbia University in 1989, the film was shown to a select audience in New York by invitation. When the scene came on – it was a scene in which Marlon Brando as the lawyer tells a state witness to turn and show the court the wheals on his back – the ANC's representative at the United Nations, who knew I was there, stood up and shouted: 'George! George! That is how George does it!' My wife Arethe was with me and when someone commented to her that her husband looks like Marlon Brando, she replied quickly: 'My husband is better looking than Marlon Brando and he speaks more clearly.'

And I write about how Nadine was part of the party of friends and family that Nelson took to Oslo when he received the Nobel Prize. I delivered the first Nadine Gordimer lecture this year.

JL: Johann Kriegler is someone else with whom you have a long association who appears from time to time in your story, from the first time you met when he administered your oath when you were admitted as an advocate. He was one of the trustees of the Legal Resources Trust.

GB: Yes. But Johann was not a Witsie. He studied at the University of Pretoria and I only met him the year after I graduated, when he administered the oath. But he became a good friend and I turned to him when Nelson asked me to go to Lusaka on his behalf. And Johann gave me good advice and accompanied me to see the minister of justice when I returned from the meeting with Oliver [Tambo].

I have another story about Johann. In the case of the Sharpeville Six. In 1988, the Greek ambassador telephoned me and told me that the European ambassadors had had lunch together and that the British and other European ambassadors would withdraw, and flights to and from the United States would stop, if the Sharpeville Six, who had been sentenced to death, were executed. They did not want to make a public statement, but they wanted to know how they could get a highly confidential statement to the prime minister that this was going to happen. I phoned Johann and said that I wanted to see him on an urgent matter. And after I told him, he immediately picked up his phone and said, 'Prof, ek wil jou dadelik sien.' When I asked him whom he was talking to, he said that it was the professor of theology at the University of Pretoria, who was also the head of the NGK [Nederlands Gereformeerde Kerk]. Johann was going to go and see him and convey the message to him in person. Apparently, the professor took the aeroplane overnight to Cape Town and went to speak to President Botha, and at 11 a.m. on the Friday, Botha made a public announcement that he had been informed that the Sharpeville Six were innocent victims of the Communist Party, and in view of the information received, he would commute the sentences to life imprisonment. And so the young people were not executed.

JL: And Arthur [Chaskalson] was on the Constitutional Court with Johann. Arthur and you really did seem to live your lives on parallel tracks that converged time and time again.

GB: Well, I write in the book how my friendship with Arthur began when he came to my rescue at university after some of the law students opposed me because of my role in insisting that black students be included in the law students' dinner. He was a year behind me – a top student in one of the most prestigious years, which included Frank Lipschitz and Joel Joffe, who would be our instructing attorney at the Rivonia Trial. He was noted for being the best goalkeeper in the soccer team, the best wicketkeeper in the cricket team and for wearing his glasses stuck down with plaster. In the middle of the debate about what the policy of the university was, Arthur, who I had not yet met, stood up and said: 'We have been debating the university policy for some time now, but the real question is surely what is right and what is wrong? I move closure.'

JL: Which reminds me of Bram Fischer, because at his trial his clarion call was 'I did what I thought was right', and this drive to do the right thing is yet another strong thread of what seems to have bound so many of you together.

GB: Yes. And I think I should mention Arthur's wife, Lorraine, here because she was a great influence on Arthur and supported him in doing what was right. She had a doctorate in literature and was always interested in the work that we were doing. I recall one weekend we were discussing, as we did during weekends, how we were to approach things. And I had a newspaper cutting of a debate between Jean-Paul Sartre and Albert Camus – Arthur was steeped in the works of Camus – and in the debate, which was about Algeria, Sartre trapped Camus and sarcastically accused him of being in favour of the black Algerians, not justice. 'Behold how speaks "the man of justice"' – because this was Camus's nom de guerre during the German occupation. And Camus replied: 'Jean-Paul, if sometimes you have to take sides between justice and your mother [his mother lived in Algeria], you will have to prefer your mother.' And I remember Lorraine remarking how cruel Sartre was. We had sympathy for Camus. In the debate between Camus and Sartre, we were on the side of Camus.

There was also a group of advocates at the Bar – Arthur, Bram, Isie Maisels and Walter Pollak – who would say, 'Hey, we are lawyers, we must do what is right', and who supported Duma taking up chambers in His Majesty's Building

JL: Like Vernon Berrangé, who was also on the team at Rivonia and something of an inspiration to you in your style of cross-examination?

GB: Vernon had the reputation of being the best cross-examiner in the country. And he also became a good friend. Duma, Ismail [Mahomed] and I were his junior counsel of choice. He had been a member of the Communist Party, but he resigned when the Stalinists came to the fore. Yet still he refused to apply for silk because he knew that it would be rejected. His father was also a lawyer and had been Paul Kruger's representative in Swaziland, and Vernon eventually moved there.

I still remember a trick he pulled in a case. One of his clients had bought stolen property and had been acquitted three or four times previously. And so the police officer said to him: 'Mr Berrangé, you got away with it a few times, but this time we have a sure case and your client is going to jail.' And Vernon said: 'Do you want to bet on it?' And the policeman said yes and so they took a five-pound bet. And then when they got to court, Vernon asked the policeman: 'Warrant Officer, do you have any personal interest in the outcome of this case?' And the policeman had to admit that he had taken a bet. And the man was acquitted.

He was very witty. He could also be terribly sarcastic, but he had a great sense of fun.

JL: And Isie Maisels?

GB: Isie was a legal giant.

We were on the Court of Appeals together in Botswana, in fact, he recommended me for appointment. We would meet for breakfast in the mornings and he would say, 'There is nothing in this appeal; let's go in and dismiss it – without hearing argument.' And the Ghanaian judge Amissah would admonish him and say, 'No, stop it, let's listen first.'

And he was our leader in the Timol case.

The counsel for the state wanted to submit a statement published by the Communist Party with the last paragraph: 'Vorster and his murderers will not halt our people when we have comrades like Archbishop Hurley, Rowley Arenstein, Vernon Berrangé, Isie Maisels, M.D. Naidoo, George Bizos and others who have been fighting with us since the days of Rivonia.' Cilliers was the Afrikaner counsel for the police. He was a man of integrity. He showed Maisels the document and said he would not hand it around out of respect for him. They may have thought that Vernon Berrangé, Archbishop Hurley and I were communists, but they could not believe that Maisels could possibly be.

And you know he was very proud that Duma was in his group. He was the chairman on the Bar Council and engaged in a lengthy correspondence with Dr H.F. Verwoerd, the then minister of native affairs, on behalf of Duma Nokwe regarding his admission as a member of the Johannesburg Bar.

He and I discussed the way that we could get Duma in by sharing my chambers, and so it was slightly stage-managed when we held the meeting of the group and said, 'Let's try to find out if there is anyone who is prepared to share', and I slowly put my hand up and he said, 'Oh Bizos, you are there? Oh good.'

JL: And so again this network. You became friends with Duma, who brought you closer to Madiba; you met Arthur Chaskalson through your university debate, who met Bram Fischer because of the association with Deneys Reitz...

GB: Arthur was a clerk to a senior partner at the firm Deneys Reitz, and the firm used to brief Bram for their mining work. Believe it or not, Bram was an expert on mining law – he taught it at Wits. So Arthur and Bram had contact with each other even before Arthur became a member of the Bar. And then when he was admitted, Arthur joined Bram's group on the sixth floor of Innes Chambers. He was not the leader. There were a number of very successful leading lawyers in the group, including Sydney Kentridge and Rex Welsh.

And Arthur and Joel Joffe were very close friends. They started doing pro bono work in political cases and became well known already in the 1960s for their defence of a group of Soweto students who were charged with contravening the Communism Act when they demonstrated outside the Coliseum Cinema.

Arthur and I did similar types of work at the Bar. One day he came to my chambers and he was pacing up and down and talking. Then he burst out: 'George, you are my senior but I want to apply to take silk. According to the rules, I have to get permission from anyone who is senior to me to give him the opportunity to take silk before me.' I told him that I was not interested in becoming a silk and that he should apply. He tried to persuade me, but I did not want to and so he applied and took silk.

As I said earlier, we were very different lawyers, Arthur and I. I once put it to a witness: 'You are either stupid or a liar – which one is it?' And the witness replied, after a pause, 'I am stupid.' And Arthur said afterwards: 'George, that was not fair – there were a number of other options – not just the two!' I think I offended his sense of fairness. He was always the gentleman lawyer – I was the bombastic and rude one.

JL: You complemented each other. I remember you and he would say that you made a good team because you liked to draw out the *facts* while he would focus on the *law*.

GB: Yes, well, we did a number of cases together over the years. The Rivonia Trial was the most famous. And what he did in the trial was excellent – the exception to the indictment was a masterpiece and it had an international effect. The United Nations and European countries called out for the release of the accused when the indictment was quashed and the accused were immediately re-arrested.

And we did the Nusas Five Trial together, as you mentioned earlier.

JL: And then there was the five-year Delmas Trial in which you and Arthur spent most of the last five years of apartheid defending over twenty accused who were charged with treason, terrorism and furthering the objects of unlawful organisations.

GB: Yes, and at my seventy-fifth birthday party Arthur told the story of how I entrapped him into getting involved in that trial. I accepted the brief, but the indictment was served a few days before I was to leave with my wife for Greece, so I asked Arthur to liaise with Zak Yacoob and Karel Tip and draft the request for further particulars. And I returned to find them drafted and a note on my desk at the LRC from Arthur to say that the indictment was *excipiable*. And so I asked him to argue the exception, which he did on a Monday. But on about the Wednesday before the argument, I said, 'Arthur, you know it would look odd for you not to have met the accused before you stand up. Can't we go over on Saturday to the jail in Pretoria?' So he agreed and we went together. Without his authority, I introduced him as the leader of the team. He could not contradict me and he was anyway really impressed with them. And so he stayed on in the case.

JL: And he argued for the recusal of the judge?

GB: Yes. He did. It was tough for him – he did not want that kind of confrontation, but he felt that there was no choice. The judge – Van Dijkhorst – had dismissed one of his assessors when the assessor told him in his chambers that he did not know why the state was spending so much time cross-examining a shopkeeper witness who had allowed a desk to be put at his shop door to facilitate the collection of signatures for a UDF petition. 'There is nothing wrong with the petition; I signed it myself,' the assessor told the judge. So the judge announced to the court that he had had the assessor removed on the basis that he was biased. I objected and warned that the whole trial may be declared unlawful. I was ignored, so we asked for an adjournment to prepare an argument. Again, I was ignored. The next day, Arthur Chaskalson came to court and argued that, as the trial had proceeded in the absence of the assessor, the judge should recuse himself and the other assessor. And the judge dismissed the application. Arthur requested that a special entry be noted and this was also refused. At the end of the trial, an appeal was requested and it was granted in mid-1989 – in September of the year that I was teaching a course entitled 'Legal Responses to Apartheid' at Columbia University. The appeal was set for November. Arthur was to argue it, but he insisted that I be present because I was more au fait with the facts and I may be required to argue. I came back, but was not called. The five appeal judges made their decision early on. The proceedings became irregular when the one assessor was removed. The five prisoners on Robben Island were released. I returned to Columbia.

JL: And your ruse in the Delmas Trial?

GB: Yes. And Arthur engineered a smart reversal of his own. After the Delmas Trial, he said, 'George, Morris Zimmerman has retired. The young people at the LRC haven't got the paternal oversight that they had during his time. Do you mind if they phone you once in a while and come to your office with their problems?' And I said yes, of course. And then he said, 'Could you agree to a regular afternoon when they could come and see you?' And I agreed to that, too. And then he said, 'George, instead of them coming up why don't you come down?' And so I did.

In 1991, Jules Browde referred a divorce case to me. The client was a rich man. He had left his wife of many years for his young and beautiful secretary. The wife did not appear at court, a divorce was granted in her absence and I was briefed to oppose her application for a *rescission* of the judgment. The wife explained to the court that she had not shown up because her hairdresser had misinformed her that if she did not arrive the divorce could not be granted. The judge called counsel into his chambers and said to me, 'Your client is wealthy and was prepared to be generous before his wife's stupidity left her with nothing. Why don't you advise him to settle?' I recommended this to the client, but he shouted at me and rudely instructed me to return to court and win the case for him, which I did. That evening I telephoned Arthur and told him that I wanted to formalise our arrangement and work with him at the Legal Resources Centre. And so I joined formally and we agreed that I would spend seven months on LRC cases and five months on private work. And my only condition was that I would not do any administration or fundraising. And when Nelson was released, he asked me whether I would like to be a member of parliament or take a position in government or as a judge, but I said no. I wanted to retain my independence and continue my work at the LRC. I did agree to an appointment to the Judicial Service Commission. So Nelson appointed me to that and then Thabo Mbeki appointed me again.

JL: And here you are, still at the LRC, working in an institution that Arthur, together with Felicia and Sydney Kentridge and others, started and worked in for many years. And from the LRC you and Arthur went into the negotiations together and on to the drafting of the constitution – as did many others from the LRC who were involved in different capacities in the early land legislation, the TRC Act…

GB: Yes, Geoff Budlender, Kate Savage, William Kerfoot, Steve Kahanovitz, Henk Smith, to name a few, were involved, and with the drafts that I was doing for the negotiations at Codesa. I got great support from people at the LRC, particularly Wim [Trengove].

JL: And this institution, the LRC, was involved in your life as well as Arthur's life, and it has touched on the edges of the core friendship at the centre of your book – you and Madiba. Did Madiba have a relationship with the LRC?

GB: Yes. Well, he gave the first LRC Bram Fischer Memorial Lecture at the theatre. And Wim Trengove was the head of the Constitutional Litigation Unit when he was representing Nelson in a number of cases, including the Sarfu case. And Wim and I were both in the death-penalty case – *S v Makwanyane* – while we were both at the LRC, but for different clients.

JL: And at the Bram Fischer lecture, Madiba used the occasion to give his Rivonia papers, which Joel Joffe had returned to him, to the LRC:

he handed them to Arthur 'for the benefit of the LRC' and then Arthur had to remind Madiba that he was at the Constitutional Court, and he then handed the papers to Geoff Budlender, who was the LRC national director at the time.

GB: Yes, Madiba saw the thread of friendship with people like Arthur, Joel, Felicia and Geoff as also linked to the LRC. He saw the LRC as a place that stood for the rights of all people.

JL: And do you think that Madiba appreciated that even under apartheid the law could be used for justice, and appreciated the work of the LRC and the reasons why the group of lawyers – the Kentridges, Arthur and others – formed it?

GB: Yes, there was criticism that under apartheid those lawyers who were trying to use the courts for justice were adding legitimacy to the regime, but I believed that it was possible for justice to prevail for those who were fighting against, or who were victims of, apartheid. The law could prevent someone from being convicted or be used to reduce the severity of the sentence. Where there was a discretion still left with the judge, the discretion could be exercised in favour of the accused. There were many examples, even in highly charged political cases, of judges who saw the conflict between the common law and apartheid, and who were reluctant to convict or impose harsh sentences. I would say that I would stop my work if the people I defended asked me to. But they never did. Nelson understood this. As he commented in that first Bram Fischer lecture in 1995: 'Bram's painstaking work on the law and above all his understanding of the vital political issues of those days played a crucial part in the defence which led to our acquittal.'

JL: And here you still are at the LRC.

GB: Yes, there is still much work for us to do.

JL: Indeed. Thank you, George.

GB: Thank you, Janet.

NOTES

1. Foreword by Nelson Mandela in George Bizos, *Odyssey to Freedom* (Cape Town: Umuzi, 2007), pp. 9–10.

2. www.wits.ac.za

3. Bruce Murray, *Wits: The 'Open Years'* (Johannesburg: Wits University Press, 1997), p. 114.

4. Bruce Murray, *Wits: The 'Open' Years* pp. 28–29.

5. John Carlin, *Knowing Mandela* (New York: Harper Collins, 2013), p. 3.

6. Murray, *Wits: The 'Open' Years*, p. 56.

7. Murray, *Wits: The 'Open' Years*, p. 56.

8. Murray, *Wits: The 'Open' Years*, p. 56.

9. Murray, *Wits: The 'Open' Years*, p. 56.

10. Nelson Mandela, *Long Walk to Freedom* (London: Abacus, 1995), p. 103.

11. Anthony Sampson, *Mandela: The Authorised Biography* (London: Harper-Collins, 1999), p. 35.

12. Mandela, *Long Walk to Freedom*, pp. 173–174.

13. Sampson, *Mandela: The Authorised Biography*, p. 79.

14. Sampson, *Mandela: The Authorised Biography*, p. 6.

15. Bizos, *Odyssey to Freedom*, p. 123.

16. The first Legal Resources Centre Bram Fischer Memorial Lecture given by President Nelson Mandela at the Market Theatre, Johannesburg, on 9 June 1995.

17. Sampson, *Mandela: The Authorised Biography*, p. 539.

18. Carlin, *Knowing Mandela*, p. 74.

19. Carlin, *Knowing Mandela*, p. 76.

20. Carlin, *Knowing Mandela*, p. 77.

21. Foreword by Nelson Mandela in Penelope Andrews and Stephen Ellmann, *The Post-Apartheid Constitutions* (Johannesburg: Wits University Press, 2001), p. vii.

22. Janet Love is the SAHRC commissioner and national director of the Legal Resources Centre.

SELECT BIBLIOGRAPHY

Andrews, Penelope and Stephen Ellmann. *The Post-Apartheid Constitutions.* Johannesburg: Wits University Press, 2001

Benson, Mary. *Nelson Mandela: The Man and the Movement.* New York: Norton & Co, 1994

Bizos, George. *No One to Blame: In Pursuit of Justice in South Africa.* Cape Town: David Philip Publishers, 1998

Bizos, George. *Odyssey to Freedom.* Cape Town: Umuzi, 2007

Brand, Christo. *Mandela: My Prisoner, My Friend.* New York: Thomas Dunne Books, 2014

Bundy, Colin. *Nelson Mandela: A Jacana Pocket Biography.* Auckland Park: Jacana Media, 2015

Carlin, John. *Knowing Mandela: A Personal Portrait.* New York: HarperCollins, 2013

Clingman, Stephen. *Bram Fischer: Afrikaner Revolutionary.* Cape Town: David Philip, 1998

Du Preez Bezdrob, Anne Marie. *Winnie Mandela: A Life.* Cape Town: Zebra Press, 2003

Hepple, Bob. *Young Man with a Red Tie: A Memoir of Mandela and the Failed Revolution 1960–1963.* Auckland Park: Jacana Media, 2013

James Smith, David. *Young Mandela.* New York: Little, Brown and Company, 2010

Joffe, Joel. *The State vs Nelson Mandela: The Trial that Changed South Africa.* Oxford: Oneworld, 2007

Kathrada, Ahmed. *Memoirs.* Cape Town: Zebra Press, 2004

Maharaj, Mac and Ahmed Kathrada (eds). *Mandela: The Authorised Portrait.* Auckland, New Zealand: PQ Blackwell Limited, 2006

Mandela, Nelson. *Long Walk to Freedom.* London: Abacus, 1995

Meredith, Martin. *Fischer's Choice: A Life of Bram Fischer.* Jeppestown: Jonathan Ball, 2002

Murray, Bruce. *Wits: The 'Open' Years.* Johannesburg: Wits University Press, 1997

Sampson, Anthony. *Mandela: The Authorised Biography.* London: HarperCollins, 1999

TIMELINE

DATE	GEORGE BIZOS	NELSON MANDELA	POLITICAL AND LEGAL EVENTS
1918		On 18 July Rolihlahla Mandela is born at Mvezo in the Transkei to Nonqaphi Nosekeni and Nkosi Mphakany-iswa Gadla Mandela. He is his father's fourth son and his mother is his father's third wife.	On 11 November the First World War ends.
1925		Rolihlahla attends primary school near Qunu and a teacher gives him the English name Nelson.	
1927	On 15 November George Bizos is born in the village of Vasilitsi in Greece to Antonios and Anastasia Bizos, the first of four children – three sons and a daughter.		
1930		Nelson's father dies and he is entrusted to the Thembu regent, Jongintaba Dalindyebo.	
1934		Nelson undergoes initia-tion and attends Clarkebury Boarding Institute in Engcobo.	
1935	George begins primary school in Vasilitsi.		

Year	George	Nelson	World events
1936			The Greek dictator Metaxas is installed as prime minister of Greece.
1937		Nelson attends Healdtown, the Wesleyan College at Fort Beaufort.	
1938	George enrols in the astiko, an intermediate school in Koroni.		
1939		Nelson enrols at the University of Fort Hare in Alice in the Eastern Cape.	On 3 September the Second World War starts when Britain and France declare war on Nazi Germany after the invasion of Poland.
1940		Nelson is expelled from Fort Hare.	
1941	On 20 May George and his father leave their home to help seven stranded New Zealand soldiers escape Nazi-occupied Greece.

George spends three months in an orphanage in Alexandria in Egypt.

In August, George arrives with his father in Durban and they move to Johannesburg. | Nelson arrives in Johannesburg.

He works as mine security before being articled to the law firm Witkin, Sidelsky and Eidelman. | On 6 April Germany invades Greece.

On 20 May Germany invades Crete by parachute.

On 14 August the Atlantic Charter is signed by Roosevelt and Churchill, committing to the principles of self-determination and the restoration of self-government. |
| 1942 | | Nelson completes his BA degree through Unisa. | |
| 1943 | George joins the Standard 6 class at Malvern Junior High School. | Nelson enrols for his LLB degree at the University of the Witwatersrand. | |

1944		Nelson marries Evelyn Mase. Together with Walter Sisulu, Oliver Tambo, Anton Lembede and Ashby Mda, Nelson forms the ANC Youth League.	
1945	George starts Standard 8 at Athlone High School.	Nelson's first son Thembekile is born on 23 February.	The Second World War ends on 2 September.
1946			The Greek civil war between the Greek government army and the Democratic Army of Greece begins.
1947		Nelson's first daughter Makaziwe is born. She dies at nine months. Nelson is elected onto the Transvaal provincial executive of the ANC.	On 15 August India gains independence.
1948	George begins his first year BA at the University of the Witwatersrand. George and his father are issued with permanent residence certificates.		In May, the National Party wins the whites-only parliamentary elections and D.F. Malan is elected prime minister. In December, the UN adopts the Universal Declaration of Human Rights.
1949		Nelson is elected to the ANC national executive committee.	The Greek civil war ends. The Prohibition of Mixed Marriages Act is passed, prohibiting sexual relations between whites and people of other races.

1950	George graduates with his BA degree from Wits. George starts working as a clerk for attorney Ruben Kahanowitz. George is elected to the Wits SRC.	Nelson's son Makgatho is born on 26 June.	The Population Registration Act is passed, requiring all people to be classified and registered according to race. The Group Areas Act is passed, requiring people to live in areas designated for their racial group. The Immorality Amendment Act is passed. The Suppression of Communism Act is passed and the Communist Party is banned.
1951	George begins studying for his LLB degree at Wits. George is re-elected to the Wits SRC.	Nelson is elected national president of the ANC Youth League.	
1952	George is re-elected to the Wits SRC.	Nelson and Oliver Tambo open the law partnership Mandela and Tambo. Nelson is elected president of the Transvaal ANC. For his role as the volunteer-in-chief of the Defiance Campaign, Nelson is convicted of violations of the Suppression of Communism Act and sentenced to nine months' imprisonment with hard labour, suspended for two years. Nelson is elected deputy president of the ANC.	The Native Laws Amendment Act and the Natives (Abolition of Passes and Coordination of Documents) Act are promulgated. The Defiance Campaign begins. Thousands of people defy apartheid laws and are arrested. Twenty leaders are convicted of 'statutory communism'.

1953	George graduates with his BA LLB degree from Wits.	Nelson draws up the M-Plan for the underground structures of the ANC.	The National Party passes the Bantu Education Act, which makes provision for separate and inferior education for blacks; the Public Safety Act, which provides for the declaration of a state of emergency; and the Criminal Law Amendment Act, which makes civil disobedience punishable by a three-year jail sentence.
1954	George is admitted to the Bar. George marries Arethe Daflos, an artist. George represents Eli Weinberg in *S v Weinberg*.	Nelson's daughter Makaziwe is born on 1 March.	
1955			The Freedom Charter is adopted on 26 June 1955 at the Congress of the People in Kliptown, Soweto.
1956	George represents Nelson in *Setoaba v Dormehl*.	Nelson is arrested for high treason and charged in the Treason Trial, which will last for five years.	The Treason Trial of one hundred and fifty-six Congress Alliance leaders begins.
1957	George's son Kimon Anthony is born on 21 May.		Ghana becomes the first African country to gain independence from colonial rule. The Sexual Offences (Immorality) Act is passed.

1958	George's son Damon Basil is born on 25 July.	Nelson divorces Evelyn Mase.	
	George defends Winnie Mandela on charges of assaulting a police officer. She is acquitted.	Nelson marries Nomzamo Winnie Madikizela.	
	George represents the Bafurutse in Zeerust and appears on behalf of Gertrude Mpekwa and two others.		
1959		Nelson's daughter Zenani is born on 4 February.	
1960		Nelson's daughter Zindzi is born on 23 December.	On 21 March at Sharpeville police station the police open fire and kill at least sixty-nine people and injure many more on an anti-pass demonstration. A state of emergency is declared. The ANC and the PAC are banned.
1961	George's son Alexi Pericles is born on 12 March.	Nelson is acquitted of high treason. He goes underground.	The remaining treason trialists are all acquitted.
			The National Party government holds a whites-only referendum on 5 October 1960 and on 31 May 1961 South Africa becomes a republic.
			Umkhonto we Sizwe is formed.

1962		Nelson leaves the country for six months.	On 5 July Algeria is granted independence.
		Nelson is arrested and sentenced to five years' imprisonment for illegally leaving the country without a passport and incitement to strike.	The General Law Amendment Act (Sabotage Act) No 76 is passed.
1963	George, together with Bram Fischer, Vernon Berrangé and Arthur Chaskalson, instructed by the attorney Joel Joffe, represent Nelson and the Rivonia accused.	On 27 May Nelson is sent to Robben Island to serve his five-year sentence.	On 11 July members of the SACP and the MK High Command are arrested at Liliesleaf farm in Rivonia, Johannesburg, and charged with sabotage. Along with other members of the ANC, including Nelson, they go on trial in October 1963.
		On 9 October Nelson appears in court for the first time together with his fellow Rivonia accused: Walter Sisulu, Govan Mbeki, Raymond Mhlaba, Ahmed Kathrada, Rusty Bernstein, Andrew Mlangeni, Elias Motsoaledi, James Kantor and Denis Goldberg.	On 12 December Kenya gains independence.
1964	George represents Laloo Chiba, Dave Kitson, Mac Maharaj, John Matthews and Wilton Mkwayi on charges of sabotage in the Little Rivonia Trial. Mkwayi receives a life sentence; Kitson twenty years; Chiba eighteen years; Matthews fifteen years; and Maharaj twelve years. Mkwayi, Maharaj and Chiba join Nelson on Robben Island.	Nelson is sentenced to life imprisonment and transported to Robben Island to start serving his sentence.	Eight out of the ten Rivonia trialists are sentenced to life imprisonment.
			On 26 April Tanzania gains independence.
			On 24 October Zambia gains independence.
			The General Law Amendment Act No 80 is passed to permit the minister of justice to extend the operation of the Sobukwe Clause in individual cases.

1965			The Criminal Procedure Amendment Act No 96 is enacted and provides for 180-day detention and re-detention. Detainees can be held for six months in solitary confinement with only state officials permitted access. There is no court jurisdiction to order the release of detainees.
1966	George, together with Sydney Kentridge, represents Bram Fischer on charges of violating the Suppression of Communism Act and conspiring to commit sabotage. Bram is sentenced to life imprisonment.		On 6 September Dimitri Tsafendas stabs Prime Minister Hendrik Verwoerd to death in parliament. Balthazar John Vorster is installed as prime minister. On 30 September Botswana gains independence.
1967	In *S v Tuhadeleni and 36 others* George, together with Ernie Wentzel and Dennis Kuny, represents Herman Toivo ya Toivo and thirty-six other Namibian leaders of SWAPO on charges of terrorism. Ya Toivo is sentenced to twenty years' imprisonment, most of the others to life.		The Terrorism Act providing for indefinite detention without trial is passed.
1968		Nelson's mother dies. He is refused permission to attend her funeral.	

1969	George's father dies.	Nelson's son Thembekile dies in a car accident. Nelson is refused permission to attend his funeral.
	George, with Arthur Chaskalson and David Soggot, defends Winnie Mandela and twenty-one others on charges of contravening the Suppression of Communism Act and the Unlawful Organisations Act, and then terrorism. They are all acquitted.	
	George is appointed to the governing body of the South African Hellenic Educational and Technical Institute (Saheti) in Johannesburg.	
1971	George appears on behalf of Winnie on charges of communicating with another banned person. She is acquitted on appeal.	
1972	George, with Advocate Isie Maisels, represents the family of Ahmed Timol at the inquest into his death in detention. Timol was detained, severely tortured and thrown out of a window on the tenth floor of John Vorster Square police station. The magistrate found no one to blame.	

George represents the family of Salim Essop who was arrested with Timol and then found comatose in a Pretoria hospital.

George visits his family and home in Greece for the first time since he left them in 1941.

1973 George represents Winnie on charges of meeting with another banned person. She is convicted and sentenced to one year's imprisonment, reduced on appeal to six months.

George represents Alex Moumbaris on charges of terrorism for assisting trained ANC activists. He is sentenced to twelve years' imprisonment.

George represents S. Hosey against charges under the Terrorism Act. He is sentenced to five years' imprisonment.

George represents Quentin Jacobsen on charges of conspiring to commit acts of sabotage and other acts with a view to overthrowing the state. He is acquitted.

1974	Saheti opens to provide and promote a Greek education.		
1975	George, together with Arthur Chaskalson and Dennis Kuny, represents the Nusas Five – Karel Tip, Cedric de Beer, Glenn Moss, Charles Nupen and Eddie Webster – on charges of furthering the aims of communism. They are acquitted in 1976.		On 25 June Mozambique gains independence. On 11 November Angola gains independence.
1976	George appears before the Cillié Commission of Inquiry into the Soweto uprising on behalf of Winnie Mandela. George defends Dexter Ronnie Mosheshle and Tiza Dlamini, charged with the murder of Dr Melville Edelstein. Charges are withdrawn against Mosheshle and Dlamini is acquitted. George represents Cyril Ndlovu and other students involved in the Soweto uprising.		Hundreds of Soweto students are killed by the police and the army during protests against the introduction of Afrikaans as a medium of instruction in schools. Unrest spreads rapidly to schools in other parts of the country.
1977		Winnie Mandela is banished to Brandfort.	On 12 September Black Consciousness leader Steve Biko dies in detention in a Port Elizabeth prison after being tortured and suffering fatal injuries to his head.

1978	George, together with Sydney Kentridge, represents the Biko family at the inquest into the death of Steve Biko. The magistrate finds that no one is to blame for his death.		P.W. Botha replaces John Vorster as prime minister.
1979	George, together with Kathy Satchwell and Raymond Tucker, defends Linda Mogale and Jimmy Mabaso on counts of murder, arson, malicious injury to property and terrorism. He is convicted on all counts but the murder charge is reduced to culpable homicide. The convictions are set aside on appeal. George, together with Arthur Chaskalson, Judge Johann Kriegler, and Professor John Dugard found Lawyers for Human Rights. The Legal Resources Centre opens.		
1982	George and Dennis Kuny represent the family of Neil Aggett at the inquest into his death. The magistrate finds that there was no one to blame for his death.	Nelson, Walter Sisulu, Raymond Mhlaba and Andrew Mlangeni, followed by Ahmed Kathrada, are transferred to Pollsmoor Prison.	Detained trade unionist and doctor, Neil Aggett, is found hanging in his cell.

	George represents Barbara Hogan on charges of treason. She is found guilty and sentenced to ten years' imprisonment.
	George represents Rob Martin and Mandla Elliott Themba. Martin is sentenced to ten years' imprisonment and Themba to five.
1983	George represents the family of Simon Tembuyise Mndawe at the inquest into his death in detention. The magistrate finds no one to blame.
	George represents Albertina Sisulu on charges under the Suppression of Communism Act for furthering the aims of the ANC.

1983 — The United Democratic Front, comprising about six hundred anti-apartheid civic, religious, non-governmental, student and other organisations, is launched in opposition to the tricameral parliament.

1984 — Archbishop Desmond Tutu is awarded the Nobel Peace Prize.

1985	George leads the defence in the Delmas Trial of twenty-two men, including three leaders of the UDF (Moses Mabokela Chikane, Popo Molefe and Mosiuoa 'Terror' Lekota), on charges of treason, terrorism and furthering the aims of unlawful organisations. They are eventually acquitted on appeal. George is appointed as a judge on the Botswana Court of Appeal. He will serve until 1993.	On 10 February in her 'My Father Says' speech, Nelson's daughter Zindzi announces his rejection of Prime Minister Botha's offer to release him if he renounces violence. Nelson is admitted to hospital for prostate surgery.	In December, the Congress of South African Trade Unions is launched.
1986	George travels to Lusaka to meet with Oliver Tambo on behalf of Nelson.		
1988		Nelson is moved to Victor Verster Prison.	
1989			The collapse of the Berlin Wall. The Delmas Trial ends.
1990	In 1990, George is appointed to the ANC legal and constitutional committee.	On 11 February 1990 Nelson Mandela is released from Victor Verster Prison after being a prisoner for almost ten thousand days.	The ANC, SACP and PAC are unbanned. Political prisoners are released.

1991	George serves as advisor to the ANC negotiating team at Codesa and participates in drawing up the interim constitution and bill of rights. George represents Winnie Mandela on charges of kidnapping and being an accessory to assault in the Stompie Seipei trial. On appeal, her six-year jail sentence is reduced to a fine and a two-year suspended sentence. George begins working as the senior counsel at the Constitutional Litigation Unit of the Legal Resources Centre.		The Convention for a Democratic South Africa brought together various political, civil, religious and community organisations to chart the future for a democratic South Africa. The Soviet Union is dissolved on 25 December.
1992		Nelson announces his separation from Winnie.	
1993		Nelson is awarded the Nobel Peace Prize jointly with President F.W. de Klerk.	In April, SACP leader Chris Hani is assassinated.
1994	George is appointed to the Judicial Service Commission by Nelson to recommend candidates for judicial office and reforms to the judicial system. His five-year term will be renewed for a further ten years by President Thabo Mbeki. George's brother Stavros passes away.	Nelson votes for the first time in his life and is elected president. On 10 May Nelson is inaugurated as the president of South Africa.	On 27 April the first democratic elections are held. The ANC wins sixty-two per cent of the vote.

1996	George leads the team for the Constituent Assembly before the Constitutional Court to certify the constitution.	Nelson divorces Winnie Mandela.	The Truth and Reconciliation Commission is established by the Promotion of National Unity and Reconciliation Act. Its theme is 'Revealing is healing'. Victims of gross human rights violations are encouraged to give their testimonies. Perpetrators of these violations can seek amnesty if their crimes were politically motivated and if they make full disclosure of their actions.
	George appears on behalf of the cabinet in *S v Makwanyane* – the death penalty case – the first case before the Constitutional Court.		
1997	George represents the family of Steve Biko before the TRC to oppose the granting of amnesty to the four policemen who killed him. Amnesty is refused.		
1998	George represents the families of the Cradock Four (Matthew Goniwe, Fort Calata, Sparrow Mkonto and Sicelo Mhlauli) at the second inquest into their deaths.	Nelson marries Graça Machel on his eightieth birthday.	
	George represents the families of the Cradock Four before the TRC to oppose the amnesty application by the policemen who killed them. Amnesty is refused.		

	George represents the families of Ruth First and Jeanette Schoon before the TRC to oppose Craig Williamson's application for amnesty for their murders. Amnesty is granted.	
1999	George appears before the TRC on behalf of the family of Chris Hani to oppose the application for amnesty of Clive Derby-Lewis and Janusz Waluś for his murder. Amnesty is refused.	
2001	George's mother passes away.	Nelson is diagnosed with prostate cancer.
2004	George represents Morgan Tsvangirai on charges of treason for an alleged plot to assassinate President Mugabe of Zimbabwe. He is acquitted.	
2005		Nelson's son Makgatho dies from complications from HIV/AIDS.

2012	George appears before the Farlam Commission of Inquiry into the tragic events at Marikana on behalf of the Legal Resources Centre.		On 16 August 2012, the South African Police Service opens fire on a crowd of striking mineworkers at Lonmin Platinum Mine at Marikana, some 100 kilometres north-west of Johannesburg. The shooting leaves thirty-four mineworkers dead and seventy-nine wounded. More than two hundred and fifty people are arrested.
2013		On 5 December Nelson dies at his home in Johannesburg.	

INDEX OF PERSONS

Photographs

14: Gisèle Wulfson; 20 (bottom): courtesy of the Mandela Collection of the Wits Archives; 42 (bottom): courtesy of the Sisulu family; 43 (bottom): Jürgen Schadeberg; 77 (top): *Drum* Social Histories Baileys African History Archive/Africa Media Online; 78: Gallo Images/Getty Images/KeyStone – France; 104: Eli Weinberg, UWC–Robben Island Museum, Mayibuye Archives; 145: UWC–Robben Island Museum, Mayibuye Archives; 146 (bottom): Cloete Breytenbach, UWC–Robben Island Museum, Mayibuye Archives; 179 (top): Peter Magubane; 179 (bottom left): Graeme Williams, UWC–Robben Island Museum, Mayibuye Archives; 179 (bottom right): UWC–Robben Island Museum, Mayibuye Archives; 180: Morris Zwi; 200: Ellen Elmendorp; 202 (bottom): EPA; 233: Greg Marinovich; 238: courtesy of Cyril Coetzee; 252: Oscar Gutierrez; 262: courtesy the LRC.

GEORGE BIZOS was born in 1928 in the Greek village of Vasilitsi. During the Second World War he escaped from his occupied homeland, becoming a refugee in South Africa at thirteen. Systematically and with determination he set about adopting his new country, graduating from Wits with legal degrees and called to the Bar. A strong inclination towards human rights brought him into contact with the legal practice of Mandela and Tambo and he acted for many of their clients in the 1950s. His legal career is associated with all the major human rights trials in the decades of apartheid. Subsequently, he acted for the ANC at the post-1994 constitutional hearings, and is on the staff of the Legal Resources Centre. Bizos has served as a temporary judge and was appointed an Ambassador of Hellenism in 2006. One of his primary concerns in this capacity is the return of the Parthenon Marbles to Greece. He is the author of *No One to Blame? – In Pursuit of Legal Justice in South Africa*, an account of five prominent trials, and his magisterial autobiography, *Odyssey to Freedom*, published in 2007.